John Pullars and Sons Ltd, Dyers and Cleaners, Perth

PULLARS
OF PERTH

by Albert W. Harding

Perth and Kinross District Libraries
PERTH
1991

ISBN 0 905452 10 0

Published in 1991 by
Perth and Kinross District Libraries
Shore Road
Perth PH2 8BH

Printed By
Cordfall Limited
Tel: 041 - 332 4640

Dedicated with much love and gratitude
to my Mother
ISABELLA SMART KEILLER
of PANBRIDE

A Famous Pullar Advertisment

Acknowledgements

Having contributed an article on "Sir Robert Pullar" to the "Dictionary of Scottish Business Biography 1860-1960", Vol. 1, Staple Industries, edited A. Slaven and S. Checkland, AUP., 1986, it seemed only logical to write a history of John Pullar and Sons, Dyers and Cleaners, Perth.

The first attempt, some 600 pages, was overlong, over-detailed and shapeless. Fortunately, John R. Hume (then of Strathclyde University) suggested the present format and this was scrutinised by his colleague, Dr. James Treble. To both of them I am much indebted.

Many others were approached for advice; far too many to list here. Hopefully, they will pardon their exclusion. However, those whose contribution was absolutely essential were Mr. Bryce, Local Studies Librarian and Mr Connelly, Archivist, Perth & Kinross District Libraries, and two former workers in John Pullar and Sons, Ltd, Mr. MacPherson and Mr. Burnett - to them all the author extends his grateful thanks.

Finally, tribute must be paid to the Thomson Educational Trust, Perth for their generous financial assistance.

The Dyer's Obligation:-

"I,_____, of my own free will and accord do promise that I shall heal and conceal all the parts and properties of Dyeing that hath been or shall be made known to me. That I shall not divulge nor make them known, shown, written, nor make legible or intelligible by any means or contrivance, natural or artificial, save only to such an one as myself, having paid for the same, in an honest and lawful manner, and whom I am well assured is such, after the examination. This I promise on honour and credit before the witnesses here present." 15/9/1711

- Burgh Laws of Dundee,
  Alex J. Warden,
  London, 1872,
  p. 568.

Contents

Abbreviations

BH	Business History
C	Perthshire Constitutional
JSDC	Journal of the Society of Dyers and Colourists
LS	Lengthening Shadows
PA	Perthshire Advertiser
PC	Perth Courier
PKDLA	PKDL Archives

Illustrations

Introduction

*"The main problem in writing any
company's history is to place the story of the
particular concern in the context."
- T.C. Barker
"Business History and the Business-Man", B.H.,
Vol. 1, 1958, p. 17."*

Some years ago an article appeared in print containing the dire warning that business history would not survive the age of high technology because its records would be lost forever in a network of computers and shredding machines.[1] While this provocative suggestion, as was intended, sparked off a fiery debate among academics[2] it does leave us with the uncomfortable question - what is the purpose of business history today? Is there any value in trying to trace the rise and fall of a commercial firm which few might even remember? Fortunately, the field's leading authorities think that there is. B.E. Supple argues that its value lies in seeking "the roots of business problems and their solutions — by an imaginative use of prosiac evidence."[3] T.S. Ashton is even more forthright: "For it is in the individual firm, rather than in the wider organisations, that we can observe the operation of economic forces at first-hand, with little distortion by politics and ideologies - the day of easy generalisation is over."[4] This view is echoed by T.C. Cochran - "Until hundreds of scholarly business histories have been written — there is very little basis for quantitative generalisation."[5] These are powerful endorsements for the worth of business history.

But immediately another question arises - how is this to be done? What evidence has to be examined? Indeed, are there any records which one might regard as indispensable for such a task? Again, the experts seem to be of one voice. To B.E. Supple it is "the ways in which firms operated, the evolution of management techniques, intra company relationships, the changing structure of enterprise,"[6] as well as "its organisation, finance, efficiency, performance and management policy."[7] K.A. Tucker thought it should cover minute books, special memoranda, shareholders' reports as well as statistics.[8] P. Matthias, on the other hand, stressed the need to examine home demand, foreign markets, technical changes, prices, labour, competitive forces, collective action by employers, changes in taste, new competing products, fiscal and legislative changes.[9] To cope with this daunting range of problems would most certainly represent "a highly specialised undertaking"[10] beyond the skills of most historians, but when few, if any, sources even exist then, "the writing of business history becomes a hazardous occupation" because one is forced to turn to what some have called "a rag-bag of external sources."[11] All too often this results in "puff stories and histories — (which) convey little except homiletic ramblings and unsubstantiated platitudes."[12] Some have even described the combination of "unmitigated praise" and "chronological lists of names and specifications" nothing more than "a perverse selectivity."[13] Many others share this judgment: T.C. Barker, for instance, describes them as "sugary romances" or "thin outlines, much of it of a nostalgic nature."[14]

All this is regrettably true of the three slim publications, totalling a mere 72 pages, which describe the history of John Pullar and Sons, Dyers and Cleaners, Perth.[15] All of these effusively "romanticise the past"[16] and unashamedly maintain "the tradition of the heroic."[17] The reason for this simplistic approach is quite clear. The "ravages of time and waste-paper drives"[18] have forced writers either to ignore or imagine relevant facts. This is made worse, as far as Pullars is concerned, by the very nature of their business.[19] Apart from the natural reticence of most businessmen[20] dyers were particularly secretive and reluctant to commit too much, in the way of confidential information, to paper. Given these comments it is only reasonable that the writer reveal his statement of intent.[21]

The author of this paper openly associates himself with the view of P.L. Payne that "regional economic history is the grass roots approach to business history."[22] Hence the emphasis that will be laid on "external sources"[23] in order to gain a proper perspective of Pullars vis-à-vis Perth and its immediate neighbourhood. Secondly, the writer is convinced that P.N. Davies was right when he said that "the personal factor is so important as to override all other considerations."[24] This is especially true of any family firm.[25] Although the writer worked for John Pullar and Sons in 1949 and had many friends who served the firm in various capacities and different levels, it was an interest in the personality of Sir Robert Pullar and his impact upon Perth which led to the composition of this paper.[26] Even in 1949, long after the Pullar family had relinquished their connections with the firm, the writer was conscious of the myths which still survived on the shop floor and which seemed "to buttress values important to its way of life."[27] Some employees ascribed to the Pullars every conceivable skill that management could possibly require: others subscribed to what T.S. Ashton and B.E. Supple have called "the Robber-

Baron hypothesis"[28] and accused the Pullars of every devious trick that management could concoct. It is the purpose of this paper, in the words of Asa Briggs, "to separate out fact from folklore"[29] and make some kind of judgment.

Of course, there are other questions that must be asked. The kind that B.E. Supple describes as "the minor methodological trouble to pose a limited and rigorous set of questions at the outset."[30] These are designed intentionally for the general reader rather than a specialist[31] and are not primarily concerned with growth. For "growth, after all, means survival and anyone in business naturally wants to survive."[32] It seems to the writer that the really significant questions are as follows - Why were the Pullars so late in switching all their resources from cotton spinning to dyeing and cleaning? How did they invest their profits and just how innovative were they in their field? What style of management did they pursue and did it vary with the personality of the chairman of the firm? Why were they unable to confront the Trade Unions and why did they eventually succumb to a merger? How did they come to dominate the city of Perth so completely and did they do so by exploiting local politics? Did they make any specific errors of judgement or was the firm simply doomed by its geography? And finally, do the Pullars fit the classical pattern of 19th century entrepreneurs? Which of these commands the greatest interest will depend on the reader.

Footnotes

1. "There is no futute for Business History", Michael Turner, *B.H.*, Vol. XX, 1978, pp. 235-239

2. "There is no future for Business History: A Reply", R. Forman, *B.H.*, Vol. XXII, 1980, pp. 100-102; "A Refutation Refuted", Michael Turner, *B.H.*, Vol. XXII, 1980, p. 103

3. "The Uses of Business History", B.E. Supple, *B.H.*, Vol. !V, 1961, p. 83

4. "Business History", T.S. Ashton, *B.H.*, Vol. 1, 1958, p. 2

5. "American Business History: A Survey", B.E. Supple, *B.H.*, Vol. 1, 1958, p.69

6. Ibid., p. 74

7. Supple, B.E., *B.H.*, Vol. IV, 1961, p. 82

8. "Business History: Some Proposals for Aims and Methodology", K.A. Tucker, *B.H.*, Vol. XIV, 1972, p. 3

9. "Business History and the Business Management Education", P. Matthias, *B.H.*, Vol. XVII, 1975, p. 6

10. "Business History and the Business Man", T.C. Barker, *B.H.*, Vol. 1, 1958, p. 17

11. "Economic Theory and Business History", Francis E. Hyde, *B.H.*, Vol. V, 1962, p. 1

12. Supple, B.E., *B.H.*, Vol. 1, 1958. pp. 70-71

13. Ibid., *B.H.*, Vol. IV, 1961, p. 84

14. Barker, T.C., *B.H.*, Vol. 1, 1958, pp. 16-17

15. *"Pullars of Perth 1824-1924"*, Sir John Fraser, Perth, 1924; *"The Story of Pullars"*, Perth, 1937; *"The History of J. Pullar and Sons Limited"*, G.H.C. Fisher, Perth, 1967

16. Matthias, P., *B.H.*, Vol. XVII, 1975, p. 5

17. "Entrepreneurship, Business Performance and Industrial Development", B.W.E. Alford, *B.H.*, Vol. XIX, 1977, p. 116

18. Supple, B.E., *B.H.*, Vol. IV, 1961, p. 83

19. Tucker, K,A., *B.H.*, Vol. XIV, 1972, p. 5; Supple, B.E., *B.H.*, Vol. IV, 1961, p. 82

20. Ashton, T.S.A., *B.H.*, Vol. 1, 1958, p. 1

21. Supple, B.E., *B.H.*, Vol. IV, 1961, p. 82

22. "The Uses of Business History: A Contribution to the Discussion", P.L. Payne, *B.H.*, vol. V, 1962, p. 17

23. *"Royal Exchange Assurance"*, B.E. Supple, Cambridge University Press, 1970

24. "Business Success and the Role of Chance: The Extraordinary Philippe Brothers", P.N. Davies, *B.H.*, Vol. XXIII, 1981, p. 208

25. "Family Firms and Managerial Capitalism: The Case of the International Motor Industry", Roy Church, *B.H.*, vol. XXVIII, 1986, p. 155

26. *"Dictionary of Scottish Business Biography 1860-1960"*, Vol. 1, Staple Industries, edit. A. Slaven and S. Checkland, Aberdeen University Press, 1986, pp. 393-395

27. Matthias, P., *B.H.*, Vol. XVII, 1975, p. 5

28. Ashton, T.S., *B.H.*, Vol. 1, 1958, p. 2; Supple, B.E., *B.H.*, Vol. 1, 1958, p.74

29. "Trade Union History and Labour History", Asa Briggs, *B.H.*, Vol. VIII, 1966, p. 39

30. Supple, B.E., *B.H.*, Vol. IV, 1961, p. 85

31. Ibid; *"Royal Exchange Assurance"*, Cambridge University Press, 1970

32. "Marshall and the Birth and Death of Firms: The Growth and Size Distribution of Firms in the early 19th century Cotton Industry", R. Lloyd-Jones and A.A. Le Roux, *B.H.*, Vol. XXIV, 1982, p. 141

Chapter I
General Summary

"Always a family firm —"
- LS 38.

The first sign of the pending Industrial Revolution appeared in Perth in 1758 when two fine-sheeting companies - the Newrow Company and the Mill Wynd Company - were established. They created a demand for weavers and rural craftsmen flocked to the town in search of work. However, industrial activity was sluggish till 1768 when local entrepreneur George Penny introduced Silesia linens. For the working weaver this was a rich trade and some were quick to purchase several looms and employ men to work them. Their cloth was sold to cloth merchants who had it whitened and sent by sailing-ship to London and from thence to the West Indies as Britannias. Nonetheless, the bulk of their cloth was despatched, still in its green state, by pack-horse to Glasgow, where it was bought by printers. The impact of Silesias on Perth can scarcely be exaggerated. The harbour, dormant for centuries, was suddenly thronged with ships from the Baltic or the Netherlands carrying flax and seed in their holds. Repairs were always necessary after a sea-voyage and in 1774 a ship-building industry developed. Soon there were innumerable small establishments producing fish-nets, ropes, sails, starch, soap and candles. Flax-dressers were in short supply and virtually every able-bodied female in the town was at work spinning.[1] With hardly any unemployment Perth was "to flourish for the next fifty years."[2]

The physical environment changed dramatically. Approach roads to the town were quickly improved and paved streets appeared 1772 - 1783.[3] Even the Old Mercat Cross was removed to stimulate the flow of wheeled traffic. But it was the completion of the stone bridge over the Tay in 1771 that proved the real spur to improvement. George Street, the fashionable approach to the new bridge, was finished in the same year and attracted professional people from Edinburgh to make their homes there. Before long, Perth was consciously trying to emulate the capital city. In 1774 the last sections of the medieval walls were demolished and two years later most of the ancient Ports disappeared.[4] Morison, a local bookseller, launched a 32 page "Perth Magazine" in July, 1771[5] and the Old Salt Vennel, full of slums and teeming with beggars, was replaced by an elegant crescent, St. John's Street, during the years 1791 - 1796.[6]

In these years of bustle and prosperity a certain young weaver, John Pullar, married an Isabella Ower in April, 1773 and started a family. No detail of his working life has survived, but he must have been busy with fine-sheetings, damasks, diapers, skirtings, heavy checks and napkins. Weavers' earnings had doubled and their purchasing power was greater than that of masons or wrights. By 1780 Perth's spinning jennies were pouring out blunts and winchies for Glasgow's printers.[7] Then, in 1782, George Penny again took the lead when he pioneered Perth's industrial advance by opening a cotton factory. The weavers were delighted; a skilled man could now earn 30/- a week and even a boy could make 3/6d. The famous Sir Richard Arkwright, who had an interest in Stanley Mill, gave his approval to the new muslin and cotton became "the rage of the monied people in Perth." The editor of the "Perth Courier" summed it up nicely: "Everybody that had any capital became a manufacturer."[8]

Perth now became the target for entrepreneurs from both sides of the Cheviots and by 1784 English machine-made cloth was flooding into the town.[9] Two years later, in 1786, the manufacture of thin linens for umbrellas began and although a light fabric was essential to take the wax for keeping out the rain, it was not long before it was found that green, stout cotton cloth was even better. Thus, umbrella gingham became Perth's main industry. By 1800 there were at least 3,000 weavers in the town earning high wages and most of them members of the flourishing Perth Operative Weavers' Friendly Society.[10] Textile agents from Glasgow and Paisley streamed into town buying and selling pullicates, calicoes, fine cambrics and light grands.[11]

One of the many who did well in these prosperous years was John Pullar, now a master-weaver.[12] The replacement of the hoop by the bustle and the contemporary trend to simplicity in dress made it an ideal time for cotton.[13] Realising the opportunity presented by the decline in linen and the increased demand for cotton.[14] John Pullar accepted a partnership in a cloth manufactory, Stalker, Greig and Company.[15] His son, Robert, who had been "well educated", obtained a clerkship with the firm in September, 1801 and married Elizabeth Black of Dunning in Edinburgh.[16] Tradition has it that there were ten children, but only three survived infancy.[17]

Industrial growth continued, stimulated by the never-ending conflict with France and many must have felt that Perth was destined to become a great manufacturing city. In 1803 a thread mill opened in Bridgend and a suburb rapidly grew on the east bank of the river.[18] To meet a middle class demand for elegance and mobility George Pentland opened the Perth Carriage Works in 1805.[19] A year later, George Smith began the manufacture of imitation silk and cotton shawls. Perth even acquired its first newspaper, the "Perth Courier", moderately Tory, whose adverts reflect the prevailing mood of confidence in the town - "the newest fashions from London brought to Perth by George Knox"; "Cheap carpets available"; "New Colours now"; "Edinburgh corsets and muffs for sale."[20] There was even a monthly column, which, amazingly, extolled everything French. New shops, some quite large, sprang up all over the town from South Methven Street to the Kirkgate.[21] The urge to copy Edinburgh intensified and the talk in the coffee rooms was of "New Town suburbs."[22] Milliners, dress-makers, governesses and school-mistresses took up residence in Perth in the hope of serving the huge military garrison and everything seemed set for a splendid future.[23]

Reality was somewhat different. Cotton had long since ousted linen from Perth and the Silesia trade had retreated to rural Perthshire and Fife. It could never return - expertise had faded and even the looms had been altered. Cotton had become so dominant that if it was ever under threat Perth would be in very serious trouble. Most businessmen must have realised that the town was far too dependant on Glasgow's economic health, especially with caseas and cambrics. Even more disturbing must have been the erratic fluctuations to which the price of raw cotton was prone.[24] This made planning virtually impossible[25] and the industry was in "constant insecurity" due to speculation buying and selling.[26] Periodically the market would flood, prices collapse, confidence evaporate with depression the result. It was made far worse for Perth by the excessive competition generated by the presence of no fewer than 70 cotton merchants and 60 manufacturing firms. This overcommitment to cotton represented a massive investment and it is fair to say that for most of the town's 16,000 inhabitants cotton was their livelihood.

Although the steep rise in raw cotton prices was first observed in 1807[27] the "shattering of the Cotton Illusion" in 1810 came as a great shock.[28] Even as late as 1853 people in Perth still shuddered when they spoke of 1810, "the bad year."[29] The immediate cause was the exclusion of UK goods from the Continent by the French. As a war-measure it was extremely effective; as a blow to Perth it was devastating. Within months the 70 cotton merchants were reduced to 10 and the 60 manufacturing firms cut to a mere 8 and these only survived because they produced

Robert Pullar (LS)

umbrella ginghams for the home-market.[30] Many, even the editor of the "Perth Courier", packed their bags and made a hasty retreat to Edinburgh. Only the intervention of a local man, Francis Morison, saved the paper from oblivion. Significantly, the first emigration advertisements appeared offering free passage to Canada from Port Glasgow.[31] Ruined men reflected bitterly on the continuing high cost of coal, the numerous bankruptcies in the town and most of all on the neglect of linen, by which "they had lost the substance for the shadow."[32] The disasters of 1810 were not confined to Perth. All the local bleachfields and printfields at Stanley, Tulloch, Luncarty and Huntingtower had to sell up.[33] Ruthvenfield Print Works was ruined and the Cromwell Park Company went bankrupt.[34] But those who suffered the most were the weavers of Perth. The Incorporation of Weavers, its members thrown out of work and unable to sell their wares, were soon bankrupt as well.[35] Neither a meeting of "the Principal Inhabitants of the Town" nor appeals to local Justices of the Peace could solve their problem.[36] The cost of living rocketed just at the time when weavers' incomes were slashed. The once proud weavers of Perth, famed for their rugged independence and high standard of living, now faced stark poverty. Many had no choice but to turn to begging.[37] Generous well-wishers opened a Soup Kitchen, but it could not cope with the hundreds clamouring to be fed.[38]

At this apparently inopportune moment Robert Pullar decided to launch out on his own.[39] In many ways he had little choice. He had a growing family to support and he was now 32 years old. But the deciding factor was probably the sudden collapse of his employment - Stalker, Greig and Company were also bankrupt. Presumably his father, John Pullar, was dead and his share of the deceased's estate may have given him the capital he needed to buy the firm. Not that he would have required a great deal because for the next ten years he had no factory. Instead, he operated as Stalker, Greig and Company had done - from a tiny office in King James V1 Hospital Building. From there, under the same company name, he bought and sold ginghams made by the weavers of Pomarium.[40] He must have known he was taking a risk, albeit, in his opinion, a calculated risk. After all, the French Wars were finally over and there was an immense feeling of relief in the land.[41] There was also an awareness that a new age was in the making - steamboats, carrying 100 passengers, now took only four hours to sail up river from Dundee and goods were arriving from Edinburgh on a regular basis at least three times a week.[42] Lastly, with thousands of men due for demobilisation from the Army and Navy labour costs would never be lower.

Most of Pullar's problems came from his work-force, the handloom weavers of Pomarium, most of whom were strong-minded individualists.[43] They had to be. In 1815 most manufacturers in the town had cut wages and this had caused intense hardship. So much so that in June, 1816 a Committee for the Relief of Suffering Weavers in Perth was formed.[44] It is interesting to note that Robert Pullar was never a member. They soon decided to investigate matters.[45] They discovered that the minimum wage needed by a married weaver was 13/2d weekly, while most barely managed 6/2d. By May, 1817 some 1,500 weavers were in receipt of free coal and meal from local charities.[46] Despite their belief that their plight was entirely due to the Corn Laws and greedy manufacturers[47] they never resorted to any kind of Luddite violence. All they did was to talk endlessly about "the Radicals coming to Perth" and how they would resolve their grievances.[48] In the continuing depression of 1819[49] the number of weavers in Perth fell to 1,900, although wages improved slightly. A mere 250 had top wages, 7/-; the remainder only 4/6d.[50] Refusing to believe that the switch to plain calicoes and heavier fabrics and the resulting competition with English goods was the root of their problem[51] they took legal action against the manufacturers and even petitioned Parliament about their low pay.[52] They also tried petitioning His Grace the Duke of Atholl.[53] Both petitions failed. Many, in despair, sought employment in Aberdeen, others emigrated to Ohio or Canada, while yet others broke stones for roads or dug ditches for farmers.[54]

Wealthier sections of the community were quite unaffected by such scenes and in the post-war period increased their purchases of Glasgow muslins, London laces and French perfumes.[55] Even cotton, as a trading commodity, became "brisker" after 1819 and it was probably this upturn in the economy that decided Robert Pullar to acquire a factory and change from cotton merchant to cotton manufacturer.[56] He was by no means a rich man. Indeed, he is not listed among the depositors of the Savings Bank of Perth.[57] The earliest public reference to him is not as an aspiring industrialist, but as Vice-President of the Perth Auxiliary Bible Society in 1817.[58] Described as "a wise and judicious Christian" he often audited the books for the Baptist Church.[59] In 1820 somewhere near the modern Kinnoull Street and on the south bank of the Lade, he opened as Robert Pullar, Umbrella and Gingham Cloth Manufacturer with "a few permanent weavers."[60] It was a very modest undertaking and did not even merit a mention in the 1822 list of Perth gingham producers.[61] Times were hard

Extract PC 23/2/1824 (New Dye Work)

for dealers and there were bankruptcies every month. Robert Pullar conducted most of his business with Perth's two main umbrella shops - John Paton and H. Mitchell, both in the High Street.[62] Competition was fierce as advertisements grew bolder, more aggresssive and unrestrained - "Bargains, truly wonderful!"; "Just arrived from Paris!"; "Observe, wonderful cheap bargains!"[63] Even the editor of the "Perth Courier" remarked on "the insatiable demand for colours, which seems to be growing stronger."[64] Middle-class ladies clamoured for coloured fans and handkerchiefs and were willing to pay almost any price for them.[65]

But it was the visit of George IV to Edinburgh that brought the colour-hunger to a climax. For weeks newspapers devoted column after column to highly detailed descriptions of the materials and shades worn by the ladies at royal receptions in Holyrood Palace. These were eagerly devoured by female readers, who then pestered their husbands for copies or besieged the town's dress-makers for "something special."[66]

One advertisement, in particular, may very well have persuaded

Robert Pullar to take the next step forward in his business plans. In March, 1823 shopkeeper David Lennox, High Street, created a minor sensation in Perth when he returned in triumph from Paris "with the very latest colours available."[67] Shortly afterwards, according to Pullar family tradition, Robert Pullar recalled his son, John, from London and set him up in a small dye-works.[68] It was destined to prove a highly important change of direction for the family firm.[69]

Premises were found for the dye-works in a narrow passage-way called Burt's Close, just off the High Street.[70] Men were hired, equipment bought and an advertisement placed in the "Perth Courier." Although it was a struggle to satisfy the public's fickle appetite for colour, a modest profit was possible every year. That was until a law-suit forced the dye-works to move in 1828. John Pullar was now compelled to develop cleaning as much as dyeing and to give more attention to rural areas, even though the bulk of his income was derived from dyeing on the hank for his father. It seems to have been this which persuaded his father to make him a full partner in Robert Pullar and Son, Umbrella and Gingham Cloth Manufacturers.

Progress in dyeing was slow as John Pullar tried to cope with a savage bout of cholera in 1832 and the premature death of his father three years later. Forced to devote most of his attention to the weaving side of the family enterprises, he took his younger brother, Laurence, into partnership in Robert Pullar and Sons, Umbrella and Gingham Cloth Manufacturers in 1838. A dyeing boom in 1840 provided the funds for the purchase of an empty flax-spinning mill in Paul Street in 1842. Laurence was placed in charge and he produced ladies' skirting. There were now three parts to the Pullar family business – a main section specialising in weaving, a growing dyeing concern and a small factory making skirting.

Unlike gingham cloth manufacturing, dyeing continued to prosper, especially in 1845 with the spread of dancing academies and the popularity of assemblies. The advent of railways two years later opened the prospect of wider markets and John Pullar, who was now able to indulge his interest in politics, took his son, Robert, into partnership in John Pullar and Son, Silk Dyers in 1848. With a flair for advertising Robert Pullar soon had a string of agencies stretching across Central Scotland. He also abandoned dyeing on the hank and concentrated on garment clothing. His great chance came in 1851 when the railways introduced a cheap parcel post rate and the London market opened up for the first time with the promise of enormous profits.

Although the Great Exhibition of 1851 was a disappointment for the Pullars, their expertise earned them a Royal Warrant from Victoria in 1852. Machinery was now installed in the dye-works and the work-force increased rapidly. Despite the fact that the findings of W.H. Perkin were not fully exploited in Perth, Robert Pullar had coped with the legislative changes of the Bleaching and Dyeworks Bill in 1856 and had captured the rail day-tripper trade. With an upsurge in working class custom he was able to contemplate a decade of expansion. In the meantime John Pullar stuck grimly to his commitment to weaving by purchasing the Keirfield Bleachworks at Bridge of Allan and placing his second son, John Pullar, junior, in charge. There were now four separate segments in the family business.

This soon changed. The Commercial Crisis of 1857 persuaded John Pullar to buy out his brother's interest in Robert Pullar and Sons and close down all weaving in Mill Street. With space now available the old dye-works was systematically converted into a modern factory. Large numbers of sewing-machines were acquired from abroad and the finishing departments enlarged. Royal events, whether funerals or weddings, provided opportunities to make large profits which went into plant investment. John Pullar even bought a small mill up river from Keirfield at a place called Ashfield, while his brother, Laurence, completed his new Balhousie Works in the Dunkeld Road, Perth.

The North British Dye Works, Perth, with James Ferguson Pullar as the latest partner, now introduced dry-cleaning. Foreign dyers came to Perth to impart their secrets, while the work-force enjoyed elaborate soirées. John Pullar, confident that his factory was in safe hands, offered himself as Lord Provost, a post which he held for six years till 1873. During this period he made a name for himself as the champion of urban re-development and a crusader against the evils of drink. Meanwhile, Robert Pullar had granted Saturday afternoons as time off for women and youths and reduced the working week to 51 hours in 1873. Laurence Pullar, at the same time, merged with Andrew Coates to form Messrs. Coates, Pullar and Company, Jute Spinners and Weavers, Perth.

The 1870's was the decade when the social life of the workers in the North British Dye Works bloomed with all kinds of clubs, suppers and entertainment. Electricity and telephones had increased efficiency and the workforce knew that they toiled in the safest environment in the city. Even the death of John Pullar in 1878 did not disturb the rhythm of production. New ideas continued to be absorbed by the management, ideas from the U.S.A. and from Germany. Trade was excellent and the profits were reflected in the splendid mansions which served as homes for the Pullar family. With the purchase of the Tulloch estate in 1882 the danger of a benzolene explosion subsided, much to the relief of the citizens of Perth. Soon there were Receiving Offices from Belfast to Brighton and from Dublin to Newcastle. London especially became the target for cut-price sales drives so essential in such a competitive area.

As the century drew to a close anti-German feeling increased with the realisation of Germany's dyeing monopoly. In Perth labour unrest intensified as trade unions made desperate attempts to secure a foothold in the city. Robert Pullar, plagued by overtime problems, successfully re-united warring Liberal groups and won the city back from the Tories. With his son, R.D. Pullar, a partner, he had the pleasure of being knighted by Victoria. With his second son, A.E. Pullar, and nephew, H.S. Pullar, also accepted as partners, Sir Robert and his wife went off to London to enjoy the delights of the Season.

The 20th century saw the North British Dye Works with a workforce of 2,600. Hot-air drying had replaced steam and vans had replaced horses. The name of John Pullar and Sons, Dyers and Cleaners, Perth was now as well known in London as in Scotland. Business, therefore, was flourishing, although there were signs, as early as 1903, that two southern rivals, Eastman and Sons and Johnson Brothers were undercutting their prices and winning their customers. Sir Robert seemed oblivious to the danger. The death of his wife left him subdued and apathetic as was shown by his clumsy handling of wage protests in 1907. Despite this he went off to London to serve as M.P. for the City of Perth at the age of 80.

Executive authority now lay squarely in the hands of R.D. Pullar and he quickly adopted the most modern ideas - holidays with pay and a 45 hour week. But a sudden upsurge in the cost of living 1909 - 1911 and the spread of militancy made his female employees restless and dissatisfied. Poor trading results meant that he could not meet their demands and he made the firm a Joint Stock Company. At that very moment the Dyers' Union decided to challenge the management on a series of issues ranging from opposition to the length of apprenticeships to the needs for an established wage-scale. The effect of the 1911 National Insurance Act and the rail disruption caused by the 1912 miner/railway strike made R.D. Pullar make disastrous errors of judgement, which were made worse by the deaths of Sir Robert and J.F. Pullar.

With their departure Pullar influence in the city declined almost overnight. H.S. Pullar resigned and even the award of a wage scale to the workers could not quell the unrest. With shop stewards demanding a National Minimum Wage and Suffragettes seeking recognition and equal pay, all that R.D. Pullar could think to do was to dismiss trade union activists. The outbreak of the 1914 - 1918 War worsened the situation. Patriotism soon wilted under a slump in trade, a shortage of dyes and coal, short-time and finally conscription. Living costs soared in 1917 and R.D. Pullar foolishly rejected the War Wages Scheme. Confrontation with the Dyers' Union was now inevitable. While R.D. Pullar journeyed to London desperately seeking a solution the North British Dye Works was besieged by a mob of 2,000. Management called in the Mounted Police and the "Battle of the Gates" was the result. For R.D. Pullar the strain was too much and he died suddenly in September, 1917. As the violence subsided the Duke of Atholl chaired arbitration talks and for a while closure seemed likely. Fortunately for Perth the works came under new management, Eastman and Sons, and the long involvement between the Pullars and dyeing in the city was over. Only the name - John Pullar and Sons, Dyers and Cleaners - was to survive.

All of these issues are probed in depth in this work. Since, however, dyeing and cleaning formed the basis of the Pullar empire, it is necessary to place the firm's development in perspective by examining in broader outline the salient characteristics of the dyeing industry itself.

Footnotes

1. *PC* 3/11/1897, 12/4/1822, 29/10/1829; *PA* 24/1/1833; *PC* 19/5/1853, 8/4/1902, 16/6/1903; *PA* 19/9/1916
2. *C* 22/4/1918
3. *PC* 8/4/1918
4. *C* 22/4/1918
5. *PC* 1/10/1889
6. *C* 28/4/1930
7. *PC* 26/6/1928
8. Ibid., 29/10/1829; *"The Growth of the British Cotton Trade 1780 - 1815"*, Michael M. Edwards, Manchester University Press, 1967, pp.2, 7
9. *C* 17/4/1918
10. *"Perth, Its Weavers and Weaving"*, Peter Baxter, T. Hunter, Perth, 1936, p.96
11. Edwards, M.M., p. 129
12. Ibid., pp. 9-11
13. Ibid., p. 35
14. Ibid., pp. 29, 32
15. *PA* 19/12/1878
16. *LS* 30
17. Ibid., 41
18. *C* 3/11/1898
19. *PA* 13/9/1877
20. *PC* 11/12/1809, 21/5/1809, 7/6/1810, 1/12/1814, 24/11/1814
21. Ibid., 30/11/1809, 24/7/1809, 11/1/1810, 15/2/1810
22. Ibid., 20/4/1810
23. Ibid., 12/10/1809, 12/7/1810
24. Edwards, M.M., pp. 22, 107
25. Ibid., p. 23
26. "Marketing Organisation and Policy in the Cotton Trade: McConnel and Kennedy of Manchester 1795 - 1835", C.H. Lee, *B.H.*, Vol. X, 1968, pp. 90-92
27. Edwards, M.M., p. 17
28. Ibid., p. 18
29. *PC* 19/5/1853
30. Edwards, M.M., p. 19
31. *PC* 12/7/1810
32. Ibid., 21/7/1814; *PA* 24/1/1833
33. *PC* 10/6/1813, 9/9/1812, 21/2/1814, 31/4/1814, 11/11/1813
34. Ibid., 9/6/1814, 11/3/1825, 25/11/1813, 14/1/1813, 3/2/1814, 7/3/1814, 9/3/1815, 30/11/1815
35. Ibid., 26/3/1810
36. Ibid., 1/10/1812, 14/1/1813
37. Ibid., 2/3/1815, 22/2/1816
38. Ibid., 9/2/1815
39. *LS* 31
40. Ibid., 32
41. *PC* 14/4/1814
42. Ibid., 7/4/1814, 19/5/1814, 24/11/1814
43. One such was Sandie Robertson, a devotee of "the fair divide." This was a simple philosophy: all wealth should be pooled and divided. When Robert Pullar explained that within a week there would be inequalities again, Sandie would reply: "Ah, but we would hae a fresh divide every Saitterday aifternun." After years of wrangling with such men Pullar would say, "Had Moses been called on to lead the weavers of Perth, instead of the Children of Isreal, through the Wilderness, he would have found them a far more factious lot! (*LS* 33)
44. *PC* 20/6/1816
45. Ibid., 10/10/1816
46. Ibid., 8/5/1817
47. Lee, C.H., p. 92
48. *PC* 23/3/1815, 18/2/1818
49. Lee, C.H., p. 91
50. *C* 3/11/1897
51. "The Decline of the Scottish Cotton Industry 1860 - 1914", A.J. Robertson, *B.H.*, Vol. XII, 1970, p. 117
52. *PC* 6/5/1819, 13/5/1819
53. Ibid., 13.1/1820
54. Ibid., 7/10/1819, 15/11/1822, 3/5/1822, 30/12/1819, 13/1/1820
55. Ibid., 1/6/1815, 17/10/1816, 24/9/1918
56. Ibid., 15/1/1818
57. Ibid., 11/5/1815
58. Ibid., 2/1/1817
59. *LS* 10; *PA* 27/10/1905
60. *PC* 25/9/1917
61. Ibid., 30/3/1886
62. Ibid., 14/6/1822, 31/10/1823
63. Ibid., 18/10/1821, 31/5/1822, 3/1/1823
64. Ibid., 4/5/1820
65. Ibid., 31/5/1822
66. Ibid., 23/8/1822
67. Ibid., 7/3/1823
68. Ibid., 25/9/1917; LS 37
69. See Chapter IV for the subsequent weaving side of the business in detail.
70. For the remainder of this chapter footnotes are omitted. These may be found in the appropriate, succeeding chapters.

Chapter II
Dyeing Techniques and Management

*"I shall heal and conceal all the parts and properties of
Dyeing that hath been or shall be made known to me."*
- The Dyer's Obligation, 1711

Of all the trades practised in Scotland over the centuries, dyeing is the
least known. Operating only in small units[1] and thus unorganised each
dyer contrived to surround his craft with a veil of mystery, and rarely, if
ever, committed his secrets to paper. Instead, they were passed on
verbally, on payment of a fee, from master-dyer to journeyman to
apprentice, each in his turn jealously guarding the key to his livelihood.
Over the years these dyeing techniques hardly changed and a 13th
century dyer would have felt at home in a 19th century dye-house, apart
from a few strange materials. Hence the simple equipment - tables, baths,
hooks and rakes.[2] Even at the beginning of the 19th century there were
no machines and the most expensive capital outlay for any dyer would
have been on the common dyes of the period - indigo (a blue dye from the
stalk of the indigo plant), madder (a red dye from a plant root) and
logwood (a dark-red dye from a Mexican tree), [3] which could be purchased
in Scotland. More important to the dyer was ready access to pure water
and the keeness of his own eye for a subtle shade.[4]

By the 1820's therefore a skilled dyer would be expected to dye, clean
and press a variety of materials: crapes (a thin, silk fabric, tightly twisted
and dyed for mournings), silks, velvets, poplins (a kind of cloth consisting
of a warp of silk and a web of worsted, with the latter being thicker to give
it a corded appearance), bombazeens (a twilled or corded fabric of silk and
worsted, or cotton and worsted), shawls, scarfs, chip-hats (a cheap hat of
Brazilian grass leaves of a Cuban palm), straw-hats, leghorn hats (fine
hats plaited in Tuscany), furniture(household goods), crumb cloths (a
cloth laid under a table to save the carpet from falling crumbs), carpets,
hearth-rugs, ladies' pelisses (cloaks with sleeves, usually silk) and
gentlemen's clothes. Apart from these there was much dyeing of silk and
worsted on the hank. The "most approved principles" of the time meant
following the recipes of the French dyer, Berthollet, and as blue and black

Dyeing Silk Yarn (National Dyes and Home Dyeing, R.J. Adrosko, New York, 1971)

were the most popular colours in 1825 these would involve the following -

"To dye silk blue:
Boil with soap and beetle at least twice; immerse in running water and then dip in a vat of indigo to which urine has been added and dry as quickly as possible.
"To dye silk black:
Boil the silk for 5 hours with soap; beetle and wash thoroughly; boil with gall-nuts and then scour well for 2 hours; add the dye in a solution of iron, vinegar and small beer; leave for 36 hours and then wash in running water."[5]

Madder has a well-known "strong disagreeable odour" and was used with huge quantities of urine, glue and sheep dung.[6] For instance, to obtain turkey Red on cotton the dyer had to steep sheep dung in a large vessel, pound it with a paste and then pass it through a hair sieve into a vat.[7] Not surprisingly, dye-houses had a deservedly bad reputation and were often the target for law-suits, especially when drinking supplies were polluted.[8] Hence most dyers were anxious to locate their premises as far as possible from householders and use large vats, tubs and stills, which were not expensive.[9]

By the end of the 1820's most dyers could handle satins, sarsnets (a thin tissue of fine silk used for ladies' dresses and linings), ribbons, stockings, gloves, table covers and bed and window curtains.[10] Dyeing on the hank had also been extended to include cotton and linen yarns. Of course, cleaning was by then receiving a greater emphasis as was the time taken to process goods. This was essential if dyers were to meet the public's demand for the latest colours and shades for display at the popular dancing academies and assemblies of the period.[11]

In 1830 chemical processes which gave fabrics "a glossy appearance" became generally available[12] and soon proved fashionable. Hotpressing was developed about the same time as was the capability of re-dyeing almost any fabric to any colour, even sheep-skins and basses (matting). Dyers also perfected techniques to renovate in situ the cloth, lace and leather interiors of carriages and gigs. Of course, pure water was still the real secret of good dyeing, but that sometimes cost the careless apprentice his life.[13]

Although most dye-works began to increase in size by the end of the 1830's the working environment had scarcely altered.[14] Certainly, there

Dyer c. 1836 (Adrosko)

Dye-house c. 1850 (PKDLA)

would be gas illumination and even a few furnaces, but these merely increased the risk of fire. Buckets of water and piles of sand would soon prove inadequate for many of them.[15] As for the dyers themselves, they were usually "dwarfish in build, hard and muscular."[16] Their labour was irregular, often slack, and then, suddenly, working continuously for spells of 3-4 days from 4 a.m. to 11 p.m., "in little light, less air and little or no space."[17] Wages for men ranged from 12/- to 16/- a week according to skill, while women finishers earned as little as 1/- a day.

With the 1840's came an increase in piece-dyeing (garments) and an extension of the range of materials which could be both dyed and cleaned:[18] merinoes (fine French ell-wool dress fabric for women), union cloths (textile fabrics made up of more than one fibre), moreens (stout woollen or cotton or woollen stuff for petticoats and curtains), damasks (figured stuff of linen, woven not printed), chintz (highly glazed printed calico with a pattern of several colours on a white ground), Cobourg (a thin fabric of worsted with cotton or silk twilled on one side), Orleans (wool and cotton cloth for dresses), delaine (an untwilled light dress material), bonnets, satinettes (cloth with a cotton warp and woollen weft), tartan, filled and printed shawls.

The Great Exhibition of 1851 stimulated the dyeing trade[19] and dyers developed techniques to cope with chair and sofa covers, mohair cloaks (fine silken hair of angora goats) and challie (fine fabric of silk and worsted for dresses). A dye-house in the 1850's therefore would usually have - boilers, casks, tubs, dressing-frames, presses, papers, indigo mills, fly-wheel ovens with plates and iron pumps.[20] Premium was now on space as machines began to appear, especially Padding Machines,[21] Wash or Dash Wheels[22] and Bucking Boilers[23] which were all used in piece-dyeing. Consequently accidents became a common feature of working life in a dye-house. Dyers' skills were now in great demand and many emigrated to improve their lot.[24] Those who remained had to master difficult techniques like dyeing "Self-Fitting Ventilator Hats"[25] or producing subtle combinations like sky-blue, yellow-red and violet-green.[26]

Dyers, as ever, were always worried about the purity of their water supplies and fearful of the danger of pollution.[27] If they could guarantee the former and avoid the latter there was always the chance of earning the dyers' accolade, a Royal Warrant, which let them be described as "Dyers and Cleaners to the Queen."[28] In an imperialistic age this carried enormous social prestige, particularly in London, and opened the door for a wide range of upper-class trade in plaids, shooting coats and evening wear.[29]

A

B

C

D

E

A. *Logwood-cutting machine - reduces blocks of logwood to usable chips.*
B. *Logwood sawdust dye tubs - logwood is soaked before put into dye-beck.*
C. *Mordanting: an alum cistern. At left center the unmordanted cloth is drawn into the cistern on the left, rolled overhead, drawn through a wringer, then stacked on the right.*
D. *Dye-beck (dye vat). A worker winds the cloth over and under a series of rollers, keeping the cloth moving continuously through the dyebath to promote even dyeing.*
E. *Water extractor on the right, finished cloth being rolled on the left.*

Processes c. 1854 (Adrosko)

By then dyers could even change the colour of a material without unpicking the seams or even dye tartan checks black.

Working conditions changed for dyers in 1855 with the Factory Act (Bleaching and Dyeing).[30] Young children were banished from dye-houses and the excessive temperatures in drying-rooms were regulated. Although dyeing was regarded as "still in its infancy"[31] and had indeed scarcely changed over 200 years,[32] there were such things as recipe books.[33] David Smith's "Practical Dyer's Guide" and John Thomson's "The Practical Dyer's Assistant" had both been published in 1849. Although both relied on no more than 20 basic colouring matters, each could offer an enormous selection of shades.[34] Smith's Guide had 300 receipts or recipes - 20 for shot cobourgs, 20 for silk striped orleans, 48 for coloured orleans and 51 for merinoes; Thomson's Assistant had 150 receipts - 43 for silk, 58 for woollens and 32 for cottons.[35] Among the basic colouring matters were - alum, annotta, archil, argol, camwood, catechu, cochineal, chrome, cudbear, chemic, fustic, galls, indigo, kermes, logwood, madder, peachwood, prussian blue, quercitron bark, safflower, sumac and turmeric. Most dyers prepared their own materials: chipping and grinding the wood before placing it in extracting kettles and boiling under pressure and running it off as a liquid. Even nuts, berries and bark as well as plants were used and chemicals refined and diluted.[36] Not surprisingly, dye-works usually emitted foul-smelling "smoke nuisance."[37]

Just at the time when Scottish dyers were struggling to meet the 1856 post-Crimean War craze for scarlet petticoats,[38] aniline dyes made their appearance. W.H. Perkin of the Royal College of Chemistry, Oxford Street, London had been trying to produce quinine from coal tar, when he observed that the slimy, black residue he had been left with produced a beautiful tyrian purple when spirits of wine was added. Before long it was found that silk, soaked in a soap bath, could hold this new dye fast.[39] Cotton was more difficult. Alum was useless as a mordant and it finally required a combination of tannin and a metallic oxide. Thus, a new method of dyeing was created which "meant a revolution in the dyeing trade."[40] Unfortunately, many doubted its commercial value and it was left to Keith and Sons, Bethnal Green, London to develop aniline dyeing.[41]

After 1857 dyeing gave way to cleaning in most dye-works with the appearance of ready-made clothing.[42] This was essentially a working-class market and it saw a huge increase in the finishing side of the dyeing trade. Some of the mystery which had so long surrounded dyeing began to dissolve with the spread of greater knowledge through the newspapers and especially with the growth of Do-It-Yourself dye kit sales.[43] Black of course was still the most popular colour for all social events.

One of the most widely-used textbooks used by dyers in the mid 1850's was "The Art of Cleaning, Dyeing, Scouring and Finishing" by Thomas Love.[44] It suggested that dye-houses should be "as open as possible" and at least 16' by 25' by 7' with flagged paving-stones and good drains.[45] Of course, there had to be plenty of coppers and a big fire-place. "The supply of water for the use of the Dye-house is of the utmost importance to the master-dyer, it is the key to his success." It also recommended plenty of big cisterns at least 6' by 4½' by 6' capable of holding 2,000 gallons of water. They should be at least 3' off the floor and be made of bricks, flat tiles and cement and have pipes and water-cocks. Cisterns intended for the preparation of nitrate of iron for dyeing silk black should be 6' by 4' by 5' and able to hold 80 gallons; the old soap cistern should be 5' by 4' by 4'; cisterns for peachwood, fustic and logwood liquors, like the green liquor cisterns, should be made of slates; cisterns for dyeing puce, lavender and crimson should be made of earthenware to protect the quality of the colours. There should also be an ample supply of copper kettles, bowls, woodern frames, scouring boards, punching tubs, winches, stoves, cockles and cradles. The Drying Room should be at least 12' by 14' by 16' close to a good store of the very best coal. Not only does the book contain methods of cleaning and dyeing feathers and all types of bonnets, but there are suggestions for dry-cleaning carpets and curtains.[46] Another popular textbook was "A Manual of the Art of Dyeing" written by James Napier,[47] which was particularly good on mordants - Red Spirits, Barwood Spirits, Plumb Spirits, Yellow Spirits, Nitrate of Iron, Acetate of Iron, Acetate of Alumina and Acetate of Copper.

Although the Victorian addiction to "sombre colours" like black[48] and brown[49] continued into the 1860's it was possible to purchase a whole range of "aniline colours, both liquid and solid, comprising blues, oranges, greens, yellow, scarlet, crimson and violets."[50] In fact, dyers were fast giving way to chemists as an 1868 receipt list clearly indicates: Humbolt's Violet, Hofman's Violet, Perkin's Green, Bismarck Brown and Nicolson's Blue. Yet, all these were produced in dye-houses with the traditional basic materials - copper and iron boilers, screw presses with plates, watering machines, tubs, winces, barrows, traces, irons and poles.[51]

Change, however, was on the way as greater contact between dyers from different countries witnessed the exchange of secrets, especially in dry cleaning.[52] Wet cleaning with soap had been known for centuries, but grease and oil stains were impossible to remove. Turpentine and camphene had some success, but both were slow to apply and had a bad odour. This was unfortunate as garment-cleaning was now such an important part of the dyeing business. It was desperately tedious; seams had to be unpicked, the parts dipped in liquor, brushed, re-dipped, rubbed dry with cloths, hung in airing rooms to dry, resewed and pressed. Benzene[53] proved to be the answer. Then, c.1880 it was replaced by Benzine[54] and eventually White Sprits, Stoddary Solvents and Chlorinated Hydrocarbons. An Inventory of 1869 shows just how basic equipment still was : 3 marble tables, 3 zinc tables, 2 wooden tables, 1 small washing machine,[55] 1 large washing machine, 3 washing coppers with taps, 3 zinc backs for same, 3 large zinc settlers with taps, 5 large tubs lined with lead each with two taps, 3 stallages for hanging goods in, 3 copper bowls for brushers, 5 zinc cans for benzene, 2 tubs for soap washing with hot and cold water fittings, gas and lamp fittings, 2 benzene washing boards.

By this time successful dye-works were huge concerns in which staffs might well run into hundreds. Often their work had to be done after daylight had expired and although electricity began to be used for illumination, in some cases as early as 1866[56], most factories relied on gas throughout the 1870's[57]. Large factories required efficient internal communications and this was achieved by the arrival of the telephone in 1878.[58] Naturally most dyers were still deeply concerned about the danger of "spontaneous ignition" in their stores of cleansing materials.[59] This was a very real threat in any congested city area and elaborate precautions were always exercised to prevent explosions. A typical Cleansing Department therefore would be a brick building, at least 120' by 40', in which as many as 16 men would work with perhaps 12 tanks of benzolene, each 5' by 3'. Some dyers sought alternative methods of cleaning stubborn stains,[60] while others kept their fluids in underground locations.[61] The most responsible tried to keep their supplies outwith urban areas.[62]

Pollution of local streams and rivers virtually became a thing of the past with the widespread introduction of settling ponds, tanks and sieves,[63] in the 1880's. New drying arrangements became available by 1894 when hot-air replaced steam. Sturtevant heaters could charge the saturated air of a drying room no less than 15 times an hour and the wet fabrics suspended from the ceiling would soon have the freshness of items dried in the open air. Incandescent electric lamps had been developed by then and the drying process could be continued through the hours of darkness, especially as the system was automatically controlled.[64]

The dream of every master-dyer was to provide a work-environment that was entirely self-sufficient, which could offer every facility from the cold dyeing of leather to the manufacture of its own packaging. In such a concept the dye-works laboratory is central. Staffed, in the main, by qualified chemists a typical laboratory by 1880 could produce azoic dyes, by 1884 dye cotton direct in "a single union dyeing" and by 1896 even make synthetic indigo.[65] With garment-dyeing the bulk of their business - suits, dresses, gloves, muslins - dyers had to have access to even greater supplies of pure water. Accordingly, huge reservoirs began to appear by 1900.[66]

With the arrival of the 20th century improvements came fast and furious. In 1900 alone machines appeared which greatly reduced steam condensation in dye-houses, while Lancashire Boilers reached massive proportions.[67] From the U.S.A. and Switzerland came new washing machines which cleaned goods by pumping cleansing liquid through them in a spray. This meant that beetling (squeezing or rotating in soap suds) was greatly improved. There were even new machines which could replait skirts and frills after dyeing. Such machines, of course, encouraged more severe competition among firms to capture the increased trade generated by the death of Victoria in 1901 and the Coronation of Edward VII in 1902. Sadly, they also carried an even greater risk of accidents.[68]

By 1903 therefore a modern, well-equipped dye-works would have a wide range of steam engines, steam boilers, steam presses, sewing machines and an enormous range of new dyes. There would be electric motors and turbo-generators which were expensive to buy and almost as costly to run. Soon, motor-vans replaced horses[69] while hat-blocking appeared[70] with "a new Parisian system of dry-cleaning."[71] Designed to reduce the loss of volatile spirits through evaporation the latter greatly reduced the risk of fire, much to the delight of the growing number of females now being employed in the various finishing trades. At the same time hours were continually being cut as master-dyers urged their apprentices to attend evening classes in chemistry to keep abreast with modern methods. That these were now very scientific can be seen from a list of cleaning agents in 1908: soap, soda, monopol, tebratol, petroleum, benzine, benzol and carbon-tetrachloride.[72] Although the introduction of Sunflower Washing Machines for gloves attracted a good deal of business in the Edwardian Age the bulk of the average dyer's work in 1909 was still with blinds, curtains, cretonnes, quilts, table covers, carpets, chintzes and even old tapestries.[73] Astonishingly, none of these large items required to have their hooks or rings removed before processing.[74]

1910 was a significant year for most dyers in that London was proving to be the most profitable market in the U.K., and a huge increase in the volume of business followed the death of Edward VII and the coronation of George V. However, there was another reason. More and more dyeing firms were forming themselves into Limited Liability Companies.[75]

Clearly a stage was approaching when only really large firms would be able to survive. Many tried to postpone the evil day by cutting costs, by devising a technique for the reuse of benzine[76] or by purchasing huge Tumbler Rotary Drying Machines[77] or enormous Super-heaters, which could cope with carpets of any size. Some wisely cut their cleaning costs on specific articles or bought the latest, but expensive, U.S. Super-heated Pressing Machines.

War brought a new dimension to dyeing. By October, 1914 both dyes and coal were in short supply[78] as thousands of skilled dyers flocked to the colours. Master-dyers, not to be outdone in their patriotism, gifted their motor-vans to the Army and their spare accommodation to the Red Cross. With fewer craftsmen in the dye-houses reluctant dyer-apprentices were badgered into evening classes. There, they tried to absorb the wisdom of the standard texts of the period: "The Practical Scourer and the Garment Dyer" by William T. Brannt, 1893; "Dyeing and Tissue-printing" by William Crookes, 1882; "Principles of Dyeing" by C.S. Fraps, 1903; "The Dyeing of Textile Fabrics" by J. Hummel, 1896; "Garment Dyeing and Cleaning" by H.G. Hurst, 1901 and "Silk Dyeing, Printing and Finishing", 1892, by the same author; "Of Dyeing as an Art" by William Morris, 1893; "Dyeing" by Antonio Sansone, 1888; "Dyeing and Bleaching" by T. Sime, 1877; "The Manual of Colours and Dye Wares" by J.W. Slater, 1882.[79] However, with the public unwilling to spend on dyeing or even cleaning, the 90 basic colours and shades which were usually in demand were reduced to 9.[80]

Eventually most master-dyers were forced to either join the National Dye Scheme[81] or to use their local herbs, mosses and trees.[82] A whole range of materials were used - birch, bracken, golden rod, gorse, ling, madder, ragwort and walnut.[83] Birch bark gave reddish-brown, but if mordanted with iron it gave purple. Bracken roots or young shoots had to be picked early in June to get a good yellow. If soaked for an hour in cold water and then brought slowly to the boil before simmering for two hours it produced "a good green" if applied to yellow wool previously mordanted with alum and cream of tartar. Broom was collected at the end of April and when mordanted with alum and cream of tartar gave "a bright yellow." With gorse, the bark, flowers and young shoots all gave yellow, as did heather. Indeed, dyers soon found that they had to consult old recipe books to discover where to find particular colours: black, for instance, was the product of meadow sweet collected in July or could also be obtained from docken root and alder bark; blue was found in elder and alum; dark-brown came from blueberries and dark galls; grey came from iris roots; red was found in tormentil; purple emerged from cup moss; yellow could be derived from bramble or bog myrtle; and green or brown could be made from whin bark and broom. Over and above all these, at least 50 lichens gave dyes from which to choose - 14 yellow, 10 red, 9 brown, 9 green and 7 purple.[84] This was entirely due to the many dye-workers who spent their leisure hours scouring the countryside for the appropriate plants and trees.[85] Old tests - permanganate of soda, chloride of lime and puriatic acid - were abandoned for simpler criteria - "fast to soap, soda and 30 days' light."[86]

By 1917 most of the dyes being used to dye khaki came directly from the U.S.A.[87] The remainder were either bought in Switzerland or captured from the Germans.[88] Costs rocketed although most dye-workers, like the general public, believed that master-dyers were making vast profits. Price - levels in 1917 were far higher than those of 1914: Belladonna from 1/6d to 9/-; Atropine 23/- to 40/-; Carbonate of Guaicol 7/- to 190/-; Camphor 2/6d to 6/-; Cream of Tartar 1/- to 3/-; Quinine 1/- to 4/-; Cod-liver Oil 75/- to 500/-; Glycerine £100 to £500; Bromide of Potash 1/6d to 6/6d; Permanganate of Potash 5d to 16/-; Aspirin 2/- to 25/-; Hydrouinone 2/- to 35/-; Acid Saliccylis 1/- to 20/-; Acetanilide 1/- to 7/-; Salol 1/10d to 47/-; Antipyrin 6/6d to 80/-; Pnenacetin 3/- to 120/-; Barbitone 20/- to 160/-; Raw Cotton 5d to 1/7d.[89] With such price-rises and the cessation of social entertaining, the War imposed an enormous strain on dyeing techniques.

Of the thousands of dyeing firms founded throughout the U.K. in the 19th century only a handful survived into the following century. They did so, not by luck, but by good and effective management, which enabled them to outmanoeuvre their competitors, to take advantage of opportunities and to keep abreast with the latest developments in their industry. The survivors then were very large firms with hundreds of employees and thousands of pounds' worth of equipment handling millions of items over the year. The transition from an obscure work-shop in a back-alley to an enormous dye-works with an international reputation required a compliant workforce, continuous profitability and a watchful eye on costs.

In the successful family firms of the 19th century, irrespective of whatsoever trade or industry, paternalism was the order of the day. Given the small size of these firms it could hardly be otherwise. Indeed, paternalism was the natural by-product of an intimate working environment which only changed slowly over the decades. It was particularly noticeable in dyeing. Master-dyers worked side-by-side with their employees whom they had to select with great care. The quality most sought after was loyalty to the firm, not to reveal work-secrets to others. This was closely followed by an ability to work hard, accept discipline and be honest and trustworthy. Not surprisingly, over the years, master-dyers began to regard their fellow-workers as almost family.

The greatest threat to 19th century work-efficiency of course was that offered by drink. The wise employer simply did not employ men addicted to drink and if any fell by the way there was always dismissal. There was also the possibility of encouraging them to drink tea as a substitute.[90] Not that temperance alone was a permanent solution. Indeed, many employers in the 1880's found that free Saturday night entertainment concert halls for their workers and their families was the best counter-attraction to the pub.[91] Paying the work-force only once a fortnight was another widely practiced trick.[92] It certainly guaranteed at least one week's sobriety.[93]

However paternalistic a 19th century employer may have been he was always in favour of long hours.[94] This was especially so in the dyeing trade in which the hours were irregular and unpredictable. Throughout the 19th century legislation had slowly forced reductions in the working day for all workers,[95] but things like tea-breaks and their length were matters left to the employers' generosity.[96] It was the same with wages. Although generally static throughout the century, most employers liked to boast that they were "liberal" in their remuneration,[97] even though "general rises" were uncommon.[98] Other methods of payment were tried, especially in the early 20th century, such as premiums for better or faster work,[99] but these were never popular and even roused resentment.[100] Even more disliked by workers was having to rely on "the master's goodwill" for any pay increment. Hence the repeated requests at the end of the century for wage scales.[101]

Paternalistic employers felt offended by such requests and responded by pointing out that they had a policy of "all promotions from the shop-floor."[102] They also stressed the value of job-security, especially if accompanied by promises of no wage-cuts,[103] even in difficult years.[104] Giving job-preferences to workers' children was another common policy.[105] Other perquisities offered were tied houses[106] and long-term pensions.[107] Then there were the apprentice-training schemes. Master-dyers took a great interest in their younger employees and tried repeatedly, often unsuccessfully,[108] to get them to attend evening classes in dyeing and chemistry. Some even purchased text-books for them or sent the most promising students off to college with all expenses paid.[109] Even mature journeymen, if very highly skilled, were sent off on courses to various continental centres,[110] or even visits to international exhibitions.[111]

Good employers tried hard to make safety at work their greatest priority. In dyeing this became the crucial issue after the 1850's and the introduction of big machines.[112] The great danger in every dyeing establishment, of course, was that of a benzine explosion. Yet, not all employers took sufficient fire-precautions.[113] Indeed, some did not even bother to have their premises adequately insured.[114] Thoughtful employers encouraged Sick and Funeral Societies by subsidies[115] and made arrangements with local hospitals for private beds for their staff.[116]

Paternalism reached a peak when employers insisted on lecturing their workers on how they should spend their limited leisure hours. Master-dyers were anxious that their employees spend as much time as possible in the open air preferably pursuing a vigorous sport. Hence their encouragement of "bathing for health"[117] as well as rowing[118] and cricket.[119] Quite a few of them subsidised swimming, football and angling teams for competitions.[120] Participation in events organised by the firm was not only expected, but demanded - excursions,[121] Departmental Suppers and Christmas Parties.[122] Such firms organised holidays on a sensible basis[123] and laid on Workers' Rest Rooms with all facilities and administered by workers' committees.[124]

Employers responsive to social change knew that they had to accept the special needs of women and they began to find a place in promoted posts[125] or in their particular interests.[126] but many employers felt uncomfortable in dealing with them.

Although paternalism is an anathema in modern society most 19th century workers welcomed it because it gave them a feeling of security.[128] These were men and women who had no other option but to spend their entire working life with one firm and they were quite happy to shelter under the patronage of their employer and develop a pride in their place of work.[129] They steadfastly refused to join any trade union[130] and looked to their master for guidance on almost every aspect of their existence. The firm was the centre of their lives and they had few friends outwith the circle of their workmates. That many shared this outlook is demonstrated by the large numbers of applicants who were eager to join them.[131]

Continuous profitability was another essential requirement for success. Although survival is the best evidence of its existence, growth must surely be another. Indeed, throughout the 19th century, as now, big firms tended to survive, small firms tended to perish.[132] Yet, no firm, whatever its size, can establish profitability without good organisation, although it is axiomatic that the larger the business the more difficulty there is in accomplishing it.[133]

Astute 19th century employers, especially master-dyers, were quick to see the value of advertising.[134] Reputation, both at home and abroad, was essential.[135] Hence the emphasis on parades and works bands.[136] Demonstrating patriotism never went amiss[137] nor did a policy of concentrating on London as the principal market.[138] Never falling foul of the law was absolutely vital as social reformers were ever on the look-out for examples of exploitation.[139] Then there was the need to make full use of the Post Office[140] and other methods of communications.[141]

Foresight, more than any other attribute, guaranteed profitability.[142] Whether it was changing direction at a crucial moment[143] or being sensitive to new ideas[144] profitability came from giving the public exactly what it wanted and quicker than any other competitor could.[145] Maintaining a consistent management policy[146] and keeping abreast with the latest developments in Science and Technology[147] were the most sensible maxims. Just as important as encouraging workers to save[148] of course was the investment strategy of every employer.[149]

Master-dyers were always aware of costs. Indeed, in the early days their expenditure was almost entirely devoted to the purchase of dyes, some of which could be quite expensive. By the mid-19th century the advent of big machines drastically altered the industry's pattern of costs.[150] A decade later most firms sought to expand and huge sums were lavished on the acquisition of land,[151] the construction of imposing premises,[152] and the maintenance and replacement of machinery.[153] As the century neared an end costs rose again with the development of telephone communication[154] and the switch to electric power.[155] The introduction of any new process required a vast outlay.[156] Unavoidable costs on new dyes, laboratory facilities, workers' amenities, fuel, transport, packaging, insurance, fire-fighting equipment continued to mount after 1900.[157] All it needed was the outbreak of War with its dye and coal shortages, short-time working and strikes, requisition of vans and horses by the Army, loss of skilled craftsmen to the colours, premises turned into military billets and the abrupt ending of most of the trade because of public apathy, to play havoc with any form of profitability and controlled cost expenditure.

It is against this unfolding backcloth that the growth of the Pullar enterprises must be set.

Footnotes

1. *LS* 34
2. Ibid., 10
3. *PC* 22/4/1830
4. *"Elements of Dyeing"*, C.L. and A.B. Bertholler, Vol. 1, London, 18-24, p. 26
5. Ibid., Vol. 2, pp. 70, 6-8, 17
6. "Essay on New Method of Bleaching", R. Kerr, Edinburgh, 1791, p. 217; Berthollet, Vol. 2, pp. 69, 112
7. Ibid., p. 123
8. The Lade was badly polluted in 1785 (*PC* 26/8/1928) and the Tay in 1814 (Ibid., 30/6/1814). On both occasions local dyers were blamed (Ibid., 8/1/1829, 22/1/1829, 12/2/1829).
9. *PC* 4/6/1829
10. Ibid., 12/6/1828
11. *LS* 36
12. *PC* 7/1/1830
13. Ibid., 13/10/1831
14. John Pullar increased his staff to 24 in 1838 (*PC* 8/6/1897). Thomas Nelson, dyer, who started work at that time reports that only six of them were actually dyers, the rest finished, sewed and repaired (Ibid., 7/7/1885).
15. The City Fire Brigade was late at Pullars' first fire 6 May, 1844 and this convinced John Pullar that he should buy the best fire-fighting equipment that he could afford. The Lade was unreliable because of droughts (*C* 15/9/1847) and spates (Ibid., 6/1/1848).
16. *PC* 31/3/1908
17. *PA* 27/6/1883
18. *PC* 20/4/1848
19. Ibid., 16/10/1851
20. *PA* 30/10/1851
21. Padding Machines were essentially frames with two rollers, either of wood with an axis of iron, or cast-iron covered in copper. By means of levers the upper roller was pressed against the lower roller, which revolved horizontally in a box containing the dye liquid. When dyed the cotton cloth was dried by hot stoves (Berthollet, Vol. 2, appendix).
22. Wash or Dash Wheels were divided into four compartments for holding garments. A stream of water flowed in through a circular slit and by rotating wheel the garments were dashed to and fro between the four partitions at a speed of 25 revs/minute for a 6' diameter wheel (Berthollet, Vol. 2, appendix).
23. Bucking Machines consisted of a fireplace, an iron boiler with a grated bottom surrounded by wooden crib, and a central iron pipe. When the alkaline ley was boiling briskly, its vapour, confined by the goods in the crib, pressed on the surface of the liquid and this forced some of the swill in a sudden stream from the top of the pipe. From here it spread over the surface of the goods and gradually percolated down through them. The alkaline ley would then cool and was reheated (Berthollet, Vol. 2, appendix).
24. *PC* 16/12/1852
25. Ibid., 12/5/1855
26. Ibid., 12/2/1852; *PA* 19/2/1852
27. *PC* 11/8/1853
28. *PA* 8/3/1924
29. *PC* 5/10/1854
30. *PA* 5/7/1855, 12/7/1855, 13/3/1856
31. *PC* 26/1/1901
32. Ibid., 3/4/1856; *"The Records of New Mills Cloth Manufactory 1681 -1703"*, edited W.R. Scott, S.H.S., 1905, p. xxi
33. Robert Pullar purchased these books in 1850.
34. *PC* 17/9/1918
35. James Moncrieff, who started as a dyer in 1852 and rose to be dye-house manager, used these receipts with his 60 dyers.
36. *PC* 7/7/1885
37. Ibid., 14/8/1856, 5/3/1861
38. Ibid., 17/1/1856
39. This was done in the Pullars' Laboratory (*PC* 17/9/1918).
40. *PA* 25/8/1917
41. "Perkin's work was not really developed in Perth (*C* 10/1/1930).
42. *PC* 8/4/1858
43. Ibid., 3/9/1861

Footnotes

44. *"The Art of Cleaning, Dyeing, Scouring and Finishing"*, Thomas Love, London, 1854. A copy was presented to the firm in 1855 by J.F. Pullar and it still survives. Heavily marked and worn it indicates constant use.

45. Ibid., pp. vii-xx

46. Ibid., pp. 227-240, 241-252, 255-274

47. *"A Manual of the Art of Dyeing"*, James Napier, Glasgow, 1853, pp. 230-234. This was also used by J.F. Pullar.

48. *PC* 5/3/1867

49. Ibid., 17/9/1867

50. Ibid., 28/1/1868

51. Ibid., 10/2/1867

52. Jean Baptiste Jolly of France is reputed to have discovered the process at the Jolly Belin Dye Works, Paris. He passed the secret on to Petitdider, who, in his turn, gave it to Wilhelm Spindler of Berlin of 1854. Robert Pullar is credited with being "Britain's First Dry Cleaner." (*The Glasgow Cleaner*, 6/4/1966)

53. Aeromatic hydrocarbon called benzol or phenyl hybride.

54. A mixture of liquid hydro-carbons of the paraffin series.

55. These were made by Summerscales of Keighley and were the very first dry-cleaning machines. By 1870 they were frequently modified by Pullars' own mechanics.

56. *C* 23/8/1880

57. *PC* 2/2/1871

58. *PA* 6/2/1879

59. *C* 18/10/1880

60. Ibid., 26/1/1893. Fuller's Earth.

61. P. and P. Campbell did this (*PA* 10/11/1881).

62. *LS* 41-42

63. *C* 14/7/1885

64. Ibid., 23/7/1894

65. *PC* 8/6/1897

66. Tulloch Reservoir, built in 1900, could hold 1,000,000 gallons (*C* 31/12/1900).

67. *C* 30/12/1901

68. The first fatality in the history of John Pullar and Sons occurred at a Dolly Blanket Machine in 1902 (*PA* 24/2/1902).

69. *C* 1/1/1906

70. *PC* 22/5/1906

71. *PA* 22/12/1906

72. *PC* 10/11/1908

73. *C* 4/1/1909

74. Ibid., 21/12/1909

75. *"The History of J. Pullar and Sons Ltd.,"* G.H.C. Fisher, Perth, 1967 - 1976; *PA* 17/5/1911

76. *PA* 17/5/1911

77. Ibid., 29/4/1911

78. *C* 7/10/1914

79. R.D. Pullar provided his student-apprentices with these books.

80. *C* 12/7/1915

81. Ibid., 11/1/1915

82. Ibid., 1/2/1915

83. *"The Use of Vegetable Dyes"*, Violetta Thurston, Dryad Press, London, pp. 18-27

84. *Celtic Annual*, 1916

85. Workers from the North British Dye Works certainly did this (*PA* 17/5/1916), while R.D. Pullar personally investigated the possibility of "peat dyes from Stornoway" (*PA* 25/1/1916).

86. *C* 4/6/1917

87. Ibid., 21/5/1917

88. *PA* 1/3/1916

89. These figures were revealed by local chemist, J.J. Forbes, at a Rotary Club talk entitled "The Effect of the War on the Supply and Cost of Drugs" (*C* 2/7/1917).

90. John Pullar did this in 1839 when he started tea-breaks in his factory (*PC* 3/1/1839). It was a clever move in that the 1,000 members of Perth's Tea-Total Society became potential customers.

91. *PC* 18/2/1883, 3/1/1888

92. Ibid., 27/2/1872

93. The drink problem was never really resolved and was particularly bad in 1916.

94. John Pullar was against granting a 51 hour week to his staff in 1872 (*PC* 9/1/1872), and it was only under pressure from his son, Robert Pullar, that he finally relented (Ibid., 8/10/1872).

Footnotes

95. R.D. Pullar granted a 45 hour week in 1908 (*PC* 7/1/1908).

96. Tea-breaks were extended from 30 minutes to 45 minutes in December, 1888 (*C* 31/12/1888).

97. *PA* 26/4/1866

98. Robert Pullar granted this in October, 1872.

99. *C* 11/2/1907

100. The Dyers' Union made a point of stressing this in 1917.

101. Wage scales were granted by R.D. Pullar in 1913 (*C* 1/10/1913).

102. This was the policy at the North British Dye Works for section foreman and departmental managers (MS 51/5/5.14).

103. *PA* 1/1/1878

104. 1878 was "a difficult year" for dyeing, yet Robert Pullar refused to have wage-cuts.

105. This was the practics at Pullars in 1911.

106. *PA* 30/5/1865

107. Fisher

108. Pullars had an evening apprentice-training scheme as early as 1852 (*PC* 16/12/1852). By 1858 it was obvious that the apprentices resented the pressure to attend (*PA* 30/9/1858). It was the same in 1908 (*PC* 22/9/1908) and even more so in 1915 (*PA* 27/3/1915).

109. R.D. Pullar did both. His best apprentices were sent to Leeds Technical School (*C* 26/2/1883).

110. In 1867 Robert Pullar sent ment to Paris, Berlin, Lyons and Zurich to master the art of dry-cleaning (*C* 3/2/1930).

111. *PA* 18/7/1901

112. Pullar's record in this area is excellent - the first death occurring as late as 1902 (*PA* 24/2/1902).

113. Pullars had the finest fire-fighting equipment in the U.K. In August, 1866 they tested the famous "L'Extincteur" extinguisher in Perth (*PA* 9/8/1866), which were so efficient that the Town Council also bought them (*PC* 14/8/1866). By 1888 these machines were replaced by Imperial Fire Extinguishers (*PC* 10/7/1888) and by 1894 there were "fire hydrants all over the building" (*C* 23/7/1894). So well-trained were the firm's two fire teams of 14 men each, that they could get to any part of the plant and be operational within eight minutes (*PC* 10/11/1896). In 1896, under a policy of "constantly updating equipment", the firm bought a powerful Shand, Mason and Company No. 2 Double Vertical Engine (Ibid., 6/10/1896). Each fireman's house was linked by telephone to the firm's New Station, built in 1898 (*C* 21/9/1898). Both Kinnoull Street and Tulloch had thousands of feet of hose on reels and cradles, not to mention handpumps, horse-carts and ladders.

114. Pullars adopted a policy of insuring everything - premises and equipment as early as 1859 (*PC* 23/6/1859).

115. In 1882 the firm's Sick and Funeral Society had 289 subscribers; by 1888 there were 540c (*C* 21/3/1888).

116. Pullars did this in 1866 (*PC* 6/2/1866).

117. *PA* 29/1/1857

118. *C* 27/9/1866

119. Ibid., 27/12/1875

120. *PC* 31/1/1887

121. In 1886 some 2,000 workers and their families went off on a summer excursion (*C* 16/8/1886).

122. *C* 27/12/1875

123. Ibid., 27/12/1876

124. Pullars introduced the facility in Kinnoull Street in 1886 (*C* 10/10/1888) and at Tulloch in 1889 (*PC* 15/10/1889).

125. Fore women appeared in Pullars in 1868 (*PC* 3/3/1868) and were quite numerous by 1896 (MS 51/5/5.14).

126. A Female Cycling Club operated at Pullars in 1893.

127. *C* 13/3/1907

128. Such workers in Pullars were Thomas Nelson, who started in 1838, received the firm's first 50-year award in 1888 and retired in 1898; Thomas Moncrieff, who started in 1852 at 16 and retired as dye-house manager in 1889; Peter Smeaton, who started in 1864 at 14 and retired in 1914; James Paterson, who started in 1867 and retired in 1931 after

Footnotes

64 years; Duncan Forbes, who toured Europe with Robert Pullar in 1883 and 1890.

129. There were other reasons. Employees of John Pullar and Sons had no difficulty in obtaining either credit or accommodation in Perth in the 19th century.

130. Even in the dramatic events of 1917 the majority of the workers refused to join the Dyers' Union because they knew that R.D. Pullar and his family would disapprove.

131. Duncan Prentice, for instance, who applied for a post at the North British Dye Works in 1893 had 14 years' service with the Co-operative Bakery (*C* 1/3/ 1893).

132. John Pullar and Sons shows this to be true. In 1866 there were 500 employees (*C* 27/12/1866); in 1868 there were 600 (*PC* 7/1/1868); in 1888 there were 1,600 of whom 200 were dyers (Ibid., 16/3/ 1889); in 1897 some 1,900 (*C* 13/2/1897) and in 1899 no fewer than 2,400 (*PC* 21/ 9/1899).

133. In 1901 John Pullar and Sons had 24 departments (*C* 21/1/1901) and in 1907 added three more (*PA* 6/3/1907). In 1848 they had 8 agencies (Ibid., 30/8/1849) and 4,000 by 1903 (*C* 19/1/1903). Their organisation was "outstanding" with directors allocated different areas - Sales, Processing, Transport, Communications and Electricity. Manual workers responded automatically to a series of electric time whistles.

134. All the Pullars demonstrated a family flair for publicity, except J.F. Pullar, whether it was horse-drawn advertising vans in 1852 (*PC* 6/5/1852), a soirée in 1856 (Ibid., 10/1/1856), a Conversazione in 1868 (Ibid., 28/1/1868), or even handling prestigious orders like ancient tapestries in 1908 (*C* 4/1/1909).

135. Royal Warrants - 1852, 1903, 1913 - always enhanced a firm's reputation in the eyes of the public, as did elections to the presidency of the Society of Dyers and Colourists for professional rivals. Contact with foreign firms was always invaluable.

136. The North British Dye Works had frequent parades (*PC* 8/8/1882) and the Works Band gave concerts in Dundee (*C* 2/3/1881).

137. All royal events were celebrated, usually with well publicised day-closures with pay for the staff.

138. By 1883 there were three offices in London (*C* 28/12/1885). The HQ at Tottenham Court Road had a dining-room, a loading bay 80' by 40', stables, sheds and a glass verandah with granite pillars. By 1897 it was linked to Perth by telephone. To meet increasing local competition in London it replaced its horses with motor vans. A move which helped the 1910 rise in trade with London.

139. Pullars was never charged by H.M.I.F. for breach of any Factory Act. Indeed, they had nothing but praise from Dr. Absolon, Royal Commissioner on Factories (*C* 19/4/1876). Neither did the River Pollution Commissioners ever find it fault with them (*PC* 20/9/1870).

140. Pullars always kept a watchful eye on parcel post regulation changes.

141. The Pullar family certainly took advantage of railways in 1847, telegraph in 1868 and telephones in 1894.

142. Robert Pullar demonstrated foresight by buying land for development in 1851, urging the use of cheap gas power in 1871, apperciating the challenge presented by laundries in 1895 and the potential of the "horseless carriages" of 1895.

143. Changing from dyeing yarn on the hank to cleaning was a major change for John Pullar and Sons as was the move to piece dyeing in 1846 and to ready-made clothing in 1857 which opened up the working-class market.

144. Robert Pullar, in particular, reacted quickly to new ideas - the Great Exhibition 1851, the "passing trade" 1853, the potential of Perkin's work 1856, dry-cleaning 1866 and contacts with Berlin in 1890 and 1901.

Footnotes

145. Pullars had done this from its early days, offering cleaning as early as 1828 together with an enormous range of colours and shades.

146. When R.D. Pullar took over from his father in 1904 he continued his father's managerial policy in every respect.

147. New Laboratories were installed in 1856 (*PC* 17/9/1918) and in 1868 (Ibid., 7/7/1868).

148. R.D. Pullar continually harangued his staff on the need for "saving for a rainy day" (*C* 5/2/1908).

149. See Chapter IV for Pullar investment portfolios.

150. Big machines were installed c.1851 - 1852, but were continually replaced as technology improved. The capital for such purchases seems to have been found in the excess profits of "boom years" like 1861.

151. Pullars swallowed up great tracts of inner Perth with the start of its Phase 1 expansion operation in 1859.

152. Not only did Robert Pullar construct a magnificent factory of great design and taste, but he had to overcome very difficult technical problems eg. building over the fast-flowing Lade.

153. Steam boilers were very costly to replace. For instance, those installed in 1865 were 20' by 6', but these were dwarfed by the three "monster boilers" of 1894 which were 30' by 7 $^{1/2}$'. In 1876 18 new furnaces were built; in 1900 Lancashire boilers were erected; in 1903 the 35,000 square yard plant had 18 steam engines, 18 steam boilers and 22 steam presses requiring an engineering force of 60 men; in 1907 high pressure boilers were ordered (MS 51/5/5.14).

154. An internal telephone system was introduced in 1878 and later much improved by the additon of Blake's Microphone Transmitters form the U.S.A. By 1885 there was a line to Dundee and by 1897 a line to London.

155. Electricity was in the dye-house by 1878; there was a Dynamo House at Tulloch 1888 running Arc and Incandescent Lamps; by 1897 the firm was spending £4,000 pa on electric power and by 1903 this had increased to £12,000 pa; by 1898 the factory was using Crompton, Gramme, Castle and Siemen Dynamos; in 1904 the firm bought 16 electric motors and another 11 in 1906; in 1906 one 300KW Parsons Turbo-Generator alone cost £2,800.

156. There were many occasions when the firm had to invest heavily in plant; in 1861 - 1862 the mass purchase of sewing-machines from the U.S.A.; in 1894 the new hot-air drying system with the construction of rooms 105' by 40'; in 1895 box-making machinery for packaging; in 1897 Globe typewriters for the clerical staff; in 1900 Wasing Machines from the U.S.A. and Switzerland; in 1906 the new dry-cleaning system which forced the complete revision of plant lay-out.

157. New dyes were very costly after 1903 as was the new Laboratory of 1905 staffed by fully qualified chemists; workers' houses were built in 1864 and a suburb developed at Tulloch in 1882; the 1886 Rest Room at Kinnoull Street cost £2,000 as did the one at Tulloch in 1889; in 1903 coal cost the company £12,000 pa; in 1905 the firm bought various types of vans - Milnes-Daimler, De Dion and Argyll for London, Glasgow, Leeds and Manchester; in 1915 Edison Electric vans were puchased aswell.

Chapter III
Development and Competition

"No business ever operated in isolation."
- T.C. Barker
"Business History and the Business Man",
B.H., Vol. 1, 1958, p. 17

Although there are oblique references to dyeing in Perth as far back as 1210, hard facts are elusive.[1] Even these are little better than scattered fragments, such as "John Tyrie of Busbie, dyer, in Perth, 1679."[2] What can be said, however, is that the dyers of Perth never achieved the status of an Incorporated Trade as had the Hammerman, Bakers, Glovers, Wrights, Shoemakers, Fleshers, Tailors and Weavers.[3]

They only begin to emerge from obscurity, at least in surviving records, in the 1790's with the agitation for Burgh Reform.[4] Dyers were particularly active under the leadership of David McLeish, "a man of unbending principle", who did much to help the poor.[5] By the early 19th century many shopkeepers were doing their own dyeing, even sophisticated dress-makers like Ann Murdoch, newly arrived from Edinburgh, who, in 1809, advertised her ability "to dye silk, muslin and hats; clean crapes, feathers, gauzes, dress laces and muslins."[6] Professional dyers had suffered as badly as any during and after the depression of 1810. For instance, Adam Ferguson, dyer, was forced to sell his premises in Canal Street to meet his obligations.[7] Bigger enterprises were also hard hit: Cromwell Park Printfield had to sell off its coppers and indigo vats in 1814.[8] Of course, there was always some brave entrepreneur willing to gamble on his skill and luck.

Such a man was Archibald Campbell, who, in 1814, formed a partnership with John Meek in a wool-dyeing establishment in Methven Street, near the open Lade.[9] Within months he had summoned Peter Campbell, a cottar from Strathtay and probably a kinsman, to be his neighbour in a ribbon and garment venture.[10] This apparently failed and Peter Campbell moved west to the Newrow where he opened "a small general dyeing and cleaning factory", later claimed to be "the first of its kind in Perth."[11] By 1819 he was back in Methven Street again with "a Silk Works on the banks of the Lade."[12] It was quite insignificant and did not even merit a

D

mention in the 1822 list of Perth dyers - "Braid and Miller, South Methven Street; Campbell, A., South Methven Street; Craigie, M., Castlegable; Harley, W., South Methven Street; McLeish, D., and Son, South Methven Street."[13] As can be seen Archibald Campbell was by then on his own, having just dissolved his partnership.[14] By far the biggest of these concerns was that of D. McLeish and Son, which was able to survive a disastrous fire in November, 1823 in which most of the stock was destroyed.[15] These were to prove formidable rivals over the next few years.

Robert Pullar had clearly long planned a dyeing career for his son. In 1816 John Pullar had left school at 13 and been apprenticed to dyer Peter Campbell in "the small dye-works in Methven Street."[16] A few years later, his grounding complete, he went to Glasgow "to work in various dye-works", one of which was McLean's Plantation Works.[17] Thereafter, he was off to London as "an improver in several houses there." Anxious to marry Mary Walker of Brahan, Ross-shire, he was only too happy to obey his father's summons to return to the town of Perth.[18] However, the two small rooms with an outside stair in Burt's Close was hardly a factory. Indeed, as the accompanying plan indicates it was little more than a workroom and shop. It was not convenient for the installation of equipment nor for ready access to the Lade. There was another hidden disadvantage. The terms of the ten-year lease from the landlord, Provost Morrison, stipulated that if the lease was abandoned at any time the rental for the whole period was immediately due. No doubt John Pullar never gave this clause a thought as he enthusiastically searched for men and materials. He was to learn a valuable lesson in the need to examine the small print in any contract.

As a working dyer himself and given his limited means John Pullar only needed two men. These he selected with infinite care - men of good character, willing to accept firm discipline and hard work and not addicted to drink. Even more important was their potential loyalty, a criterion that was to become paramount for the Pullars in the future. In return the men were guaranteed steady wages and secure employment. Of course, they had to be skilled dyers as well, "men who could judge shades."[19] Equipment was easier to find because it was so simple, just a few small tables, baths, hooks and rakes. There were no machines and thus little chance of serious accidents. The main capital outlay would be for dyes and these were probably bought from John Deas, dye agent in Perth, who specialised in indigo, madder and logwood.[20] As there were anything up to 25 dyestuff mills in Scotland at this time they were readily

Burt's Close (PKDLA)

available.[21] Finally, everything was ready.

On 23 February, 1824 John Pullar placed his first advertisement in the "Perth Courier."[22]

"New Dye Work
Burt's Close
129, High Street, or 19, Mill Street
J. Pullar respectfully intimates that he has commenced business in the above central situation, where he carries on the dyeing in all its branches.

Crapes, Silks, Velvets, Poplins and Bombazeens dyed and dressed on the most approved principles.

British and Foreign Shawls and Scarfs cleaned without injuring the most delicate colours.

Chip, Straw and Leghorn Hats dyed and dressed, Cloths dyed, and Furniture of all kinds cleaned and renewed; Crumb Cloths and all sorts of Carpeting and Hearth Rugs cleaned and renovated to look like new.

Ladies' Pelisses and Gentlemen's Clothes cleaned, re-dyed and dressed.

J.P. having been lately employed in some of the first Dye houses in London, as well as in Scotland, and having acquired considerable knowledge and experience in his business, he hopes, from the style in which he executes his work, together with strict attention and punctuality, to secure a share of public patronage."

It could not have been long before John Pullar realised that he had been over-optimistic in his expectations, in view of the wide range of services he had offered. Middle-class customers did not flock to his shop and as he later confessed, if it had not been for the contract to provide his father with yarn dyed on the hank, he would, almost certainly, have gone under.[23] It was a time when businesses collapsed almost daily[24] due to continual changes in fashion and John Pullar had to learn to respond quickly to them. For example, in 1825 the popular colours in Perth, as far as the ladies were concerned, were blue and black;[25] in 1826 carrick hats were all the rage, but in 1827 it was waterproof hats and leghorn bonnets.[26] Not surprisingly, John Pullar was often to remark in later life, "Growth was slow - very slow."[27] Still, the profit margin was enough to marry in 1826 and make a home in Burt's Close, near his place of business.

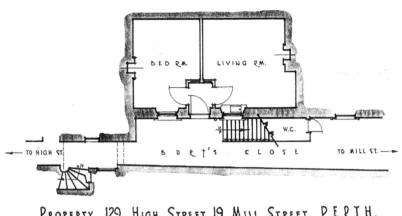

PROPERTY 129 HIGH STREET, 19 MILL STREET PERTH.

SCALE OF FEET.

129 High St (PKDLA)

The "fashionable dancing schools" that sprang up all over the town in 1827 and the students' frenzied desire to get "the latest colours" seemed to guarantee prosperity.[28] Then came a crisis. The residents in Burt's Close complained to the authorities that the dyeing premises were a "nuisance" and that they should be moved. No details of the ensuing lawsuit have survived except that it was long, bitter and expensive. John Pullar's livelihood was at stake and he fought hard to safeguard it, but to no avail. On 19 February, 1828 the very day after the birth of his first child, Robert, he lost his case and was served notice to quit.

John Pullar was suddenly faced with two problems - paying six years rent to Morrison and finding new accommodation. No doubt he turned to his father to help with both. He certainly had little money of his own and his later comments on his "modest means" at that time suggest that his father helped out. The second problem took at least three months to solve. Luckily, a piece of vacant ground "near the remains of the Black Friars Monastery" became available and here he set up his "very small works."[29] By all accounts the premises were bigger than those in Burt's Close and he probably had to buy more vats, tubs and stills, which were, in fact, cheap to buy at that time.[30] One enormous advantage of the move was being much nearer to the Lade, thus solving, for the moment, the problem of water. The only snag was the approach to the works. It was over the open Lade by "a narrow wooden bridge with green palings on both sides."

Finally, there was the matter of a new flat for his family which he found in Mill Street. Although John Pullar was viewed by his contemporaries as "shrewd, masterful and hard-working" he described this stage in his life as "uphill work which needed great attention and steady perseverance."

By June, 1828 John Pullar was settled in his new premises and he soon advertised the fact.[31]

> *"John Pullar*
>
> Grateful for the Patronage he has hitherto experienced, begs respectfully to intimate to his friends and the Public that he has now *Removed* his *Dye-Work* and shop to his new Premises *Mill Street,* opposite Cutlog Vennel, where he continues to *Clean* and *Dye* all kinds of Silk, Woollen and Cotton goods viz. Velvets, Satins, Sarsnets, Poplins, Canton Crapes, Bombazeens, Bombazetts, Shawls, Stockings and Gloves of all sorts; Blacks changed to other colours; Ribbons Dyed and Watered.
>
> *Ladies' Cloth Pelisses* and *Gentlemen's Apparel Renovated*, in so superior a manner as to look new. Bed and window curtains, table covers, crumb cloths, cleaned, redyed and pressed; carpets and hearthrugs cleaned; silk, cotton, woollen and linen yarn dyed any colour and shade.
>
> Orders from the country executed with the greatest punctuality and despatch."

Two changes of emphasis are obvious in this advertisement compared to that of 1824. Stress was now laid on cleaning and more attention was being paid to rural districts. This was a wise move in view of the increasing competition in the town. A new shop had appeared in St. John's Street and there Hugh Smith offered "to renovate clothes."[32] From Spittalfield in London to the same street came Hugh Small who even offered "starching and glazing facilities."[33] Fashions, of course, were as unpredictable as ever - in 1828, furs, exotic silk turbans, Gros de Naples and Baraige.[34] 1829 on the other hand, saw the "New Invented Hats."[35]

Although the bulk of the business was still dyeing on the hank for his father, John Pullar continually sought to offer a wider range of services to the public. For instance, his advertisement in January, 1830 contained the following[36] -

"Silk Dye Work

Ladies' and Gentlemen's Apparel Renovated in Mill Street, opposite Cutlog Vennel.

John Pullar

All kinds of Silk, Cotton, Woollen and Linen Goods Cleaned, Dyed and Dressed - velvets, satins, sarsnets, poplins, canton crapes, bombazeens, bombazetts, British and India shawls, gloves and stockings of all sorts.

Ribbons dyed and watered.

Gents' clothes Renovated in a very superior manner by a chemical process, which not only preserves the cloth from injury but greatly improves it, while it receives a new glossy appearance.

Ladies' cloth pelisses cleaned, dyed and hot-pressed in the best manner.

Table covers, crumb cloths, Bed and windon Curtains cleaned, redyed and pressed.

Carpets and rugs cleaned.

Sheep-skins dyed various colours for Rugs and Basses.

The cloth, lace and leather of the linings of carriages and gigs renovated to look like new, without being taken out.

Silk, cotton, woollen and linen yarns dyed every colour and shade."

This was a considerable advance on the 1828 offering - chemical processes to give a gloss, hot pressing, re-dyeing and carriage furnishings cleaned in situ.

It must have impressed rival Peter Campbell because he began to advertise as well his particular emphasis on his "Calendar and glaze."[37] Three of the other competitors tried a new tack - improving their social image in the community: Andrew Mills had himself appointed Water Commissioner[38] while James Braid became a Police Commissioner and a member of the Guildry.[39] The most successful was James McLeish - Captain of the High Constables,[40] member of the Town Council[41] and Commissioner for the Navigation Act.[42] Within a year he was also a Bailie and a Police Commissioner and making a name for himself with donations to the Infirmary.[43] The two other local dyers had not done well: W. Harley had disappeared and Robert Craigie had fallen out with the police.[44] Unfortunately, John Pullar was unable to compete; he had fallen sick with cholera in 1832, so sick, in fact, that he nearly died.[45] For a whole year he lay on a sickbed, nursed by his wife, while his father struggled to keep the dye-works viable. Ironically, despite the intense suffering of "Cholera Year", fashionable balls continued in the town and the demand for exciting new colours actually increased.[46]

As John Pullar slowly recovered from his near-fatal illness he seems to have decided to play a bigger part in local affairs. He must have assessed the free publicity given to his rivals as they competed for prestige. While trying to meet the 1833 craving for "fashionable yellows" and the 1834 insistence on the "New Invisible Green,"[47] he took time off to have himself elected Water Commissioner in November, 1834.[48] The lesson was not lost on Peter Campbell either. He also plunged into local politics and was soon Police Commissioner, then Guildry member and finally candidate for the Town Council.[49]

The sudden death of his father in 1835 interrupted John Pullar's rise in society and left him with a heavy responsibility. The weaving side of the family business would require all his attention and it seemed as if his working dyer days were over. Indeed, dyeing was now virtually neglected and no advertisements were issued for several years. It was the same with communal affairs, apart from the post of Water Commissioner, an office vital to his interests.[50] This must have been frustrating as his competitors continued their race for recognition in the town: James M Leish was now Dean of Guild[51] and James Braid was in the Town Council[52] although his premature death soon followed. The greatest, as far as dyeing was concerned, came from Archibald Campbell, who, despite a serious fire at his Mill Wynd Silk Works[53] was able to open new premises and make a bid for the town's funeral trade.[54]

It was not till 1838 that John Pullar revived his interest in dyeing. On one of his many trips to London[55] he discovered that English dyers were making a higher profit from dyeing cloth rather than yarn and he decided to do likewise.[56] No sooner had he increased his dye-works staff to 24 than he had a good piece of fortune due to a change of fashion. In July, 1840 it was found that umbrella cloth when woven white could be taken to a printfield and a printed border added which could then be dyed any colour without affecting the border pattern.[57] This resulted in a huge rush of orders and a steep rise in profits which enabled him to purchase furnaces. Unfortunately, these carried a fire-risk as John Pullar found out to his cost on 6 May, 1844.[58] Nonetheless, it was a profitable and satisfying period despite constant criticism from the "Perth Courier"[59] that the Tay was being polluted. Indeed, what may be described as "a second dyeing boom" took place in 1845 with the advent of new dances - La Polka and

La Valse à Deux Temps[60] and the rise of many new dancing schools[61] which created an enormous demand for new colours. It was this that convinced John Pullar to move to piece-dyeing ie garments and to extend further his activities in rural areas.

Of course, there was also a more practical reason - the emergence of what was to prove to be the greatest threat to the Pullar business interests, P. and P. Campbell, Dyers. Young Peter Campbell, born in 1824,[62] apprenticed to his father at 12, had learned his trade in London, Paris, Liverpool and Ireland. His dynamic energy was soon displayed in his advertisement[63] offering piece-dyeing through agents located at Crieff, Auchterarder, Dunning, Stanley, Bridge of Tilt, Blairgowrie, Errol, Newburgh, Auchtermuchty, Strathmiglo and Falkland as well as by his provision of tenements for his workers.[64] The other competitors were less of a challenge - Peacock, silk-dyer, Methven Street, whose firm was continually plagued by accidents;[65] James McGregor, High Street, whose expertise was limited to "fast dyed hats";[66] the Berlin Wool Establishment, George Street, which only "cleaned bonnets";[67] John Drysdale, dyer and local Radical leader, who spent most of his time organising demonstrations against the Corn Laws.[68] The only irritant was the "Hints to Readers" column in the "Perthshire Constitutional" which revealed some of dyeing's most closely guarded recipes every week.[69] Clearly, the anonymous contributor was a trained dyer.

For many years John Pullar had argued for a rail link to the port at Dundee[70] which would give Perth industries an opportunity to export their goods to a wider market. Its completion in May, 1847[71] was a triumph for his courage in facing up to the powerful river-harbour interests in the town. He soon extended his argument for a link to Edinburgh and the Fife and Lothian coalfields;[72] his view that cheap coal would be the main benefit soon won the day[73] and earned him a place in the Town Council in November, 1847. Although this guaranteed wider business contacts it meant less time in the dye-works. As might have been expected a notice soon appeared in the press[74] - "John Pullar begs to return his best thanks to his Customers, for their liberal support during the 25 years (1823) he has carried on business in Perth as a SILK DYER and to intimate that he has now taken into Partnership his Son, Robert Pullar, who has been his Assistant for several years bypast. He trusts that the arrangements now made will facilitate attention to the orders of employers, and that the Firm will enjoy the public patronage with which he himself has been so long favoured."

Born in 1828 and apprenticed to his father at 13 the twenty year old Robert Pullar had already spent seven years in the dyeing trade.[75] As far as his father was concerned his great strength was his vitality as a young man especially as the business was so small. In fact, its capital value in 1848 was only £500.[76] Like his father Robert Pullar was convinced that the future lay with the railways[77] and that they had to look beyond dependence upon local dancing academies for trade.[78] But first, he determined to widen their base of operations. Within a matter of months he had agents at Auchterarder, Dunkeld, Newburgh, Auchtermuchty, Coupar Angus, Alyth and Blairgowrie[79] Although he purchased machinery for winding yarn[80] in 1849 to please his father, it was not long before he persuaded him to give up yarn dyeing completely.[81]

Dyeworks 1850 (The Story of Pullars, 1837)

There were plenty of problems demanding attention: the continual loss of life in the Lade[82] the source of their water supply and even a serious drought in the summer of 1850.[83] There were also disappointments, one of which was the failure to win any awards in the Great Exhibition of 1851.[84] Still, in the wave of Exhibition fever that hit Perth[85] Robert Pullar used horse-drawn advertising vans to increase business[86] and encouraged his workers to take advantage of the subsidised rail fares to London.[87]

By some means or another his products were drawn to the attention of royalty and in 1852 he was awarded with the prestigious Royal Warrant - Dyer to Her Majesty the Queen.[88] However, it was the introduction of a cheaper parcel rate to London in March, 1851 that opened up a vast, potential market in the south.[89] Robert Pullar was quick to appreciate that a reduction from 3/6d a parcel to 1/9d would allow him a substantial profit if he could increase the volume of goods. So great was the increase that John Pullar had to resign from the Town Council[90] in order to assist with the paper-work. A whole range of new cleaning and dyeing machines were bought and installed in the dye-works.[91] This was a huge outlay in capital as well as carrying a high risk of accident.[92] The Pullars were well aware of this and their meticulous attention to safety procedures gave them the lowest accident rate in the city. Space had now become a matter of urgency and Robert Pullar tried to buy as much land as he could in and around Mill Street.

Naturally, staff had to be increased and by 1853 there were 80-100 employees, of whom 60 were actually dyers.[93] It was not long before they complained of long hours and the increased amount of work caused by "the passing trade from rail trippers."[94] This led to Robert Pullar offering them early closing at 7pm from 13 December, 1852 to 1 May, 1853.[95] With greater expansion came the problem of water supplies[96] and with the growth of emigration came the problem of losing key workers to the Colonies.[97] But, at that particular moment Robert Pullar was much more concerned with an "Advertising War" with P. and P. Campbell, his main rival in Perth.[98] With each issue of the local papers both firms waxed eloquently on their "improved methods and machines" and their "speedy delivery" and "careful workmanship."[99] Although this costly paper conflict lasted the whole of 1854 John Pullar and Sons clearly had the edge with the Royal Warrant. Nonetheless, it was a useful exercise in that the 1849 agent network was enlarged to include Dundee, Kinross and Milnathort. Significantly, all these were burghs on railway lines.

In mid-summer 1855 the newspapers were filled with criticisms of the dyeing industry.[100] Many felt that conditions were far too hot for overtime working with temperatures often 130° F in the drying rooms. They argued that 11 years rather than 8 years should be the minimum for children who worked and that night-work generally should be greatly reduced. Soon there was a Bill before Parliament to regulate "the labour of young persons under the age of 18 in dyeing."[101] Briefly the details were as follows - No children were to be employed after 1, February, 1856 and that females and young persons could only work from 6am to 6pm on weekdays and till 2pm Saturdays. Breakfast was to be 30 minutes and dinner 60 minutes. However, if meals lasted 2 hours then they might work to 6.30pm without notice to H.M.I.F. Any kind of "after-work" had to be entered in a book and under no circumstances should a female or young person work more than a 10 1/2 hour day or a 60 hours week. Many in Dundee opposed the Bill, especially bleachfield owners who claimed that their work was irregular and had to be done at speed even if it meant long hours for the workers because of the weather.[102] By early May, 1856 the Bill was printed and H.M.I.F. appointed.[103] It stated that after 1 November, 1856 "no child could be employed in any bleaching work in preparing, cleaning, scouring, bleaching, dyeing, calendering, finishing, mangling, dressing, embossing, tambouring any woven fabric, twist or yarn in packing, carrying or conveying or aiding in any other labour or process connected with bleaching, dyeing or finishing." Only in the home could children do such work, otherwise it was a penalty of £10 for each offence. This Bleaching and Dyeworks Bill aroused great agitation in Perth and 700 citizens petitioned their support.[104] The Pullars made it obvious that they too were in favour of the changes.

With the end of the "Advertising War" in March, 1855 John Pullar and Son, Dyers, Cleaners and Finishers continued their emphasis on "improved methods of Cleaning, Dyeing and Finishing with extensive business by machinery."[105] They aimed particularly at a fast turnover - "Our work being finished by Machines we are enabled to do it in much shorter time than usual."[106] This met with a great response and to celebrate the firm held its first soirée in January, 1856 in the Mill Street Dyeworks "decorated with laurel, evergreen, holly and coloured drapes" with 100 participants.[107] It was to prove to be a very successful year. Scarlet petticoats were all the rage in Scotland and were much flaunted at dancing schools and assemblies across the land.[108] The conclusion of the Crimean War brought a flurry of gaiety and a stampede for some new colour in which to celebrate.[109] Meanwhile, Robert Pullar was hard at work developing the parcel-post side of the business for the lucrative day-tripper trade.[110] Some statistics reveal its potential - in July, 1855 some 2,000 arrived in Perth from the Falkirk Iron Works;[111] in September, 1855 came 1,400 Lochgelly miners;[112] in May, 1856 appeared 700 Alloa miners;[113] while in August, 1856 Perth was visited by 1,600 Edinburgh and Leith bakers, 700 Airdrie miners and 600 Mearns farmworkers.[114] Then, in July, 1857 came a tidal wave - 6,000 day-trippers from Dundee.[115] Of course, rail traffic could work both ways and Edinburgh and London dyers sought to find markets in Perth. Gowans and Godlet of Edinburgh tried to capitalise on the popularity of black and offered to dye any material in that colour.[116] F. Smith, dyer, Mount Street, Grosvenor Square, London was a firm founded in 1818 which specialised in dyeing shawls, mantles and dresses.[117]

There were also the local competitors. Andrew Miller, despite his proud boast of being able "to capture any shade",[118] was more interested in organising a campaign against Roman Catholics. Peacock's Silk Works, South Street was still dogged by a series of unfortunate accidents[119] while Peacock and Imrie, Silk Printers, South Methven Street were crippled by a serious fire.[120] Another, Robert Craigie, dyer, Castlegable died in May, 1859.[121] Indeed, the only significant rival was still P. and P. Campbell, especially after Peter Campbell, Jnr., was made a partner in 1851.[122] Adding Dundee, Dunkeld, Auchterarder and Tayport to his agencies his aim was to dominate rural Perthshire and Fife.[123] He also began the development of a new dye-work site in the Dunkeld Road in 1852[124] and advertised his firm as Silk Dyers and Shawl Cleaners stressing quality work and low prices.[125] Although troubled with minor cistern explosions their expansion into the Glasgow area and their vigorous "Don't Fling Them Away!" advertising slogan was an ominous reminder of their challenge.[126]

Robert Pullar's willingness to examine new ideas was demonstrated in the summer of 1856 when he invited the young chemist, W.H. Perkin, to Perth to explore the possibility of developing his newly discovered aniline purple dye.[127] For several weeks they worked in the Pullar's Laboratory[128] and even visited calico printers in Glasgow to assess its commercial prospects. Unfortunately, the verdict was negative and Perkin turned elsewhere. Strangely, a myth grew that aniline dyes were first processed in Perth. This was not so.[129]

Of more immediate interest was the problem of "smoke nuisance."[130] In 1856, 1858 and 1861 there were dozens of complaints from Mill Street residents about the smoke and smell from the dye-works. Another headache was the reluctance of apprentice dyers to attend evening classes to study chemistry and the new field of synthetic dyes.[131] On the other hand, 1857 saw the end of weaving at Mill Street and the family's devotion to dyeing and cleaning. With the new trend in "ready-made clothing"[132] dyeing now appealed to working-class customers. Hence the premium put on space.

The opportunity to obtain more space came unexpectedly in June, 1859 when a fire at the corner of Mill Street - Kinnoull Street in an upholsterer's shop destroyed a school and Pullar's Old Weaving Shed.[133] The damage was estimated at £6,000, but Pullars was insured.[134] The site was rapidly cleared and the first phase of building expansion began.[135] The Town Council were not too happy about this and complained about pollution of the Lade[136] and the excessive use of Tay water by the firm.[137] The local Tory newspaper, the "Perthshire Constitutional" took up the matter and launched a "Filthy State of the Lade" campaign against John Pullar and Sons.[138] Not long after the Town Council sued John Shields, local manufacturer, for taking water from the Lade for his pumps.[139] John Pullar quickly rose to his defence by making the point that water should be free if it brought employment to the city. His own section of the Lade he always kept in "good repair."

The Lade continued to be a problem into 1861. It was an effective barrier to an integrated work-unit and John Pullar applied to the Town Council for permission to build over it.[140] Meanwhile Robert Pullar faced a distasteful situation - the large-scale theft of shawls, silk dresses and scarfs.[141] Fortunately, their discovery in various pawnbrokers and simple detective work led to the arrest of the culprits whose sole motivation had been to get money for drink. They were dismissed. More serious was the "DIY craze" that swept Perth in 1861.[142] A London firm, Judson and Sons, had made significant inroads into the city by selling bottles of dyes from 6d to 1/6d and many thought to take advantage of this offer. Another passion which gripped Perth in the same year was the Cheap Gas Movement by John Shields.[143] Mass meetings were held to demand a reduction in price and the excitement nearly spilled over into violence. Although equally anxious to benefit from cheaper fuel bills John Pullar was much less strident than other employers and advocated moderate tactics.

With the 1860's came a tremendous increase in the volume of business and this is reflected in the physical growth of the firm. On 19 December, 1861 H. R. H. Prince Albert's death was announced in the press and important segments of the nation entered a period of deep mourning.[144] Throughout the land the "respectable classes" frantically tried to lay their hands on mourning attire and consequently every dye-works was committed to long hours for many weeks. It also gave Robert Pullar a chance to seek agencies in England. Another event which produced a dramatic upsurge in business was the wedding of H. R. H. Prince of Wales with H. R. H. Princess Alexandra of Denmark when bright colours became the order of the day.[145] The dye-works was decorated with evergreens, banners and even "a gas illumination of the Brunswick Star and the Star of Denmark."[146]

Management was becoming more complex and James Ferguson Pullar, third son of John Pullar, was made a partner at the age of 27.[147] Often referred to as "the silent figure" he had also joined the works at the age of 13 in 1849. Profits were now "high" and Robert Pullar bought the most modern fire-fighting equipment that money could buy. It was soon needed, first at a fire in the Public Baths[148] and then at a £4,000 blaze at Murdoch and Sons, Tanners and Curriers.[149] Other large outlays involved the purchase of the latest U. S. sewing-machines for the finishers.[150]

The excellent trading position allowed Robert Pullar to begin the next phase of his extension plans in May, 1864 when he finally received Town Council permission to build over the Lade.[151] This had taken a long time to achieve and was only won in the face of stiff opposition from those who feared a narrowing of the streets. Official consent was the signal for a massive transformation of the dye-works, especially in its lavish interior.[152] Naturally, it was not plain sailing - there were many thefts by building workers,[153] the new 160' chimney stack collapsed in a storm,[154] old machines ad to be ripped out and replaced[155] and the high rate of accidents among construction teams continued.[156] By the end of 1856 this phase was complete and the City Hall was hired for a celebration attended by at least 500 guests.[157]

Now that the dye-works covered a huge area and employed some 400 workers personal control was no longer feasible. Management had to be tightened and something had to be done about absenteeism through drink at the festive season. Accordingly, Robert Pullar issued a statement deploring "the great inconvenience and immorality arising from the protracted series of holidays commencing at Christmas and only ending on Auld Hansel Monday." As an alternative he offered to close the works down for one day with pay.[158] There were plenty of applications for jobs especially after the death of Archibald Campbell in 1865 and the steady decline of his firm.[159] "Good character" was still the basic requirement to win"the liberal wages of a dyer."[160] Competition to do so was fierce given the life-long security offered by Pullars. One life-long employee was Peter Smeaton, who was taken on as "a temporary clerk" from school in 1864 and retired after 50 years in 1914.[161] Workers regarded John Pullar and Sons as the safest factory in the city because of its many fire appliances[162] which were often tested in public.[163] Everybody in Perth knew that the Pullars strongly disapproved of drink[164] and were keen on physical fitness through swimming and rowing.[165] Then again, if any worker was injured there was always a "Pullar bed" available in the Infirmary with all expenses paid by the firm.[166]

In 1866 the Drainage Question arose. Was this gigantic dye-works in the middle of the city slowly polluting Perth's water-supply? No-body knew. Since 1858 the throwing of rubbish from windows and the use of cess pits had been banned and a main drain had been installed.[167] Even then many of the poorest inhabitants kept pigs and butchers' backyards were a well-known health hazard. Not surprisingly, cholera was a frequent visitor to the city and there were deaths in November, 1866[168] Most of the letters in the newspaper correspondence columns openly blamed the dyers.[169] It took the 1868 Police Act to stop people from throwing refuse into the Lade or into open ditches and sewers. As for the Lade itself it continued to take a dismal toll of drowned victims[170] which, John Pullar said, would only end when the waterway was entirely covered.

While most Perth workers agitated for shorter hours or better pay[171] those at the North British Dye Works (as the factory was now called) enjoyed a soirée attended by 720 guests, of whom at least 100 came from other parts of the country.[172] Robert Pullar well knew the value of publicity and he used Perth's First Conversazione to widen his firm's reputation.[173] More than 1,000 citizens flocked to the City Hall to examine a wide range of telegraph instruments, electric experiments, lantern slides, microscopes and aniline dyes as well as a model of the latest extension in Kinnoull Street which had cost £15,000.[174] The firm's new settling ponds, tanks, sieves and laboratories were the talk of the town.[175] Always conscious of the dramatic Robert Pullar announced at the 1869 soirée and ball that Saturday afternoons would henceforth be free for children, young persons and women.[176] Against this backcloth of industrial power smaller rivals simply withered away. For instance, A. Hay, dyer, South Methven Street, sold out to Patrick Robertson[177] who, a few months later, also gave up business.[178] Only P. and P. Campbell provided meaningful competition.

Not everybody shared the enthusiasm for technology. When Robert Pullar installed electric bells and hoists[179] some members of the public complained about the noise.[180] Others said that "the vapours from Pullars are particularly offensive in the locality and threaten to prove injurious to public health."[181] Investigation by the police established that these came from a tanner's yard.[182] Some even quoted the British Medical Journal[183] to the effect that aniline-dyed clothing next to the skin was harmful to the wearer. What these critics did not know was that John Pullar and Sons had been conducting secret experiments on dry-cleaning.[184] Given the details of the process from the Spindlers of Berlin Robert Pullar had determined to learn all he could about it. Picked men were sent to Paris, Berlin, Lyons and Zurich to assess their progress, while expert foreign dyers were invited to Perth.[185] The marriage of James Ferguson Pullar to Adelgunde Spindler in 1867 cemented the bond with Berlin.

During the years John Pullar was Lord Provost of Perth 1867-1873 the task of running the dye-works fell to Robert Pullar. With some 30 years' experience as a dyer he had almost an instinctive awareness for the moment when "Black is in great request"[186] or when "Brown is in vogue."[187] Limiting his involvement to a daily inspection of the factory John Pullar watched him handle the day-to-day problems of a dye-works' owner: continual pressure from the Town Council to fence off the Lade;[188] constant increases in the cost of water[189] and gas;[190] complaints about "smoke nuisance";[191] competition from Judson's Dyes, now in 18 colours and fast in 10 minutes;[192] loss of key craftsmen to England in search of higher pay.[193] Even phase 3 of the building programme was delayed by strikes in March, 1869 and again in March, 1870[194] as well as by far too many accidents[195] the most serious of which was the bursting of a boiler.[196] Trade Union activists tried hard to exploit the situation, but Robert Pullar responded by arguing for "worker collectivity" and encouraging the development of the Working Men's Association.[197] One problem, however, did require his father's intervention. In October, 1870 the River Pollution Commissioners came to Perth to investigate an allegation made by Colonel Sandeman of Springlands that the river was badly polluted by dyes.[198] It was only by proving that the pollution came from Ruthvenfield Print Works and by offering inspection of his dye-works and processes that John Pullar saved the day. Later attempts by anonymous complainers to reopen the issue all failed.[199]

It was a strike by 700 female workers in John Shield's textile factory in November, 1871 that sparked off labour unrest in Perth.[200] A few minor

E

employers, to avoid a confrontation, reduced their working week to 51 hours.[201] By October, 1872 the restlessness had spread to the North British Dye-Works. A mass meeting of employees was held in Parliamentary Close Hall, a committee appointed and demands made - [202] a 51 hour week, weekly payments on Saturday and overtime till 7pm at 1 1/4 rates, thereafter at 1 1/2 rates. John Pullar was astonished and angry. As recently as January, 1872 he had extended breakfast by 15 minutes, dinner by 15 minutes and given a pay rise as well.[203] He therefore offered the following package - a 54 hour week from 1 January, 1873 with weekly payments, but only if another lying-day was accepted, but not on Saturdays. Finally, he absolutely refused any change in the time system.[204] The workers met again and decided to accept the 54 hours and the extra lying-day, but were adamant on the need for better overtime rates. It seemed as if a head-on collision was inevitable. At this point Robert Pullar took the lead. He offered "a swift and generous compromise"[205] - a 51 hour week from 1 January, 1873, dinner from 1pm to 2pm, wages fortnightly on Saturdays at 1pm, changes in overtime and a further "general rise in wages." This was an astonishing volte-face for a major employer and the workers appreciated it. At a Festival, in January, 1873 to celebrate the 51 hour week, 1,000 people in the City Hall heard the manager, John Moncrieff, thank John Pullar "for the reduction in hours and the liberal increase in wages maintaining your exalted position among the most advanced and generous employers of labour at the present time."[206] John Pullar's reply is an insight into his philosophy: "Permit us to say that no shortening of hours can prove of real benefit unless the greater leisure is employed in mental improvement and useful pursuits, as well as harmless recreation, and increased wages can only give increased comfort when the money is wisely spent, and on better food, clothes and houses. Lastly, not forgetting to put something in the Savings Bank for a rainy day." P. and P. Campbell had no option but to follow suit.[207]

Social life in John Pullar and Sons bloomed in the 1870's. Workers in the Office and Warehouse Department held their first Christmas Party in 1872,[208] while the Framing Department held theirs in 1875[209] and the Mechanics, Firemen and Examiners did the same in 1877.[210] Dye house workers met regularly in the Royal Exchange Hotel[211] while excursions were common[212] as were cricket matches between the married men and bachelors.[213] The work itself was considered "not exceptionally unhealthy"[214] as the "Perth factories are very conscientiously conducted" according to the Factory Act Commissioners.[215] As for the management they were in the throes of phase 4 of their building plans which found their two-acre site valued at £730 per annum.[216] An increase in Lade drownings 1873-1874[217] led to the firm voluntarily taking on the cost of covering the entire North Methven Street section. Agencies had continued to spread: in 1856 they were established in Edinburgh and Stirling and by 1874 they were to be found in London, Leeds, Bristol and Birmingham.[218]

The huge extensions to the dye-works led to several clashes with the Police Commissioners who were troubled by the number of juveniles in the building trades who were injured by lathes[219] and by the "dangerous scaffolding" that always seemed to be blocking the streets.[220] The worst clash came in 1875 when the Commissioners refused to collect any more ashes from the factory under the terms of the 1862 Improvement Act.[221] Given that there were now 20 large furnaces in the dye-works the daily production of ash was enormous.[222] But it was the fact that this ash was not saleable that annoyed the Commissioners. John Pullar took the case to the Court of Session[223] where he won his case with costs.[224] The furious Commissioners appealed, but lost again in July, 1876.[225] However, it did have an effect on the firm's expansion policy - additions were postponed and difficulties[226] were encountered when it was proposed to build a road near the Lade later that year.[227] Renewed agitation over pollution in the Tay and the Lade[228] and competition from Glasgow Rainbow Dyes at 3d a packet seemed minor in comparison.[229] Still, the parade in August, 1876 by 1,400 excursionists off to St. Andrews with bands and banners summed up the general mood of confidence.[230]

P. and P. Campbell had their problems too, especially thefts of goods on transit by rail to Manchester and Leeds.[231] Accidents too had increased with the greater use of machinery and some were very serious.[232] Still, nothing was allowed to hinder the expansion programmes of 1874[233] and 1877.[234] Large sums of money were involved in all these operations. For instance, the new Furnishing Department alone cost £3,000 in 1875.[235] Soon telephones were installed[236] and as prosperity increased a large building, henceforth called the Perth Dye Works, was erected near the Lade.[237] With the latest designs in heat and ventilation controls it cleverly had its benzolene tanks placed underground. Unfortunately, even this was no safeguard against a fire in 1881 which cost almost £3,000.[238]

December, 1878 delivered a heavy blow to the North British Dye Works with the death of John Pullar.[239] For over 50 years he had guided the firm from a humble beginning to a mighty industrial concern. His estate, valued at £122,561, is a measure of his achievement. Robert Pullar took his death badly and went off to the U.S.A. and Canada for a holiday. The dye-works, in his absence, although in phase 5 of the building programme, ran like clockwork - drying sheds rose in Blackfriars' Wynd[240] and more walls along the Lade.[241] On his return Robert Pullar was a hive of activity with fresh ideas for improvements to the telephone and electric bell systems.[242] Trade was very good[243] and business profits plus his inheritance enabled him to purchase the splendid villa of Tayside House and its beautiful gardens.[244] Eager to find new lines he toured the dye-works of France and Germany with his chief mechanic, Duncan Forbes, and sent his son, Rufus Daniell Pullar, to study dyeing at Frankfurt-am-Main.[245] The perennial problems were still there - smoke nuisance complaints,[246] a benzolene tank explosion,[247] a diarrhoea epidemic in the city which revived allegations of pollution,[248] a £600 benzole fire which cost a worker his life[249] and a sudden upsurge in drunkenness.[250]

The most serious problem was the storage of unstable cleaning agents. This was made worse by the heavy congestion around Mill Street[251] despite having absorbed 3 churches, 2 schools, a gas-works, a weaving factory, a tannery, a slaughter-house, a drill hall and a coach-builder's yard. Everybody in the city awaited in dread the inevitable big explosion.[252] A solution came quite unexpectedly in 1882 with the 112 acres of Tulloch Bleach Works coming on the market due to the sudden death of its young owner.[253] Robert Pullar moved quickly and purchased it, cleared the site and began to build a factory for dry cleaning, especially gloves and lace curtains and storing 50,000 gallons of cleaning fluid in safety.[254] Before long Perth had acquired a new suburb with houses, school and even a farm whose sole function was to attend to the recuperation of the firm's sick carthorses.

The year 1882 saw another change in G.P.O. regulations which brought a huge increase in business in London.[255] A Central Parcel Depot was immediately opened in Perth and parcel postage was reduced to 3d and 1/-.[256] All 11 departments in the dye-works had to work out how to cope with the massive daily inflow of garments for dyeing and cleaning.[257] Fortunately, the firm's heavy investment in electric power made it just possible.[258] Robert Pullar appreciated the efforts made by his workers and he encouraged them to save their wages through the Working Men's Building Society.[259] He subsidised their various clubs - bowling, swimming, cricket, football and angling[260] - and even bought musical instruments for a works' band.[261] He laid on free musical concerts[262] to keep them from shebeening (illegal drinking).[263] Holidays with pay were given for special occasions, like the Queen's Jubilee[264] and the 1884 Reform Act celebrations.[265] One thing he failed to do - he simply could not persuade them to attend evening classes to further their study of dyeing.[266]

By the mid-1880's John Pullar and Sons were known the length and breadth of the U.K. There were 18 Receiving Offices, including Brighton, Bath, Birkenhead, Liverpool, Manchester, Newcastle, Glasgow, Greenock, Dublin and Belfast.[267] London alone had 3 offices - at Chenies Street, where there was a staff of 70; Finsbury Pavement and Sloane Street. In 1885 the head London Office was located in a modern six-storey building at Tottenham Court Road, where the loading bay was regarded as an architectural wonder.[268] All these were linked by a complex system of distribution vans and controlled by trunk calls.[269]

Naturally, such power excited envy. In 1883 a legal action "to restrain the use of a trade name had to be brought against a John Pullar, linen draper, Shepherd's Bush, London, who tried to capitalise on the name.[270] In 1884 a new dye-works appeared in Perth on a 3 acre site at Friarton bought from Sir Robert D. Moncrieffe.[271] It was not long before the laird regretted the sale - his revenue from his fishing stations on the Tay fell drastically and he took the Friarton Dye Works to the Justiciary Court.[272] It was not long before John Pullar and Sons were involved, but expert witnesses soon established that any pollution could not have come from the North British Dye Works because of its highly efficient system of settling ponds, tanks and sieves manned by 1,600 watchful staff. The decision of Lord Trayner was important for all dyers using the Tay: "The water is quite clear and fit for domestic purpose." Thus Moncrieffe lost.[273]

P. and P. Campbell tried hard to keep apace with John Pullar and Sons. They also had a Mutual Improvement Society[274] as well as a wide range of clubs and excursions.[275] Indeed, the installation of electric lights in 1882 made their building "the most brilliantly lit works in Perth."[276] Of course, they also had trouble with dubious firms. In 1883 they brought an action against Andrew and James Reid of Perth who traded under the name Campbell and Company, Campbell's Dye Works, Perth.[277] The deception was almost plausible in that Andrew Reid's wife was the niece of Archibald Campbell who died in 1865. As one might expect P. and P. Campbell won their case with ease. To celebrate P. Campbell went off on a world cruise 1883-1885 leaving his sons, Peter White Campbell and Edward Campbell in full charge as partners.[278]

By 1886 Rufus Daniell Pullar, aged 20, was a partner in John Pullar and Sons.[279] The best educated of the Pullars he was a product of Edinburgh and Leeds Universities[280] and was determined to keep up the tradition of being in the forefront of modern management. With his father he encouraged membership of the firm's Sick and Funeral Society, saw off 2,000 excursionists in 1886, the largest group ever to leave Perth,[281] presented the first gold watch to Thomas Nelson, first employee to complete 50 years' service,[282] maintained the finest fire-fighting unit in the country,[283] opened Workers' Rest Rooms at Mill Street and at Tulloch[284] and extended tea-breaks to 45 minutes.[285] He also had his problems - a benzene fire a Tulloch,[286] a £2,500 blaze in Foundry Lane[287] and even a drought in 1887.[288]

This was nothing to the troubles experienced by their competitors. P. and P. Campbell were sued over a missing dress in the famous Bennett Case,[289] fought a right-of-way dispute over the Lade,[290] challenged a compensation for injury claim in the Winton Case,[291] suffered serious embezzlement by a clerk,[292] competed with new laundries not covered by any Factory Act[293] and had a £300 fire.[294] It was much the same with the Friarton Dye Works - fined for employing children under the age of 10,[295] a logwood extractor explosion and a strike in 1890.[296]

The 1890's brought a period of profound unrest in Perth. Works' excursions dropped off dramatically as their popularity waned.[297] But it was the rail strike of December, 1890 that triggered off real discontent.[298] It soon had an effect upon Pullar's London trade and for the first time exposed the firm's fatal vulnerability if communications with the south were disrupted.[299] Violence too soon flared up[300] and this at a time when Robert Pullar was very ill after a visit to Berlin.[301] As usual the trouble began at Shield's Wallace Works when female workers were asked to accept a series of wage cuts.[302] They called in the Rev. H. Williamson, President of the Dundee and District Mill and Factory Operatives' Union, who strove to enlist as many women as he could.[303] John Pullar and Sons with its 1,700 female employees was a natural target.[304] Despite a full-scale Trade Union onslaught in 1892-1893[305] with a considerable amount of accompanying violence[306] and visits from Tom Mann[307] and Ben Tillet[308] the workforce at the North British Dye Works did not respond, not even when insinuations were made that the Pullars were pro-German.[309]

Then, in 1895, came an issue which divided the management of the dye-works and nearly cause a split in the family - "The Overtime Crisis."[310] The Factories and Workshops Bill was intended by the Liberals to ban overtime to all under 18 "under any circumstances" in a dye-works and to limit it for all others to a maximum of 3 days a week or 30 days a year.[311] Robert Pullar was called to London to consult with Asquith and vaious Factory Inspectors. However, William Whitelaw, M.P., Unionist, called a meeting in Perth at which he suggested that the Bill was "harmful" in that dyeing was "an irregular trade."[312] He also suggested that the work itself was "light and easy" and that if the Bill were passed major dyers, like Pullars, would pay off in the winter. Robert Pullar was furious and even considered a libel action against Whitelaw. Instead, he sent a memo to Asquith advising him that overtime to 8pm was "hopeless" as it sent up the sick list the following day. In his opinion working from 6am to 6pm daily Monday to Friday and from 6am to 1pm Saturday was "more than enough." He suggested that any legislation had to include laundries which were "trying to cut out dyers." John Pullar and Sons never had overtime at Christmas and he was glad to be "slack" in January, because it was so cold, hence the 9am start. He argued that dyeing was "fast becoming a regular trade" and that the work was anything but "light and easy." There had been no winter pay-offs since 1865, at least half of his employees were on full-time and all of them had a 48 hour week. He expressed his dislike of long hours for the young and pointed out that the maximum overtime allowed was only 12 nights per annum. He condemned Whitelaw for speaking only to the workers at P. and P. Campbell, a mere 150 out of Perth's 2,500 dye workers, in other words only 6%. Finally, he warned that laundries were after more overtime and that every English dyer was opposed to Whitelaw's view. The latter was quick to respond. He suggested that the age-level be placed at 16 and quoted J.F. Pullar as "one of his supporters", especially in regard to "the poor wages in the trade."[313] Immediately a rift appeared between the two brothers. It widened when J.F. Pullar went to London with a Tory deputation to see the Home Secretary. Most writers to newspapers were opposed to Whitelaw and these together with embarrassing disclosures in the House of Commons persuaded J.F. Pullar to drop his activities. Amid the excitement of an election he made a discreet departure to the Spindler Works in Berlin.[315] Needless to say, Whitelaw was ousted from his Perth seat.

As usual, the other firms also had their troubles. Friarton Dye Works, which had operated under the name of Campbell and Company, had, by 1894, an outstanding debt of £9,500.[316] The owners had no option but to sell.[317] The late manager, Thomson, offered £4,000 when an agent, J.B. MCCash, mysteriously offered £5,700 "for a client."[318] No sooner was the purchase completed than "the client" sold it to Thomson at a loss of £1,700 on condition that "he refrained from operating under the title Campbell and Company." Now all was clear. P. and P. Campbell were the mystery buyers anxious to eliminate any further confusion over names. At P. and P. Campbell itself, although still troubled by a stream of accidents,[319] they had succeeded in introducing cold-dyeing for leather, box-making machinery and a new Receiving Office at Bath.[320] Hamilton's Steam Laundry was even more unfortunate as a missing blanket legal case resulted in a court's condemnation of their "poor marking system."[321]

In contrast, at the North British Dye Works, Robert Pullar had just received a knighthood.[322] With the works decorated and the city church-bells ringing[323] no fewer than 23 managers from all over the U.K. gathered in Perth to present Sir Robert with an illustrated address on vellum.[324] The celebrations obscured an ominous demand from the Trade Unions for higher wages for dyers.[325] Nonetheless, there was good reason to laud "this vast employer of labour."[326] With the bulk of the work now devoted to cleaning suits, dresses and gloves[327] the dye-works employed 1,900 staff and was organised on a departmental basis with specialised sections under managers and foremen and forewomen who had all risen from the shop foor.[328] The Works Fire Brigade units at Kinnoull Street and Tulloch were far better equipped than the City and County Fire Brigade,[329] while the works' laboratories were able to produce synthetic indigo. Every year more than £4,000 was spent on electricity[330] and many of the better-paid staff actually had electricity in their homes.[331] The Sick and Funeral Society, founded in 1880, guaranteed its 1,300 members at least 11/- a week if ill at a cost of 2d weekly.[332] Indeed, the dye-works was even a tourist attraction and was visited by many prominent people including Prince Herman of Saxe-Weimar and His Grace the Duke of Marlborough.[333] Technical groups, like the Chemical Industry Society, were there almost every week.[334]

The century drew to a close for Hamilton's Steam Laundry with a move to the Dunkeld Road area.[335] P & P Campbell had a serious fire in 1899 [336] and great difficulty in installing a new boiler.[337] Thomson's Fair City Dye-works was having great problems with the dyeing of silks.[338] At the North British Dye Works, Sir Robert, despite illness,[339] celebrated his Jubilee in 1899 by making his son, Albert Evans Pullar and his nephew, Herbert Spindler PUllar, full partners in the business.[340] The works was closed for a week with pay and the workers were secure in the knowledge that they had a job for life. Once they had completed 30 years' service they were entitled to time off without pay and Christmas holidays now stretched

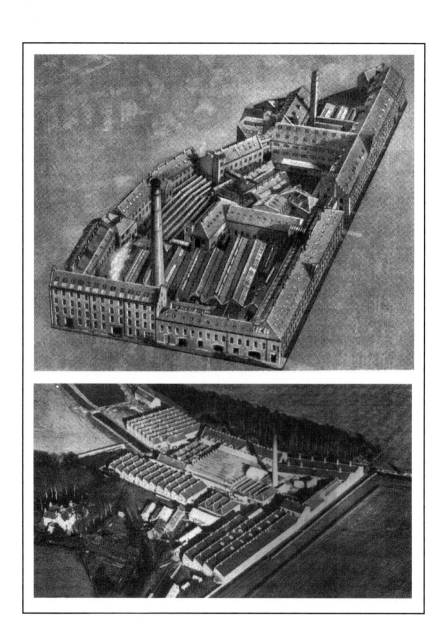

The Two Factories

from 22-27, December.[341] In fact, the 2,400 staff were even allowed off to watch the Barnum and Bailey Circus Parade through Perth.[342]

John Pullar and Sons entered the 20th century with supreme confidence. With Sir Robert as Chairman and J.F. Pullar as Deputy Chairman the actual management was in the hands of Rufus Daniell Pullar and H.S. Pullar, who dealt with Sales and Processing, and A.E. Pullar, who supervised Transport, Communications and Electricity.[343] With 24 departments to control they had a mammoth task on their hands, but even their most bitter rivals had to admit that "they were very well organised." In 1901 these departments were listed as follows:[344] Engineering, Stationery, Cleaning, Silk Dyeing, Mechanics, Glazing, Finishing, Electric, Coloured Silk Dyeing, Silk Framing, Silk Ironing, Ribbon Finishing, Examining Room, White Ironing, Large Cylinder, Curtain, Parcel Post, Office, Stoves, Shawl Frame, Hat, Folding, Picking and Skirt Finishing. There were also 9 sets of tradesmen in the dyeworks: Boilermen, Blacksmiths, Slaters, Joiners, Plumbers, Engine-men, Time-Keepers, Dyers and Engineers. The last category alone numbered 60.[345] The other statistics were staggering - 90% of the staff of 2,600 were full-time;[346] £12,000 was spent annually on electricity; 12,000 tons of coal were used every year; there was a 180' chimney stack; there were 300 branches and 4,000 agencies. There was even talk that the work-force would soon rise to 6,000.[347] Those who did work in the North British Dye Works admitted that they had "the best wages in Perth"[348] and it was common knowledge that "the Pullars' girls were the best dressed women in town." In fact, Pullars' workers found it relatively easy to find credit if they so wished. In July, 1900 R.D. Pullar selected his 60 best workmen and sent them off, all expenses paid, to the Paris Exhibition.[349] A week later another 13 followed.[350] Managers were sent regularly to Germany to absorb the latest ideas, while J.F. Pullar did the same in Paris.[351] Sir Robert and R.D. Pullar spent two weeks visiting dye-works in Berlin, Frankfurt-am-Main, Aix-la-Chapelle and Roulaix.[352] Not surprisingly, the firm soon received a Warrant of Appointment as Dyers to King Edward VII.[353] Even the traditional work-environment was changing as the introduction of hot-air drying did away with the accustomed clouds of steam.[354] More and more of the Lade was covered and built upon[355] despite enormous technical difficulties[356] and a huge parcel post warehouse appeared.[357] Within the fabric itself was to be found every modern machine known to dyeing and cleaning.[358]

The smooth running of this industrial empire received a jolt with the drain of men off to fight in the South African War.[359] One of those was H.S. Pullar who won a battlefield commission[360] and whose exploits were avidly followed by readers of the Works' Bulletins.[361] Sir Robert, always patriotic, allowed Volunteers to attend summer camps whenever they wished.[362] Even on the death of Queen Victoria and the Coronation of Edward VII, occasions when dyers normally worked full out, he closed the works and gave his employees full pay.[363] On two issues Sir Robert must have experienced great satisfaction. Smoke nuisance allegations turned out to be caused by the Water Works[364] and investigation into the discovery that the Lade was "poisoned" turned out to be the fault of Lumsden and Mackenzie, who had been releasing lime waste.[356] On the other hand there was the death of a man operating a Dolly Blanket Machine, hitherto considered safe;[366] a near disaster with a benzene explosion at Tulloch;[367] a scarlet fever outbreak which left many sick;[368] and an increase in Sabbath drinking which led to heavy absenteeism on Monday mornings.[369] Far worse was the threat of increasing competition both at home and abroad.[370] At home, by 1903, the competition for trade was "fierce",[371] particularly for the London market, where, it was calculated, some 660 dye-works were fighting for existence.[372] But it was the vigorous growth and aggressive sales policy of two English firms which worried the Pullars most - Eastman and Sons, Acton Vale[373] and Johnson Bros., Bootle.[374] Abroad, it was becoming increasingly clear that Germany had a virtual monopoly in dyes.[375] Anti-German feeling was quick to grow[376] especially when it was discovered that the Germans were cleverly exploiting the British Patents Act.[377] Soon there was talk of industrial spies[378] and before long there were demands for punitive tariffs.[379]

P. and P. Campbell also continued to expand with particular emphasis on curtain-cleaning.[380] As coal became more and more costly fuel-savers and automatic-stokers were purchased. Machines which could replait skirts and frills after dyeing were bought in the U.S.A. and Switzerland. So busy were they that they even worked through the mourning period of Victoria's death.[381] However, as recompense 1,200 workers had a paid holiday at the Glasgow Exhibition.[382] Accidents were still numerous[383] and one led to a Workman's Compensation case.[384] After the retiral of Peter Campbell, Snr.,[385] his son, P.W. Campbell, went off to Paris in search of new ideas.[386] He returned with French dyers and then reorganised his entire works on "Parisian lines."[387] Plans were made for a hat department, a new navy-blue colour was produced and an advertising campaign - "We can dye ANYTHING black in 24 hours" - was launched. Unfortunately, their dry-cleaning area was gutted by fire in 1906.[388] Fire also played havoc with two of Perth's three laundries - the Perthshire Laundry, Caledonian Road, which had opened as recently as March, 1900[389] and was destroyed in a £4,000 blaze.[390] Craigie Laundry had a £2,000 fire in 1905[391] and only Hamilton's Laundry, with its small staff of 60, was doing well.[392] With branches from Kingussie to York it was well ensconced in Fife and Forfar, while its 1 1/2 acre site had several Summerscale washing-machines which could boil and rinse 150 shirts at a time. The Friarton Dye Works struggled on to perfect its "direct dyeing."[393]

Sir Robert's health was poor in 1902[394] as was that of his wife in the following year; but her death in February, 1904[395] marks a watershed in his skill as a chairman. Married 45 years her absence was a shattering experience and he seemed unable to concentrate on business. Restless and subdued he sought consolation in long holidays abroad - 1904 Switzerland, Mediterranean, North Africa, Lisbon and Egypt;[396] 1905 Teneriffe;[397] 1906 South Africa, New Zealand, Australia and Japan.[398] Proof of his fading ability was his neglect of a wage complaint by the girls of the Ironing Department.[399] It was a bad sign for the future. This was not obvious at the time as R.D. Pullar bought Horse Cross Mills[400] and a large part of the Castlegable for further expansion.[401] 1905 was a specially good year[402] for the North British Dye Works with the addition of bright, new dining-rooms, new experimental laboratory and a new gate-room. Motor vans were now rapidly replacing horses and A.E. Pullar bought Milnes-Daimlers, De Dions and Argylls A potentially bad fire at Tulloch[403] and the death of a painter killed in a fall[404] did not dampen spirits, although excessive drinking had flared up again among the work-force.[405] Around the Castlegable R.D. Pullar had several street widened for better access to the works while the steamplant lay-out was revised and boilers replaced.[406] Vans now operated in London, Leeds and Manchester and reports indicated that they were giving excellent service[407] while three new departments had been added to the firm's structure - Drawing Office, Urgent Department and Starching Department.[408] At the same time all District Offices throughout the U.K. had been remodelled to a uniform design.

Unfortunately, there was increasing evidence as to just how powerful the two rising English competitors had become. Eastman and Sons, Acton Vale had suffered a terrible fire costing £25,000.[409] Complete collapse of the firm was anticipated; instead they reduced the working week to 50 hours and devised new work-schedules - 8am to 12.30pm and 1.30pm to

The North British Dye Works Lab (PKDLA)

6pm.[410] Johnson Bros. at Bootle had a high standard in dry cleaning and a massive organisation of 75 departments administered by 150 clerks.[411] Their staff enjoyed excellent pension and bonus schemes together with gardens and libraries.[412] Sir Robert seemed blissfully unaware of this threat as he sallied off to London as Perth's new M.P. It was different for R.D. Pullar - Canada continued to lure his best workers with glowing advertisments[413] while Spotted Fever was rampant in Perth.[414] The immediate problem however was unrest among the girls in the Ironing Department who wanted more money.[415] These very same girls who had agitated a year before claimed that 11/- a week was "not a living wage." Sir Robert was silent, but R.D. Pullar responded by stressing job-security and the long-term advantages of working for the firm. He pointed out that men with 30 years' service and women with 24 years' service were entitled to an automatic week's holiday with pay every year.[416] Further, women with 33 years' service were guaranteed a minimum wage of 75/- a month, whereas all workers were to be paid for a 45 hour week, whether they worked that or not.[417] Thus, the central cause of the unrest - low wages for younger women - was ignored.

At Thomson's Fair City Dyeworks, Friarton they were so busy after 1906 that extra staff had to be hired.[418] Emphasising their speed of turnover[419] they specialised in light shades and glove-cleaning.[420] Not surprisingly, their 1908 Annual Report assessed the year as "very prosperous."[421] Trade also improved for P. and P. Campbell in 1907.[422] A new system of premiums for better and faster work kept the workforce contented, even though they were refused any breaks between August and Christmas, the busy season.[423] Capital outlay was considerable with better finishing machinery and new offices in Portobello, Birmingham and three in Glasgow. The former, unfortunately, resulted in a death[424] and there were further difficulties with workers leaving without notice[425] as well as a few fires.[426]

During this period women of all classes were growing steadily restless with their status in society. In April 1908 a Women's Freedom League branch opened in Perth, but attracted few workers from the North British Dye Works.[427] The Guild Hall debate in November, 1908 on "Suffrage for Women" was different - it was attended by many women from Mill Street and Tulloch.[428] The Pullar family however were unaware of pending social change. Sir Robert was off to Egypt[429] and then Belgium and Holland[430] while J.F. Pullar was in France.[431] All that R.D. Pullar could do was to push the P.S.A. Movement as a solution - Pleasant Sunday Afternoons. The real warning came in March, 1909 when there was a sudden rise in the cost of living.[432] All that management would admit was that there was "a trade depression"[433] and that consequently "trading results were poor for 1909."[434] R.D. Pullar, struggling with a heavy sick list due to Diphtheria and Scarlet Fever,[435] placed his hopes on a new curtain cleaning process developed by his chemists,[436] as well as winning prestigious orders such as restoring 300 year old tapestries. There was one problem which seemed insoluble - the loss of key workers through age.[437] With their departure the hard core of devoted staff slowly withered away. Sir Robert, despite his retiral from politics, seems to have offered little advice and even less help - he was off to France again on holiday.[438]

One positive response however by the Pullars was the decision made in 1910 to incorporate John Pullar and Sons under the Companies Act 1908.[439] The five partners, Sir Robert, J.F., R.D., A.E. and H.S. Pullar "agreed to sell the firm for the considerable sum of £200,000 - 20,000 shares at £10 each" to form John Pullar and Sons, Limited. They were then declared Directors of the new Company. Unknown to anybody was the fact that the change carried a malicious thorn which was to cause a change of direction for all. By March, 1911 the new Joint Stock Company of John Pullar and Sons, Dyers and Cleaners had been formally registered in Perth with the object of being "general dyers and cleaners, launderers of ladies' and children's clothes, household materials, beating, bleaching and colouring." The first subscribers, naturally, were the five Pullars.[440] The work-force were quite unaware of the significance of the change.

R.D. Pullar was now legally in complete charge of the firm and he made all the decisions.[441] Although two General Elections "were not very good for business"[442] the death of Edward VII brought "a rush for black." The Coronation of George V was even more profitable with the staff engaged till 8pm for three nights a week in a frantic attempt to meet demand.[443] All the laundries were equally busy: Hamilton's Steam Laundry, Scone Laundry, Ltd., and the Perthshire Laundry Company, St Catherine's Road[444] although the latter fell foul of H.M.I.F. for breach of overtime regulations.[445] They were well able to cope with their new Tumbler Drying Machines and electric motors which had replaced shafts and belts. They could even reprocess benzine and use it again and again, an enormous saving in costs. Further, they had opened new outlets at Liverpool, Southport and Walsall.[447] Only a £3,000 fire in the French Cleaning Department blotted progress.[448]

But, in the summer of 1911 food prices again rose dramatically[449] and the workers' social problems multiplied.[450] With the Labour Party now entrenched in Perth[451] the S.T.U.C. decided to send Alderman Hayhurst, J.P., Secretary of the Amalgamated Society of Dyers and Bleachers to the city.[452] With him came three organisers, George Dallas, Mary Macarthur and Agnes Brown, dedicated to their task and destined to earn themselves a niche in Labour history.[453] Dallas quickly held meetings in the I.L.P. Rooms and stated his aims: to raise wages, cut hours and improve working conditions. He also saw to the opening of a branch of the Dyers' Union. Mary Macarthur and Agnes Brown concentrated on the female workers urging them to join the National Federation of Women Workers, whose Organising Agent, Miss McLean, had also arrived in Perth. Within a week many of the female employees in P. and P. Campbell had joined.[454] The August, 1911 rail strike, which virtually paralysed Perth, showed the potential power of the Trade Unions.[455]

The 83 year old Sir Robert made no comment being more interested in his award of the Freedom of the City of Perth.[456] Unlike his father R.D. Pullar struggled to reduce cleaning costs in view of the increasing competition and he committed the Company to huge expense by purchasing carpet-cleaning machinery. No doubt he thought that this was a better indication of the future than the announcement in December, 1911 that the N.F.W.W. was the biggest Trade Union in Perth.[457] If he did, he was wrong. The proof came with the Miners' Strike of March, 1912.[458] Railwaymen joined them and the price of coal jumped from 1/6d to 1/9d a cwt., ie from 30/- to 35/- a ton.[459] Short of coal and with no incoming goods R.D. Pullar faced "the saddest day I have spent in business" when he prepared a notice for his staff - "If the coal strike continues it will be necessary on Saturday to give final notice to all workers." On the 9, March, 1912 this was done and 2,000 were made idle.[460] By 15 March, 1912 all 2,500 men and women at the North British Dye Works were no longer working. Thomson's Fair City Dye Works did not suffer at all.[461] With astonishing foresight they had stockpiled coal and with the purchase of Collar Machines had switched the bulk of their work to laundering.[462] It was otherwise at P. and P. Campbell where they had hardly any coal left.[463] Perth Dye Works, now a Limited Liability Company too, had concentrated on faster dyeing with the purchase of expensive superheaters when news broke that Peter Campbell had died at the age of 88 leaving an estate valued at £50,781.[464] Fortunately, for all concerned, the coal-rail strike did not last long.

Then on 26 May, 1912 the Perth branch of the Dyers' Union announced that it was "an approved society under the National Insurance Act" and that from henceforth they would strive for "solidarity and a common scheme of protection and enforcement of aspirations towards betterment."[465] This wordy pronouncement probably meant little to most workers at the North British Dye Works. They were waiting for 1 June, 1912. Since the year 1882 the firm had announced annual rises on that date and everybody looked forward to the news item in the local press. To their amazement there was nothing. The Dyers' Union took the opportunity to announce that they now had 200 members in Perth and that their funds totalled £50,000.[466] They also issued a statement condemning seven year apprenticeships for dyers which ended with a mere 22/- weekly and especially the system by which annual increments "depended on the goodwill of the masters." They thought that the top wage rates of 28/- and 30/- were "inadequate" for the hours worked and therefore they demanded "a stab wage" ie an established scale. The management passed no comment. The workers in the Finishing Department held a meeting and sent a delegation to the Directors.[467] R.D. Pullar explained to them that because the firm was now a Limited Liability the financial year ended in

November, not June, and that they would just have to wait till then. He also explained that rises were "not automatic" but would be "considered." He said that there was no alternative due to the increased cost of coal, the losses sustained during the strike by the miners, the rail dislocation and the payments under the National Insurance Act. However, he said that he would grant an immediate rise to the poorest paid ie all those under 18 years of age. By this time rumours were rife in the Glazing Room to the effect that the deputationists were to be sacked and that there would be no rises for anyone. Trade Union activists among them argued that annual rises for 30 years made it a matter of "use and wont." As a result some 200 men, mainly apprentices, and 40 women, walked out. The Directors immediately ordered the closure of all gates. The strikers assembled on the North Inch and organised pickets, but few of their colleagues at Tulloch would join them. Eventually, a deputation of eight, half of them from Tulloch, took their demands to the Directors - 6/- at 14 yrs; 9/- at 15 yrs; 11/- at 16 yrs; 14/- at 17 yrs; 16/- at 18 yrs; 18/- at 19 yrs; 20/- at 20 yrs; 22/- at 21 yrs; 24/- at 22yrs; 25/- at 23yrs; 26/- at 24 yrs; full time at 25 yrs; 27/- at 26 yrs; 28/- at 27 yrs; no rise at 28 yrs; 29/- at 29 yrs; and 30/- at 30 yrs. The Directors were coldly polite, but did not even look at the written demands. Activists claimed that this was "a direct challenge" and 200 walked out of the Ironing Department. That afternoon Councillor Stewart of Dundee and George Dallas came "to organise the strikers." The former confirmed that the deputationists were indeed dismissed. News of the arrival of "these outsiders" angered the Directors and they telephoned the police asking for protection for loyalist staff. That evening local newspapers published special editions condemning management insensitivity and deploring "the first strike in the long history of the firm." Next day, 4 June, 1912 there was a mass meeting at which Councillor Stewart called for "the support of other workers" while Dallas urged a strike roll. Later, they conferred with the Directors while the Tulloch picket marched to the North Inch "watched by thousands" to hear rousing speeches form Agnes Brown and David Bruce, President of Perth Trades Council.

It was raining on 5 June, 1912 but there were large pickets at both Kinnoull Street and Tulloch before 5.30am. Discipline was good, but their "friendly persuasion" had little success with those determined to work. Some of the strikers, fearing that the Directors might cancel the 45 hour week, tried to return to work, but they were refused entry by the gate-keepers. Another deputation was unsuccessful too. R.D. Pullar then

F

posted a notice: "It is much to be regretted that the amicable relations which have hitherto existed between the employers and the employed in Pullars Dye Works have been interrupted." He pointed out that workers were required by law to give notice of strike action and as they had not done so he assumed that they had "given up their situations." He assured them that nobody had been sacked and promised that nobody would be victimised. All those under 18 years of age would get an immediate rise and "the rest will be considered in November as liberally as the resources of the Company will permit." R.D. Pullar then summoned a press conference and described how "Trade Union organisers were pouring into Perth from all over" and that "it was strange how quickly the strike had spread." Apart from hinting at a plot he reminded his listeners that John Pullar and Sons never paid off at a slack time as they might have done. He suggested that the female workers were "agitated because of the Suffragettes and the N.F.W.W." and revealed that only one dyer was actually on strike. Finally, he told how all the demands of the dyers' apprentices would be met as they were "key workers." By this time female strikers must have felt that the struggle was lost and the arrival of Rushton from the Bradford Dyers' Union did nothing to uplift their spirits. The 500 strikers were now hopelessly divided, most blaming the dyers whom they accused of pushing for bigger differentials. Then came a further statement from the management: "If you stay off work without one week's notice it is the same as resigning and means you have left." That decided it for most of them, they demanded a vote. Out of the 500 strikers only 201, a mere 40%, took the trouble to attend and of these only 50, just 10%, wanted the strike to continue.[468]

Next day the workers streamed into work early. The Directors, wisely, did not gloat over their victory, but announced a new programme of expansion.[469] To their astonishment business had actually increased during the strike and they now felt that their reaction had been the correct one. The strikers felt differently: they were convinced that they had been cheated and many enlisted in the Dyers' Union for the first time.[470] Female workers were especially aggrieved and Agnes Brown enrolled 500 of them in one night to form a second branch of the N.F.W.W. Clearly, the Trade Union movement had suffered a defeat in Perth, but the Dyers' Union vowed to continue the fight.[471] At the end of the month they sent their two best men to the city to rally the faithful - Hayhurst and W. Rushworth, their Scottish Divisional Secretary. Clumsily the Directors played into their hands by announcing that the firm's Sickness Benefit

Society would probably lapse because of the National Insurance Act.[472] To the workers this seemed a mean form of retribution. A few days later the Directors announced their arrangements for the Midsummer Holidays.[473] To make up for lost production the summer break was to be cut drastically and would only be from Friday afternoon till Monday at 10am. To most of the staff this seemed a miserly allocation given the fact that other factories in the city were to have a whole week off. To them it was another piece of spite and revenge. For years this reaction was to fester and slowly destroy the long-established trust that had once existed between management and workers. However, normality, in the meantime, slowly returned to the factory.

Sadly, there was to be no normality for either Sir Robert or his brother, J.F. Pullar. The two old men, frail and ill, felt betrayed by what had happened and with the harsh winter of 1911-1912 taking its toll they sickened and died within days of each other.[474] With the death of Sir Robert on 9 September, 1912 an era came to an end.[475] Perth was conscious of the fact and the 85 year old man's body was escorted to the cemetery by more than 2,000 mourners, the biggest funeral ever seen in the city. Despite the many gifts he had bestowed on the poor and the city he left a personal estate valued at £519,675. J.F. Pullar, who died on 19 September, 1912, was a man who loved his privacy and accordingly his funeral was in private. His son, H.S. Pullar, equally disillusioned with the work-force, retired early. With these deaths Pullar influence in Perth rapidly began to fade.

One would have thought that P. and P. Campbell would have tried to take advantage of their rival's predicament. If they did, they failed. A huge fire in the Benzine Department[476] forced its complete reconstruction. Another legal case, a worker suing the firm for blood poisoning at work, attracted unwelcome publicity.[477] Far more serious was a dispute with the Assessor at the Perth Valuation Court over rates which ended in the Court of Session.[478] The Assessor wanted £2,100, but "as dyeing is not flourishing" the Court decided on £1,300. After this lucky escape new American pressing machines speeded up work in the Finishing Department, but sewage seepage[479] and an outbreak of typhoid made it an unsatisfactory trading period.[480]

At the North British Dye Works G.D. Pullar and R.M. Pullar replaced two of the three Directors. In their joint view the key departments were Dyeing, Cleaning, Ironing, Glazing and Warehouses.[481] Although they did not admit it publicly they also had two problems - and excessive number of females in the Hat, Ironing and Warehouse Departments and a standard pay rate in the latter which was the root of much envy in the works. However, the honour of "Royal Tradesmen to H.M. GeorgeV" overcame all doubts.[482] even the continual drainage of skilled men to Canada - 70 in one month.[483] Behind the scenes the Directors had had "a friendly expression of views" with Rushworth of the Dyers' Union and had decided "to meet the recent demand put by the workers."[484] The following was the new agreed scale for journeymen dyers - 24/- at 20 yrs; 21/- for others; 25/- at 21 yrs; 23/- for others; 27/- at 22 yrs; 24/- for others; 29/- at 23 yrs; 25/- for others; 30/- at 24 yrs; 26/- for others; 31/- at 25 yrs; 27/- for others; 32/- at 26 yrs; 28/- for others; 33/- at 27 yrs; 29/- for others, if skilled; 34/- at 28 yrs; 30/- for others, if skilled. These were good wages for dyers and other skilled workers, but for the mass of female workers higher differentials were worse than useless. Many felt that they should have had something in view of R.D. Pullar's statement that "there was better trade in 1913,"[485] as well as the firm's purchase of a fleet of 3-ton Commer vans and 15 cwt Albions.

The N.F.W.W. co-operated with W. Rushworth and held "enthusiastic meetings" for female workers at the North British Dye Works.[486] Noted for his eloquence he won "large numbers of recruits." Some of the newspapers remarked on this and asked "How long till a Labour M.P. in Perth?"[487] Certainly all the signs indicated that the workers were abandoning Liberalism in droves and moving left politically. Miss Sloan of the N.F.W.W. announced that "Perth was the most costly place in the U.K."[488] The "Perth Courier" checked her figures and found them to be accurate[489] - since 1906 rent, food, fuel and clothing had gone up by 10% while wages had only risen by 3% in Perth. The conclusion was obvious - "Perth has the highest food costs and the lowest pay." This revelation spurred the Dyers' Union to demand standard wages throughout the U.K.[490] They clarified their demands - a national minimum of 36/- a week for all dyers, finishers, cleaners, dyehouse labourers and apprentices, with an extra 2/- a week for all on a fixed wage for a 51 hour week and with all overtime at 1 1/2 rates. Other workers in Perth were equally strident in their demands, sometimes violently.[491] The Suffragettes too added their own particular brand of unrest.[492]

The pressure on R.D. Pullar was severe and he and his Directors decided to strike back. Apparently, a Henry Gloag, elected Shop Steward, asked R.D. Pullar about the non-payment of advances.[493] He was told that his services were no longer required as he was "unsuitable." Angered by this constant prodding R.D. Pullar instructed managers "to prepare lists of men no longer required" as they had more dyers than they needed and business was slack. The managers took the hint and they sent in the names of the leaders in the recent strike. Rushworth was furious and called "a mass meeting."[494] He told his audience that "the most prominent Trade Unionists in the firm had been selected — for dismissal purely on the grounds of their activity." He reminded them that James Wilson had worked competently in the Benzine Department for 13 years and could hardly be described as "unsuitable." Another 9 listed men had actually entered the firm's service as boys and that almost all of the recent Strike Committee were included. What was worse, advertisements were already out for replacements. Seething with anger the meeting resolved that "We ask the *right* to discuss the case of any worker dismissed."[495] The Directors' response was shallow: "Work is slack and it is desirable for such men to have wider and more varied practical experience than can be gained in any works." They added that "there was no victimisation" and that the replacements were not dyers, but "specialists." Significantly, of the 27 men finally dismissed by the firm in February, 1914, all but one were trade unionists. As the editor of the "Perthshire Advertiser" described it: "A feeling of fear pervades the Works." Rushworth called another meeting of his 600 members[496] at which he described the move by management as an attempt to lower production costs by taking on cheaper labour and "to crush the recently formed Union, which in 18 months had won a standard scale." Again, irritated by such comments, R.D. Pullar circulated a Petition of Loyalty to the Firm which was signed by 1,671 of the 1,947 work-force, but 276 bluntly refused. When arbitration was suggested R.D. Pullar refused on the grounds that 80% of the staff had signed the Petition "spontaneously." The "Perthshire Advertiser" analysed the situation[497] - "Due to changes that have taken place in recent years the same relationship does not exist now between masters and men." The editor blamed the fall in the value of money which forced the workers to ask for higher wages. The Directors, although they protested that they were not opposed to Trade Unions, clearly discouraged them. Trade Union activists complained that there were too many overseers and that "the Directors knew too much about the workers' private affairs." Once again the Dyers' Union had no option but "to let their grievances sleep."[498] They had suffered yet another defeat.

This was R.D. Pullar's second victory over the Trade Unions and perhaps it was no accident that he was almost immediately elected President of the Society of Dyers and Colourists at Bradford.[499] Apart from some concern over possible sewage pipe repairs[500] he had much to feel pleased about in that the Royal Commission on Housing in Scotland had lavishly praised his model cottages at Tulloch which stood out in glaring contrast to the squalid slums of the Cow Vennel, Meal Vennel and Thimblerow.[501] Other employers were struggling unsuccessfully to combat Trade Union demands and may well have sought his advice.[502] Thomson's Fair City Dye Works was not really "a hygienic Laundry"[503] and the Perthshire Laundry Company was continually being fined for overtime offences.[504]

Suddenly, on 4 August, 1914 came War. On the first day of hostilities 100 men from John Pullar and Sons rushed to the colours, while the firm donated 3 of their largest motor vans to the military and a large hall to the Red Cross. The Directors bought a large stock of wool and encouraged their girls to knit comforts for the troops in slack periods. The mass of the workers joined in to collect money for ambulances.[505] The Pullar family did not shirk either: H.S. Pullar went to the Scottish Horse, G.D. Pullar to the 6th Black Watch and J.L. Pullar to the 4th Black Watch.

At first the Directors expected a vast increase in business from the Army - cleaning mattresses and blankets, dyeing uniforms - and for a short spell this was so. But rail traffic dislocation caused by troop trains soon compelled the firm to go on short time.[506] By October, 1914 a more serious problem had emerged - "a famine in dyes."[507] Few people appreciated how vital aniline dyes were for the national economy, nor how widely they were used - in cotton and woollen fabrics, wall-papers, carpets boot polish, straw hats, feathers, paint, leather, hemp, ink, soap, jute and linoleum.[508] At Manchester, Lord Moulton summed up the situation: "The U.K. is at the mercy of Germany as a source of dyes and will be even after the War."[509] Imports were £2,000,000 a year for an industry producing £200,000,000 per annum and employing 1,500,000 people. On 10 November, 1914 the Board of Trade met at Manchester "to devise methods of increasing the supply of synthetic dyes with the help of H.M.G." A Committee of six was elected to form a joint stock company "to make and supply synthetic colours" and these were - R. Lennox Lee, Calico Printers' Association Limited; Milton S. Sharp, Bradford Dyers' Association Limited; H.W. Christie, United Turkey Red Company; Charles Diamond, English Sewing Company Limited; G. Manchetti, John Crossley and Sons, Limited and R.D. Pullar, John Pullar and Sons, Limited. Essentially, their plan was to set up a Limited Company under the Companies Act with a £3,000,000 share capital of 3,000,000 shares of £1 each. On allotment 2/6d per share would be paid and a further 5/- on 30

R. D. Pullar (PKDLA)

June, 1915. The remaining 12/6/d would be paid at 2/6d a call every six months. H.M.G. would advance £1,500,000 at 4 $^1/_2$ % interest secured on assets and an undertaking to repay in 25 years. The interest on the advance and a Sinking Fund for its repayment were "to be payable only out of the net profits of the Company which are to be cumulative." If £3,000,000 were subscribed then H.M.G. would advance £750,000 and another £750,000 on the 5/- call. H.M.G. would also appoint two Directors with "power to vote any undue encroachment on the business of British Manufacturers' products other than dyes or colours" and these would be Sir Gilbert Calughton, London and North-West Railway Company and Sir Frank Adam, C.I.E. Of course the Company would remain British. Five years after peace consumers would only take supplies if they were of "good quality and at reasonable prices" and these would be determined by an independent referee. Ree, Holliday and Sons, Limited, a Colour Works, would be "taken over" and their plant extended; other companies would follow. Any company would be allowed to trade with the Swiss and the Company's Board would consist of "businessmen who are not in dyeing." An Advisory Committee of Dye Users would be set up with access to experts. Alcohol, for the Company, would be free of duty and German patents could be ignored. With this as a basis queries were sent out to assess support especially how much capital would be subscribed? And would users only buy from the Company?

By January, 1915 reactions came in[510] with both R.D. Pullar and P. Campbell for it. Some felt that the scheme needed more capital and suggested that H.M.G. should find all the money; others felt that H.M.G. should not be involved and that tariffs should be placed on dyes. The important Bradford Dyers' Association Limited was even more direct in its criticisms.[511] It condemned the "faulty structure" and urged H.M.G. to give another £500,000 immediately and grants-in-aid for 10 years. At this point Milton S. Sharp and Lennox B. Lee resigned.[512] For H.M.G. this was a crisis.[513] Most critics had advised an enlarged Board and this was duly accepted. It met for the first time in London on 28 January, 1915 and consisted of the following[514] Sir A.F. Firth, D.L., J.P., President, Association of Chambers of Commerce, U.K.; Sir Frank Hollis, Chairman, Horrockes, Crowden and Company, Limited; Sir Mark Olroyd; H.W. Christie; J. Clarkson; Charles Diamond; Kenneth Lee; G. Marchetti and R.D. Pullar. In a short time they accepted the modified Treasury Scheme, "The National Dye Scheme", which suggested an initial share capital of £2,000,000 with £1,000,000 issued at once and H.M.G. undertaking to equal the amount subscribed up to £1,000,000 as a loan for 25 years. Interest would be 4% on net profits and only become cumulative after 5 years. There would be no compulsory Sinking Fund but dividends and shares would be limited to 6% per annum on paid-up shares so long as the Government advance was outstanding. Research would receive £100,000 per annum for 10 years from H.M.G., which would nominate two Directors. On 10 February, 1915 R.D. Pullar spoke to Glasgow Chamber of Commerce[515] urging them to accept the new scheme which was "more insurance than investment." They agreed.[516] London also agreed[517] as did Manchester.[518] The new company therefore was called British Dyes Limited and "reasonable prices" were promised. However, it still had a difficult hurdle to pass - Parliament. In the debates of February, 1915[519] it was described as "a mix-up of everything, a miserable compromise."[520] The absence of a Sinking Fund was called "slack finance" and H.M.G. nominees "mere spies." Even Sir W. Ramsay, 1904 Nobel Prize Winner in Chemistry, called it "a fraudulent scheme." At Manchester the Users of Synthetic Dyes were not enthusiastic and they listened impatiently to Mr. Eastman argue that "In the national interests the scheme should continue." At Bradford R.D. Pullar argued likewise.[521] In fact, R.D. Pullar was inundated with work for the scheme as a member of the Dye Users' Committee based at Huddersfield[522] and as President of the Society of Dyers and Colourists at Bradford.[523] He was constantly on the move, arguing, cajoling and persuading.[524] The First Report for the Shareholders of British Dyes Limited in August, 1916 showed that he had not worked so hard in vain.[525]

At the North British Dye Works great efforts were being made too. There were "Treats for Belgians" and "Smokers for Troops"[526] and part of Kinnoull Street Workers' Rest had been turned into a Black Watch Club with gramophone, piano and hot meals. The Works Fire Brigade horses had gone to the Army[527] and the firm had to buy a tractor. Edison Electric vans were also purchased to speed up the distribution of goods. Sadly, casualties began to be reported steadily.[528] By August, 1915 it was clear that the War was not going well and cold reality replaced wild enthusiasm. From March, 1916 R.D. Pullar served on the Tribunal Appeal for Perthshire[529] and occasionally had to appear on behalf of his own employees.[530] His policy was consistent - "not to appeal for anyone." Left with old men and the unfit it was not long before dyers became scarce[531] as more and more of them died in France.[532] With the decline in dress and household goods cleaning the factory had to go on short-time in 1915.[533]

Yet, unknown to the public the Engineering Department "produced munitions and mechanics made shells" on a small, but specialised scale. Full-time working was restored in May, 1915 with the countryside being scoured for herbs, mosses and lichens to use as dyes[534] while staff adopted POW's held in Germany. In July, 1916 the award of War Bonuses of up to 7/- weekly to dye workers in England caused a wave of restlessness in the factory.[535] It even attracted more attention than the news that charabanc outings were cancelled because of the petrol shortage[536] or the fact that 409 men were serving as "Pullars' Battalion" in the Army.[537]

There were good reasons for the workers' interest in more money. In the first six months of the War prices had risen by 30%[538] while coal was scarce[539] and clothing had risen by as much as 70% in price.[540] Almost every section of the community, even police, was threatening strike action[541] as the 1899 £ fell in value to 16/3d. The air was thick with rumours of huge profits being made by dyeing firms and the workers wanted their share in the form of War Bonuses.[542] Drink was an ever-increasing menace both to society and the war-effort,[543] so much so that a National Patriotic Pledge Campaign Against Drink was launched.[544] Drink prices were raised[545] but had no effect "because there was so much excitement in the air."[546] So serious was the problem that in 1915 Defence of the Realm Acts had to be use to close pubs at 7pm.[547] Soldiers' wives, in particular, were noted as "heavy drinkers."[548] Many turned to prostitution and a "Moral Watch" patrolled the streets at night.[549] Care-playing on the Inches[550] and "juvenile cigarette smoking" increased dramatically.[551] In this spiral of despair more and more workers came out on strike.[552] By February, 1917 the cost of living had risen by 89% in Perth[553] and even the humble loaf sold at 1/1d.[554]

At P. and P. Campbell full-time working continued throughout 1914-1915, although 25% of the men had gone to the colours.[555] Dyes were scarce and expensive and the Cleaning Department had almost ceased to exist with the collapse of the city's social life. The distilling plant however had been improved despite two pollution scares in 1915.[556] The latter was "a very difficult year"[557] and the firm was glad to acquire "a substantial holding" in British Dyes Limited.[558] Part of the dye-works was occupied by Royal Engineers and Leonard Rigg, manager, was continually before the City Tribunal[559] pleading for his skilled men - "If we lose more qualified dyers, the doors of the Works will be closed - for ever!"[560] But the War Machine was insatiable and by 1917 not only was Peter Campbell in uniform, but so were 70% of his men. Thomson's Fair City Dye Works, with its staff of 150, was "prosperous" 1914-1915, especially in laundry contracts for military hospitals.[561] Thereafter, matters deteriorated and the firm was "hard-hit" in 1916 and "a disastrous conflagration" in 1917 totally destroyed the Dye Works and caused damage to the value of £15,000 to the laundry wing.[562]

The Amalgamated Society of Dyers, Bleachers, Finishers and Kindred Trades managed to secure "a cost-of-living rise" of 3/- per man and 1/9d for women and boys on 20 June, 1916. However, the various branches reported that this "was not enough." In August, 1916 therefore they appealed to H.M.G. and the Board of Trade for help. These refused. The Dyers' Union, in November, 1916 then held a Conference in Glasgow at which it was agreed to demand another 10/- per man and 6/- for everybody else in the industry or they would strike by November, 1916.[563] Some, indeed, in the west of Scotland did strike. In Perth there was fear of what the Dyers' Union might do.[564] Many felt that the demand was unreasonable given that the workers already had a War Bonus of 7/- per man and 4/8d for others. The Directors of John Pullar and Sons were quick to respond. They explained that their costs had risen steeply due to the rise in the price of dyestuffs, coal, packing materials, rail delays, etc., while the volume of trade had fallen.[565] The Dyers' Union decided to take the matter to arbitration and in January, 1917 the Arbitrator, Sir Thomas Munro, decided for the Trade Union against ten of the country's most famous firms - United Turkey Red Company; Messrs W. Fulton and Sons; Messrs. A. Hamilton and Sons; Bowling Bleaching Company; Messrs. Wallace and Company; Messrs. J. McNab and Company; Eastwood Bleaching Company; Messrs. Pollock and Cochrone; Messrs. J. McLardy and Sons; and Messrs. A. Robertson and Sons. They had refused to accept a decision made in Glasgow on 9 December, 1916 that all timeworkers over 18 years should have "war wages" of 8/- and that girls and youths should have 5/-; that piece workers under 35/- weekly should have a rise of 22 1/2%; that piece workers earning 35/- to 45/- weekly should have a rise of 17 1/2%; that piece workers earning over 45/- weekly should have a rise of 15 1/2%; that all these would be payable by 11 December, 1916. Five big firms had accepted at once - Messrs. W.G. Mitchell and Company; Messrs. Crawford Easton; Messrs. J. Lean and Sons; Messrs. D. Macfarlane and Sons; and Hogganfield Bleaching and Finishing Company. Only one major firm stood apart - John Pullar and Sons, Limited, Perth. The Dyers' Union decided to launch an all-out war against them.

The opening shot was fired on 30 April, 1917 when William Rushworth,

General Secretary, wrote to the Directors of the North British Dye Works[566] suggesting "an advance to all workers of 10/- per week over pre-war rates" due to "the enormous increase in the price of food-stuffs." One sentence in the letter especially annoyed R.D. Pullar: "Your workers have become the lowest paid workers in Scotland." Apart from the fact that such rises would have put another £60,000 per annum on the wages bill without any increase in production, it was the cheap labour insult which was most resented. The Directors replied on 3 May, 1917 - "The statements contained in your letter do not apply to the workers in our employment." The Dyers' Union responded in turn by calling a meeting in the Lesser City Hall, Perth on 8 June, 1917. There were 5 speakers - Town Councillor and President of the Perth Trades Council, baker David Bruce; young war-widow, Mrs. Jessie Jardine, who accused Pullars of "pleading poverty every time";[567] John Teevin, Chairman of the Glasgow District Council of the Dyers' Union; Hugh Sinclair, gas worker and J.M. Rae, Secretary to the Perth Trades Council, who declared that "Pullars are hanging back."[568] The "spirited meeting" then elected a Committee. A week later Rushworth hired the City Hall on 14 June, 1917 and addressed a huge turnout of 1,500.[569] He told them that there were now 1,000 in the Union and he cleverly assessed the Pullar family: "This firm has been a good firm. There is no doubt about that. It was one of the best firms in Scotland. But times change. The late Mr. Pullar felt a certain responsibility towards Perth and his people. He decided firstly that there should be a living wage paid to his workers, but when he passes away his children began to grow up and they began to launch out. They took unto themselves wives, and they took big mansions. Where did they get them from? Out of their earnings. That was the most important reason why they are pleading poverty today. There is more profit being made now in dyeing and cleaning than in any trade in Scotland. They might pull the outsider, but they cannot pull you. They pulled you for five years, but they cannot pull you all the time." Often he waxed lyrical: "Capital has no conscience. The employer is only concerned as to what profit he is going to get. We are not here to create trouble and we have had enough talk about charitableness. We have had enough of the talk about gold watches at 50. We want no more of it. We have got past that stage. Once upon a time we felt we were serfs, today we are free men and women. We want to tell them to give us the money and we will buy our own watches!" He finished on a note which brought a thunderous ovation. "Why do men get 30/- and women 16/- for the same work? This will have to be sorted out after the

War." That night he again wrote to the Directors appealing for an independent arbiter. Their reply was brief - 1916 had seen "a heavy loss" and their geographical position was a serious disadvantage for trade. They said that they had not drawn any salary and had lost "a substantial portion of their capital." They urged the workers "to stop the present harmful agitation" and offered to show their books to an accountant to verify their claims. The editor of the "Perthshire Advertiser" made a valid point:[570] "Perth as a city is deeply - too deeply for its own good many think - concerned with the dyeing industry — a very large proportion of the city workers now find themselves at the edge of the precipice whither they have been brought by the 'one industry' dependence of Perth. They are shackled to a trade which is, in its essentials, a non-productive one."

At this stage Rushworth looked for wider support. In the City Hall on the evening of 21 June, 1917 some 1,500 people gathered to hear Councillor Bruce, Mr. Simpson, Scottish Organiser of the Amalgamated Union of Co-operative Society Assistants and Mr. Farquhar, Railway Workers' Union.[571] Bruce began by pouring scorn on wages in Perth's dyeing trade especially that of girls on 13/- a week. He quoted the case of a male foreman cleaner at Campbells with 30 years' experience and described by Mr. Rigg, manager, as "invaluable to the firm" at the City Tribunal Appeal, yet earning "a miserable 32/- weekly." He then made the interesting proposal that H.M.G. should subsidise wages while the War lasted. Farquhar spoke next pledging the support of his Union. His enthusiasm tended to overreach itself when he ended with the cry, "We are also exploited by Pullars!" Simpson's contribution was an attack on the "loyalists" - "We want all non-unionists cleaned out of the dyeworks in Perth once and for all!" Rushworth, as usual, was more pragmatic. He began by telling his audience how a carter in Perth earning 18/- a week in 1914 could now get 47/-; that a Glasgow firm had just given a blanket rise of 6/- a week to all its employees; that a Barrhead laundry paid its workers 38/- a week. He made the point that even Campbells had given rises of 1/- to 4/- recently, while Pullars had given nothing. He therefore issued a challenge to the Directors of John Pullar and Sons, Limited - a two months' trial with 10% rises to all employees and if their business fell by 10% then the money would be returned. Failing that, he offered to meet "any or all of them in public debate before the citizens of Perth." He mocked a Pullars' advertisement: "We are the patriotic firm; we have been working for no profit throughout the War; and there lies our case as to why we should clean you suit and have your custom at a minimum

price. The prices are so light that even the Directors do not get any salary."
After the laughter died down Rushworth commented acidly - "The
hardest pressed men and women in the dyeing trade in Scotland are those
employed at Pullars (applause) - in Perth there has been too much respect
for the Pullars; had there been less respect for them, the workers would
have been better off today! — They speak of 'harmful agitation'. The
Directors can afford a year without pay, but not the workers. The firm has
said that we can send an auditor to audit the books, but whilst the
accounts of a public company are published, those of a private company
are not, and one could make out any balancesheet of the kind he wanted.
— We do not imperil the firm and its interests — we believe there is not
a person in Britain who would refuse to pay the trivial extra changes to
cover the cost of war wages. We want to put our case before the Government
Board of Arbitration, and whatever decision it gives we will abide by it.
We do not want a dispute, but we do want an advance in wages. If the firm
are prepared to do that, things can go smoothly. The Glasgow workers got
a rise. Their firms charge 4/9d for work while Pullars charges 6/6d to 7/-.
We are to win! Nothing can stop us!"

Next day Rushworth again wrote to the Directors[572] suggesting that "a
small tax be placed upon all goods" which could be used to increase wages
for a three months' trial period. "If at the end of such a period the tax has
proved harmful to the firm, your workers agree to forego any increase
from that date." If refused then he again asked for arbitration. R.M.
Pullar responded with a veiled threat of closure and a reminder that wage
rises had been given in December, 1915 and in December, 1916. He also
urged the Union to note that the firm was paying generous allowances to
the dependents of a large number of serving soldiers. It now seemed as if
in impasses had been reached, but, behind the scenes Joseph Hayhurst
was making renewed efforts to find a solution. First, he wrote to the
Employers' Association of the Dyeing and Cleaning Trade in Scotland
urging a meeting.[573] Then he wrote to the Board of Trade in London giving
them the statutory 21 days' warning that "a dispute is imminent."[574] Finally,
there was a note to the Directors of John Pullar and Sons that under
D.O.R.A. and the Munition of War Act he was giving them the 7 days'
statutory warning also. During the lull that followed the editor of the
"Perthshire Advertiser" was again very perceptive;[575] "For the first time
in the existence of labour in this Perth industry, the wages problem has
ceased to be a local and has become a British trade dispute." He made the
salient point that there was English support for the strike and that strike

pay would probably be available. Another significant fact was that there were now 1,400 in the Dyers' Union.

Then, on Wednesday evening, 18 July, 1917 over 2,000 "enthusiastic workers" crowded into the City Hall for the Dyers' Union's fourth rally.[576] The platform party consisted of Rushworth, Mrs. Jardine, Mr. Munro of the N.U.R. and Mr. Baker, Organiser of the Shop Assistants' Union. Mrs. Jardine began by saying that Perth had "some need of alternative employment to dyeing", preferably munitions work and she even hinted that Pullars might be responsible for its absence. But it was Rushworth that people had come to hear. He did not disappoint them. He told them that the Masters' Association had refused to negotiate and that the Directors had turned down his request for a rise three times. He described how the lowest paid, unskilled female in Glasgow had 19/- a week, while workers in Pullars and Campbells averaged 16/- a week if over 20 years and only 13/- if under. He reminded them that a lb of butter was 2/2d, a dozen eggs 2/9d and a loaf of bread 1/6d "and for this they work from 6am to 5pm - for a lb of butter, a dozen eggs and a loaf! How do they pay the rent? Remember, the pre-war £ is now worth only 3/6d." Some 90% of the dyeworkers were in the Union, but when he went to Tulloch he could not get "a single man to stand for fear he would lose the house he lived in." Then he warned them - "You have not joined the Union for a bit of fun. If there is anyone afraid to sign that paper, if there is anyone from now not prepared to give the master 7 days' notice I advise them to leave the Hall and their Trade Union." None did. "If you are on strike then go berry-picking! I have been in 14 strikes and I have won 14 times!" He ended with his customary, dramatic flourish: "There is more in this than an advance in wages. This movement is an awakening of the intelligence of Perth." That night each worker had to decide whether he or she would sign the ballot paper and give 7 days' notice.

In fact, the Dyers' Union were anxious to avoid a strike and they asked their members to delay handing in their notices while Hayhurst and Rushworth made a dash to London to consult with the Board of Trade.[577] P. and P. Campbell's Directors had not been inactive. They sent an open letter to the newspapers in which they claimed that their workers were "satisfied" because they had had a rise in June, 1917 and always got overtime when busy without having deductions in slack spells. They also posted a Works Notice[578] stating that "It took years to bring the dyeing trade to Perth, before there were any large works in the South. Now there are many well-equipped garment dyeworks in England, employing non-union labour, and if the trade is driven to them it can never be brought back." It warned that munition-making would not outlast the War and was therefore not the answer. It asked them to await the judgement of the Board of Trade.[579] During the waiting period the Dyers' Union delayed notices for a second time[580] but doubts began to grow by 6 August, 1917 when these were expressed at an N.U.R. rally on the North Inch by Robert Smillie, President of the British Miners' Federation and John Marchbank of the N.U.R. Equally puzzled by the delay were Campbell's Directors - "The masters are really compelled to consider the matter of winding up the business of the firm, that is if the strike notices of the workers are given in — a temporary stoppage would mean a breakdown of the industry and the nature of the trade is such that it could not be stopped and restarted."[581] Some of the men at Campbells may have changed their minds when they heard that closure would mean conscription for 102 men.[582] Many others had made up their minds. On 18 August, 1917 some 681 workers at Pullars and 211 at Campbells handed in their notices, a total of 892, far short of actual Union strength. Bluntly, the facts, as the public saw it, were these - some 900 dyeworkers intended to strike for a rise in wages; Pullars refused even to discuss the matter and Campbells "having given a small concession" threatened to close down.[583]

On 21 August, 1917 the Directors at P. and P. Campbell released details of rises given to 21 groups of workers since June, 1914.[584] They ranged from 3/- to Feather workers to 12/- for Stenters. They also announced an immediate rise of 2/- per week to all those whose previous rise was less than 5/- and a further 1/- for those over the 5/- a week. Mr. P.W. Campbell asked staff to meet him on 22 August, 1917 to discuss these details.[585] The meeting did not last long. Mrs. Jardine's comment, "They are trying to get behind the Union," guaranteed that. All the workers gave the same reply: "We want to work through the Union!" That very day Pullars also launched their counter-attack on the Dyers' Union.[586] They issued a statement repeating their previous views with a clear threat - "We do not see our way to carry on longer under present unsatisfactory conditions. Every worker who is paid fortnightly will not be needed after Thursday, 6 September, 1917 and every worker paid weekly will not be needed after 1 September, 1917. A statement containing the new conditions of employment will be issued in the course of next week, and everyone employed at present will be eligible for re-engagement and is invited to make application." Most dyeworkers were stunned by this announcement and blamed the long delay by the Board of Trade

Officials. Perth Trades Council sent a report and a protest to the Minister of Labour and appointed a Committee of Twelve "in case of a strike" as well as formally asking the City of Perth Co-operative Society "to come forward with material help, such as augmenting the Union allowance."

For some time Hayhurst and Mrs. Jardine had suspected that Campbells were the weaker of the two dyeing firms and much more likely to yield under pressure. This was indeed what happened on 24 August, 1917 when both parties "after a frank discussion" agreed that there would be no strike and that they would go to arbitration. This must have been a heavy blow for the Pullars' Directors, but they were quick to react. They released a notice stating that they Dyers' Union had induced 31% of the men and 60% of the women to tender notices to terminate their employment. This was an opportunity to introduce "the new arrangements" which, hopefully, "may mark the beginning of happier days for workers and Directors alike." They suggested that those who wanted to work present themselves at noon on Tuesday, 28 August, 1917 and although there would be no steam or power there would be plenty to do, preparing what had come in and despatching what was left on Saturday. "If intimidation in any form is in evidence, we advise you not to enter the Works, but to go home and write to us that you presented yourself prepared to work. In that event you will be paid as if you had been working the full day." Old and faithful servants were told not to worry and that "we promise that those who occupy our houses will not be disturbed within a reasonable time, even if any of them decide not to re-engage under the new conditions."

The Dyers' Union realised that they had to act swiftly. That night "a densely packed meeting in a demonstrative mood met in the Co-operative Hall. Rushworth, who received his usual "enthusiastic reception" was "temperate" having just returned from the Board of Trade in London. He was scathing in his attack on "Pullars' Circular 2" which said that "the firm will pay full wages to those that blackleg!" He urged each worker to write to Pullars, "the autocrats", to demand that work should only be offered to trade unionists. He had asked the Directors for lying time on Saturday, but this had not been rejected. "Don't accept your Insurance Cards — When you do strike — Pullars will remember it!"[587] Next day it was learned that R.D. Pullar was off to London with details of his "new reconstruction" which included a 48 hour week for all departments, including parcel-post and warehouse, with a start at 6.30am; full-time for all employees; and a Bonus Scheme to be worked out. The editor of the "Perthshire Advertiser" described it as "the first real crisis in the history

G

of dyeing in Perth" and mused sadly: "Is the fabric of the country's diligence to be ruthlessly torn down in an hour?"

Monday, 27 August, 1917 was a public holiday and Rushworth's train was met by "hundreds of well-wishers" who formed a procession and led by Mrs. Jardine marched to the North Inch "singing defiant protest songs." That evening 2,000 people, "a record attendance", crammed into the City Hall.[588] Councillor David Bruce was first to speak - "The railwaymen have unanimously resolved to levy themselves in connection with the dispute and strike in sympathy if necessary." This, he explained, was why R.D. Pullar had been summoned so urgently to London - fear of a rail strike. He told them how R.D. Pullar had said he disliked arbitration and did not accept that workers had the right to Trade Unions. Bruce then delivered his battle-cry: "Tomorrow will be the Battle of the Gates - it will be your Bannockburn (applause)!" Mr. Sime, Organiser of the Jute and Textile Workers, Dundee told the audience that this dispute was like that in Lochee when the workers challenged Cox in 1911. "You have to teach the Pullars the lesson we had to teach Cox in 1911." James Taylor, who presided, reminded his listeners that the Finishing Department had a bonus scheme a few years ago. It started at 12/-, but after three weeks it was cut to 8/- and eventually it was reduced to 4/-. Thus, "Bonus means Blood Money!" He urged them to remember that Campbells would never have yielded without enormous pressure from Rushworth and Mrs. Jardine. "We should have 8 hours a day and 8/- a day" he said amidst gales of laughter and applause. From the body of the Hall a Mr. Roy stood and voiced the feelings of the majority - "The 48 hour week is so much bunkum - we practically have it already. I think this reconstruction scheme is a scheme to get behind the Union and we should denounce it for that; we want our negotiation conducted through the proper channel in the Union." He then proposed "That this meeting of the Dyers' and Bleachers' Union resolves to stand by their previous demand, feeling that the new proposals were indefinite and were not conducted through the proper channels." This was carried unanimously. Then it was Rushworth's turn. He told them how Pullars and Campbells in 1913 had agreed to pay 16/- to girls at 18 years of age. Campbells had only done so for the last six months. "The Messrs. Campbell had been robbing the girls — no wonder Perth had been the black spot of Scotland for the last 30 or 40 years." Campbells had now agreed to arbitrate, "but was this simply to grab Pullars' trade? For the past five years Pullars had not been too bad, but now they had produced these half thought out proposals. For nine weeks

Pullars have played hide and seek with the Union, and then, in 24 hours, drafted a new agreement!" He condemned the fact that there were too many supervisory staff, "one cause of the trouble," and he savaged the bonus scheme proposal: "The bonus system is the curse of the trade - a brutally scientific method of piece work by an employer to get 12 hours' work out of a person in 9 hours. It should have been fought and killed years ago!" He ended with a fighting cry - "You are going to tell the people of Scotland and England that Perth is no longer a black spot, but one of the most advanced cities in the country."

Next day it rained, but the constant drizzle did not dampen the high spirits of the strikers. That Tuesday morning, 28 August, 1917 pickets were out and greeted loyalists with a chorus of boos at Tulloch. At Kinnoull Street the eight gates were guarded by police. At first there was only "good humoured chaff" but things soon changed when a group of about 100 loyalists appeared.[589] These were mainly older workers who were "not in sympathy with the strike." Their arrival sent a wave of anger through the strikers, especially the women, who "acted hysterically - coats were torn, a policeman was slapped and another had his helmet knocked off by an umbrella." Trade Union officials rushed around trying to discourage "the forceful picketing" and begged their members not to use force. All this had been seen by A.E. and R.M. Pullar from their windows and they decided to act. At 9am precisely a notice was posted at both Perth and Tulloch - WORKS TO CLOSE TILL FURTHER NOTICE. As the loyalists streamed homeward they were received with howls of derision. The strikers then asked for their lying time and when this was refused they paraded through the streets and held open-air meetings.

They were back next day banging empty tins and demanding their money which was given to them under the watchful eye of "bodies of Constables in the vicinity." Money in their pockets quietened them and they dispersed. The following day, Thursday, 30 August, 1917 they held sports on the North Inch. This was very peaceful apart from "some hostility" shown to a Director foolish enough to venture on the Inch to see what was happening.[590] The succeeding two days were also quiet, although there was the astonishing news that R.D. and A.E. Pullar had gone to Inverness on holiday. More interesting to the strikers was the news that Councillor David Bruce, foreman pastry baker, had been dismissed by the Co-operative Society and the Perth bakers were threatening strike action in sympathy. "Could it be victimisation?" asked the "Perthshire Advertisier."[591] Before any reaction could be assessed the Directors published their reconstruction scheme:

"To The Workers
On Saturday, 25 August, 1917 we said that our proposals include
(1) a 48 hour week (2) full-time (3) a bonus system.

1. (a) the 48 hours per week arrangement will begin at 6.30am on Monday, 17 September, 1917 as follows: 6.30-9.00; 10.00-1.00; 2.00-5.—; Saturday 6.30-9.00 and 10.00-1.00.
   (b) the hours for those who are unable to work at 6.30 will be 43$^{1/2}$ hours per week beginning 8.45am on Monday, 17 September, 1917 as follows: 8.45-1.00; 2.00-5.30; Saturday 8.45-1.30.
2. Full-time for all workers from Wednesday, 22 August, 1917.
3. Bonus. The Chairman, when in London on 28 August, 1917 saw the originator of the system, which we hope to adopt in our industry.
4. Wages. We ask you to elect a Committee of Women and Men to assist the Directors in preparing new scales with our new conditions.
5. Re-opening. We estimate that all who are willing to give our proposals a fair trial may resume work at his or her usual hour on Wednesday, 5 September, 1917 without any formal re-engagement.

This notice was read by "a considerable crowd" and although there was no demonstration there was a mood of sullen resentment that the Union was still ignored. That afternoon the strikers paraded the streets headed by a Charlie Chaplin!

By Tuesday, 4 September, 1917 "the air was electric with pent-up feeling."[592] Detachments of police from Forfarshire and Dundee had been seen at the Police Station while Mounted Police from Lanarkshire rode out of the Railway Station.[593] Rumour had it that at least 40 had arrived in the city. The strikers, after formally rejecting the new proposals, massed on the South Inch and 800 of them led by a brass band and waving banners and escorted by "many N.U.R. men" marched through the streets "to the cheers of thousands."[594] That night they assembled in the City Hall where there was not even standing room and hundreds were turned away. James Taylor spoke of the "great support" from Glasgow; "The citizens of Perth are not fighting for material or pecuniary gain to themselves, but merely for a standard wage given throughout the United

Kingdom and in asking it they are only asking for their rights and self-protection." Councillor David Bruce told how the Manchester Union of Dyers had sent representatives to Perth as far back as 1877 to set up a Trade Union branch, but Pullars had "sabotaged this by starting full-time. Pullars dominates its workers. It is said that Pullars made Perth. That is a lie. Perth made Pullars and Pullars has brought the condition of the citizens to the verge of starvation." J.M. Rae denied that the strike was the outcome of outside agitation - "nobody can live on pre-war wages!" Mrs. Jardine's contribution was a slogan: "It's better wages we want!"

Then Hugh Sinclair gave a short, fiery address and ended with the cry: "I would rather be a hooligan than a blackleg!" When Rushworth appeared he was greeted by the Dyers' Strike Song and an excited ovation. He began by saying that Pullars was trying to starve them back to work, but "as contributions were pouring in strike pay would probably be doubled." He defined hooliganism as bringing strange police into the city. "Messrs. Pullars are not fighting Pullars' workers, but the citizens of Perth. If they brought the Devil from Hell they would not beat the workers." He explained why he was against an N.U.R. boycott of Pullars for the moment. "Messrs. Pullar and the Police must remember this, we are not a deteriorated remnant of the Trade Union army, we are a regular part of the Trade Union army of Britain." He poured contempt on the fact that the Directors had gone off to Inverness on holiday. "They can go to Monte Carlo if they wish. Did they go there out of the losses they had sustained for the last three or four years? Messrs. Pullar never touched a single garment sent there to be cleaned. They touched nothing but the money at the end of each period — The Union had done more for Perth in a week, paying 10/- to each man, than the firm of Pullars has done for half a century." Then he laughed at the idea that girls paying 10/- a week for digs from 5/- strike pay welcomed a strike. Men had been more fortunate with their strike pay scaled at 8/- to 9/- a week. Cheques were coming in from sympathetic businessmen and there was tremendous support from the N.U.R. and the bakers. The evening ended with the battle-cry from James Taylor - "Tomorrow will be fought our Waterloo!" That night the strikers paraded the street singing and shouting till the small hours.

Wednesday, 5 September, 1917 dawned, "the day that the Battle of the Gates became a reality." A few, brave loyalists managed to sneak into the works at 3am, long before the mass of strikers were even awake. By 5am however they were at the homes of well-known nonunionists trying to persuade them to stay off work. Those courageous enough to reject the veiled threats were escorted to Kinnoull Street to a chorus of abuse. One was even physically assaulted and locked in a cellar. By 5.30am it was still dark as 65 police arrived to take up position - two to each corner. Before long "a very large crowd" gathered at the corner of Mill Street - Kinnoull Street to greet each loyalist with shouts of "Blackleg!" Many of them turned for home "after some pretty rough handling." Female strikers tore the hats off four women and one manager had to be protected by no fewer than twelve policemen before reaching his office. Several loyalists were carried bodily into the works and one of these collapsed, seriously ill. At 6am another wave of demonstrators arrived to make "an enormous and aggressive crowd" and "the booing, hissing and jostling intensified." At the main gate alone there were at least 500 strikers. Suddenly, three Lanarkshire Mounted Police galloped up Mill Street. Their appearance made the crowd "very hostile" as they tried to form a cordon in Mill Street, opposite the Sandeman Library. By this time only 24 female loyalists had actually gained entrance to the works through the howling mob of some 2,000 outside. Observers noted that even the curious onlookers were now "clearly on the side of the strikers." Precisely at 7am "another body of strange Police appeared, jeered at by the hilarious girls." One of the police seized a male demonstrator who had deliberately jostled him and flung him to the ground. "The mob became infuriated and blows were exchanged with the Police as the scene of disorderliness continued." Missiles - fruit, skins, apples, stones, old shoes, rings, oily waste and even iron punches were hurled at the horsemen."[595] One hit a sergeant's horse, it reared and darted into the crowd. "There was a mad scramble for safety with much screaming on the part of the women and at least four people were knocked down." Matters were fast getting out of control and Chief Constable Scott called on the Trade Union leaders to control their supporters. Taylor pleaded for "no rowdyism" and Rushworth begged for "peaceful protest." When asked to disperse the crowd he did so, reluctantly. At 8am they were back to block the entry of the warehouse and clerical staff. Again there were scenes of fighting and pandemonium. One clerk was felled by a blow and a female office worker fainted. For almost an hour the mob seethed to-and-fro in a constant see-saw battle with the police. Chief Constable Scott had by now decided that a more vigorous policy was needed and four youths and a woman were hauled from the melee and arrested. Another arrest followed and missiles were thrown at the police again. All this had been witnessed by frightened workers in the dyeworks and at 9am some of them decided to stop work and go home. They had to run a gauntlet of baying demonstrators. By 10am the crowd was even greater and it was apparent that the most vociferous group were about 100 N.U.R. men. Suddenly, the mob began to break up. They reassembled at the Co-operative Hall at 11am where James Taylor denounced the use of horses and warned that unless they were withdrawn he would call for a General Strike. Rushworth also deplored the use of mounted police. Despite this, both men felt that the Union "had won a great victory." That afternoon the strikers gathered on the North Inch to be told that they had succeeded in their aim as less than 100 loyalists had actually got to work and these had all left early. Conscious of "having won the fight" they marched through the city in a mile long procession with a brass band and fluttering banners singing -

"If it wasn't for the gallant little Union
Where would the dyeworks by?"

Even the "Perthshire Advertiser" described it as "a catchy refrain." Late that night the exhausted police told their Chief Constable that if the confrontation was repeated on Thursday they "would draw their batons." Somewhat alarmed, Scott immediately told Sheriff-Principal Wilson, K.C.[596] He, in his turn, acted swiftly. A meeting was held with Scott and they agreed to summon more Mounted Police to Perth. Then, together, they called on James Taylor and "roused him from his bed." He agreed to do what he could to keep the peace and he sent word to the N.U.R. at once ordering them to stay away from the dyeworks. This done, a visit was paid to R.D. Pullar and after some discussion he decided that he had no alternative but to close down the works.[597]

At 5am on Thursday, 6 September, 1917 notices were posted at Perth and Tulloch -

"To All Workers
At the request of Sheriff Wilson, the Sheriff-Principal of Perthshire, and in order to maintain the peace, Messrs. Pullar have agreed to close their Works, September 5, 1917."

During the night word had been passed to all non-unionists to stay away from the works and when over 1,000 strikers gathered at the gates at 6 am they were "startled to read the announcement." Who had taken the initiative? The Sheriff or R.D. Pullar? The notices were soon "mutilated and defaced" and wild talk of "pressure" was on every lip. Fortunately, James Taylor appeared, tired and drawn: "I was invited to co-operate, but this is still a Union victory. No worker will enter the Works!" Slowly and quietly the crowd dispersed and by 6.30 am the street was deserted. In fact, they had gone to Tay Street to the Burgh Police Court where an ironer was fined £1 "for striking a Constable on the face with her open hand." When she left the Court she was applauded by hundreds. That evening there was a "Victory Dance" in the Co-operative Hall and next day a picnic at Buckie Braes. Behind the scenes the Perth Trades Council had written to A.F. Whyte, M.P., "complaining about the use of Police which has led to the riot," as well as to the Secretary of the Parliamentary Committee of the Trades Union Congress at Blackpool asking for assistance. The editor of the "Perthshire Advertiser" described "the silence of the great Works as almost eerie" and told of "hundreds roaming the streets idle." He added a piece of sound advice – " Let us have more of the human touch, as in the old days, and mindful of changing conditions, less of the vanity which precedes a fall or the violence which alienates sympathy and brings its own Nemesis." There was also sad news - the dye-worker taken ill while trying to get to work had died. The Dyers' Union had to date distributed almost £400 to the strikers, 10/- a week for men and 7/- for women. Finally, the rumour that R.D. Pullar was ill was confirmed; he had suffered "a serious nervous breakdown" and this was the reason he had gone on holiday to "get a rest."

A kind of stalemate now ensued as both sides waited to see what would happen. The six young persons arrested on a charge of "being part of a riotous mob" were remitted to the Sheriff Court and released on bail. Interestingly, only two of them were trade unionists. At last on 12 September, 1917 it was announced that the arbiter in the Dyers' Union vs P. and P. Campbell dispute was to be Sir James Urquhart of Dundee. To some extent the city was returning to normal. But, in fact, many dyeworkers had left Perth convinced that Pullars would never employ them again. Others had gone to work for Campbells who were"amazingly busy" and were glad of skilled workers. They had no other choice as overtime was not allowed by the agreement with the Dyers' Union. Meanwhile, rumour had it that Hayhurst and A.E. Pullar had been called to London by the Ministry of Labour in view of the fact that industrial unrest had now spread to the Wallace Works and to the Balhousie Works.[598] On the 15 September, 1917 a Press Bureau was announced in Perth - "The Ministry of Labour has had a long interview with Mr A. E.

Pullar and his Manager, and has arranged for a conference to be presided over by the Duke of Atholl, Lord Lieutenant. The employer will select his own representatives, not to exceed six, the workpeople to appoint six representatives, who may be Unionists or non-Unionists and may include persons not employed by the firm." The strikers were delighted. It seemed as if their sacrifices had been worth while.

Their hopes were dashed when notices appeared at Perth and Tulloch on 17 September, 1917 –

"To All Workers
As suggested by the Ministry of Labour, these Works will be re-opened under the old conditions on Wednesday, 19 September, 1917 at 19 am."

This was "a bombshell to the workers and their Strike Committee."[599] Their assessment quickly turned to anger and bitterness, especially against the Dyers' Union. They were furious and felt betrayed. Neither Hayhurst nor Rushworth could be found to explain the situation. In fact, they were with Mrs. Jardine in the City Chambers at the Campbells' Arbitration Inquiry. Sir James Urquhart had the chair and their opponents were solicitors from McCash and Hunter, Perth, agents for Pullars. For hours the argument dragged on, but no decision seemed possible. During this time the entire Strike Committee went to the Station Hotel to see the Duke of Atholl and urge him to obtain from A.E. Pullar clearer guarantees as to what was in his mind. At 4 pm the strikers crowded into the Co-operative Hall to discuss the notice, but in the absence of their leaders the meeting was postponed till 7pm. At last, after seven hours of fruitless bargaining the Campbell Inquiry came to an end. The firm's offer had been refused and the dispute was now, officially, to go to avizandum. Hayhurst and his two colleagues rushed to the Co-operative Hall where "a very large gathering" awaited them. It was hostile. Nevertheless, Hayhurst began by saying that he "sincerely trusted that Mr Rufus Pullar would very quickly be restored to good health and again resume his duties as a Captain of Industry in the city." He then read the Strike Committee's Report: "The whole of your Strike Committee met today with the Duke of Atholl as intermediary between you and the Messrs Pullar and we have got such guarantees, explanations and assurances (approved by Messrs. Pullar), that we have no hesitation in advising you to resume work." This was met by "a chilly silence." Immediately, "a shrill female voice cried -

"We're no gaun in!" Rushworth, sensing opposition, was quick to reply: "You must trust your officials. We have won two great points - arbitration and recognition of the Union." He ended with an appeal to reason. "Your employers are autocrats. They have originated from a bygone age. They are still living in times 100 years ago, when the employer was entitled to own the machinery and the men and the women inside the works. You have got to break that down. You *will* break it down by reasoning, not by bludgeoning and pistolling!" Sullen and resentful the strikers dispersed quietly.

A crowd gathered at the factory gates on Wednesday, 19 September, 1917 and "they showed great reluctance to enter and some did not enter at all."[601] The Dyers' Union officials were now worried about the health of R.D. Pullar and expressed their concern to A.E. Pullar who assured them "that the illness was not linked to the strike troubles."[602] That very night, Rufus D. Pullar died in an Edinburgh Nursing Home from "severe strain and pneumonia." He was only 56 years and his son, R.M. Pullar, was by his side to the very end. His funeral was private and in striking contrast to the pomp and civic pageantry of Sir Robert's funeral. The "Perthshire Advertiser" described him as "clever and cultured"[603] while the "Perthshire Constitutional" called him " a man of kindly acts, great determination and enthusiasm.[604] The most accurate analysis came from the "Perth Courier" - "He had strong convictions and he was never afraid to stand by them - absolute integrity of purpose — punctual and thorough."[605]

On Monday, 24 September, 1917 at precisely 11am the Duke of Atholl opened the conference of the two sides at the Station Hotel, Perth.[606] The management side was led by A.E. Pullar and consisted of two other Directors and three non-unionists; the Dyers' Union was led by Mr Hayhurst and consisted of five other prominent trade unionists. At the very last moment Atholl allowed ten other unionists to be present, but only as spectators. The atmosphere was "generally friendly" as Atholl began by reminding them that work had ceased on 25 August, 1917 and that twice the firm had tried to re-open and twice disturbances had occurred.[607] The Minister of Labour had called A.E. Pullar and Hayhurst to London and suggested that the workers return as soon as possible while a settlement was sought. A.E. Pullar had insisted on the phrase "old conditions" and this had led to more unrest. A vote of condolence to Mrs R.D. Pullar was then passed and a formal letter from A.E. Pullar was read to the gathering and thereafter released to the press. Briefly, it was to the effect that he "intended to sell and if no buyer could be found he would close down."[608] He hinted that "negotiations were underway", but warned that any settlement reached that day "must be purely temporary and not binding on any buyer." No doubt the Dyers' Union side were taken aback by this declaration and it must have made them more amenable to the firm's proposals for a settlement. The unionists promised to examine these carefully and it was agreed to meet again on Thursday, 27 September, 1917 at 11.30am. Then A.E. Pullar spoke: "Before we part, will you allow me to say that personally, and to the other Directors, it is a matter of gratification– that we are no longer in a position of controversy with any section of our employees. We are not and have not been, regardless of the fact that the increased cost of living has pressed heavily on many employees. If that had been the sole point involved, there need never have been the necessity for the kindly intervention on the part of your Grace. But we had to take the wider view. Neither the present management, nor the management of past generations, we think, ever tried to press heavily on employees, or to disregard the interests of the community in the business which formed part of the industrial interests of Perth. But that spirit we know did not result in the organisation of our business being continually modernised regardless of the interests of individual employees - in accordance with the changing and developing conditions of industrial life. This was being born upon us by the facts and results even before the War, and the effects of the War, with the inevitable largely increased expenditure, even irrespective of wages, enforced the recognition of this. We had to consider the nature, and even the traditions of the business. We feel that, in order to get into harmony with modern labour conditions, there must be taken a course of reorganisation which, in our case, would amount almost to a revolution. This may, indeed, prejudicially affect individual employees, and might involve steps which would be distasteful to myself and my connections. It was with these feelings - well meant towards the employees - that my late brother sought earnestly some method of reorganisation, in which the employees might have a part. In these efforts he had the entire concurrence of his colleagues, and although these may have, unhappily, proved ineffective, I mention the matter, as disproving altogether the notion, that any unkind feeling existed, or exists, between the management and the employees, or any part of them. Circumstances prevent myself, or any members of my family, from undertaking the reorganisation of the business and hence there exists only the alternative course announced, namely the disposal of the business or its cessation. We all hope that the former alternative may be accomplished." These words were spoken with great emotion. Hayhurst realised this and kindly said that as "Mr Pullar was under very great strain he did not want to go deeply into the contents of the statements Mr Pullar had made."[609] There, the conference ended.

Ironically, while the Trade Union leaders were analysing the settlement proposals, Dundee Trades Council were considering an application by Perth Trades Council for financial aid for the Perth strikers. One member argued that "the Dyers' Union was very wealthy and as the strikers had only been off for two weeks the application was ridiculous." He went further: "These large organisations in particular were apparently prepared to agitate, and promised anything to get members into the Union, and after they got them in, they gave nothing to support them. There had been no trouble with the dyers, as far as I know for 100 years, and surely these people should be able to keep themselves for a fortnight if the worst comes to the worst." Nonetheless, the application was recommended to the Dundee trades. As for the citizens of Perth, the news about Pullars "fell like a bombshell on commercial Perth."[610] Some 2,000 men and women were employed there and although most bought their food and household goods through the Co-operative Society the loss of their purchasing power in the city would be "catastrophic." That this was clearly so is seen from the fact that the firm's annual wage bill was almost £150,000. Then there were the many pensioners who feared for their weekly benefits as did the host of relatives of the 430 workers who had gone to War. All these might very well lose their income. Then there was the tremendous loss to the city itself in rates and the subsequent increases for others. Amidst all this near-panic only the editor of the "Perthshire Constitutional" was perceptive enough to see that Pullars had been placed in their dilemma by ever-increasing competition from the south and by Perth's geographical situation in the north.[611]

The Thursday meeting on 27 September, 1917 saw the full agreement of the two sides as to the settlement and this was released on Saturday, 29 September, 1917.

"Settlement

It is agreed that an emergency bonus be paid as follows -
(1) To those who receive at present not more than 38/- weekly and are 18 years or more 5/-
(2) To all women 18 years or more 4/-
(3) To all under 18 years 3/-

These payments will be from 19 September, 1917 and are an emergency bonus and only payable by the present arrangement."

By this stage all those involved in this fierce and passionate industrial dispute were emotionally drained. Although there must have been intense disappointment felt among the mass of the strikers this is not reflected in the local press. Everybody seemed stunned by the death of R.D. Pullar and it was as if a feeling of guilt had diffused throughout the city with everybody reluctant to comment on the events of the past few weeks. Then there was the desperate sense of apprehension as to what would become of the works over the succeeding days. Would the North British Dye Works close down completely? If so, what would happen to the work-force? Or would the works be taken over by another firm? If so, would there have to be another round of strikes to establish wage-levels? The questions must have seemed endless. Obviously, it was a time to say little. No-one will ever know what bitter arguments of recrimination went on between strikers and loyalists at the work-bench, but according to those who were in the works at the time it took years for the scars to heal. As for the Pullar family the confused and disjointed words of A.E. Pullar speak for themselves. They could not understand how a work-force for whom they had done so much could have betrayed them in such a fashion. Although they said otherwise in public they did feel that the "Battle of the Gates" had been directly responsible for the death of R.D. Pullar. Because of this they wanted to wash their hands of the works and mourn in private. One point was made in the press - the work-force was changing. Fewer and fewer were long-serving craftsmen who prided themselves on belonging to a family firm. Those who did were fast disappearing.

While the seven remaining persons charged with "riotous behaviour" were either admonished or fined[612] Sir James Urquhart's Report on P. and P. Campbell was published.[613] He flatly rejected the original 10/- demand, arguing that Campbells had introduced a scale of wages in October, 1913 for men and one for women in April, 1914. When the War began in August, 1914 most women were paid on a higher rate than the scale, but the wages of men ranged from "well above" to "well below." During the War there had been many rises, some automatic according to the scale, some on "merit" and some due to War conditions. However, there had been no general rise. Since 1 August, 1914 the average rises for a 51 hour week were 3/6d for journeymen dyers, 4/7d for wet cleaners, glaziers, finishers and 2/10d for females. But it was vital to appreciate that during the period

1915 - 1917 the firm was "unprofitable." Still, the Report said, "pre-War wages were too low." Accordingly, Urquhart awarded 4/- to journeymen dyers, 3/- to other men over 18 years of age and 2/- to boys under 18 years; women earning 14/- or more would get 3/- and other women 2/-. Piece workers would get a 10% rise, while overtime would be unchanged. On the other hand, the existing bonus of 1/- a week, paid half-yearly, would be added to wages and paid weekly. But Urquhart gave a warning: "All of these are temporary increases of remuneration, intended to assist in meeting the increased cost of living and are to be recognised as due to the existence of the abnormal conditions prevailing in consequence of the War."[614] Most people in Perth believed "it is bold and generous and shows a somewhat sympathetic leaning towards DEMOS as the rises will cost at least £5,000." Not surprisingly, the end-of-year report reflected this: "No opportunity for adding new plant due to enormous increase in cost of dyes, cleaning agents, coal and labour."[615] R. Hamilton at the Perth Steam Laundry got the message and gave his workers a 5% rise.[616]

While John Pullar and Sons did not issue an Annual Report for 1917 the Dyers' Union was quick to recover from A.E. Pullar's shock announcement and they decided to flex their industrial muscle. Early in January, 1918 they held a "Perth Dyeworkers' Rally" in the Lesser City Hall.[617] There, 600 members heard their local President, James Taylor, talk on the subject of "Non-Union Workers." It was unanimously resolved "That an Earnest effort be made to get non-unionists in the dyeing industry to join the Union. That those outwith the organisation, joining by Monday first, be admitted on the usual terms and conditions, but that thereafter a graded increase be imposed for each succeeding week of non-membership." There was no comment from the management at Pullars, who had enough on their hands with a fire at the Tulloch.[618]

The first hint of a buyer for Pullars came in March, 1918.[619] Although there was no hard information, a London firm, Messrs. Eastman and Son, Limited were reported "to be interested." The Dyers' Union decided to act. On Tuesday, 12 March, 1918 they held their A.G.M. in the Lesser City Hall.[620] In "a crowded hall" James Taylor announced that the Union now had 1,300 members in Perth. Then a two-hour discussion on wages followed. Male dyers were the most vocal and they passed a resolution that they wanted 20/- a week over the prewar rates. At this point the female workers in the Ironing Department stridently demanded higher wages as well. After a noisy debate it was resolved that all females in the works, over 18 years, should have a minimum wage of 25/-. Next day, to

8th March, 1918.

From J. PULLAR & SONS, Ltd., Cleaners and Dyers, Perth.

To their Employees.

We have to inform you that Eastman & Son (Dyers and Cleaners) Ltd., Acton Vale, London, have acquired a controlling interest in this business as from 31st December, 1917.

For a time some of the members of the Pullar families will retain an interest in the business, but will not have any responsibility in the management.

Messrs. Eastman have been established in London since 1802, and have always been known for high-class Cleaning and Dyeing. Their reputation as a firm of high standing is well established, and their relations with their employees have always been of a friendly character. Their business has been rapidly developing under enterprising personal management, and at the present time is nearly equal to that of " Pullars."

Mr. Frank Eastman, the eldest son of the present head of the Firm, has left London to take charge of the works at Perth, and Mr. A. Wotherspoon Fisher, a Greenock man, with a long experience of the Cleaning and Dyeing trade, both in England and Scotland, and lately manager of the Chemical Cleaning and Dyeing Company, Argyll Street, Regent Street, London (Eastmans' Wholesale Branch), has been appointed Commercial Manager, superintending the Branches, Agencies, and Postal Trade in all parts of the country. The organisation and methods of business now existing will be maintained, and the Perth processes, and the quality of the work depending on them, will be carried on as heretofore, except in some cases where improvements derived from London practice will be introduced.

One of the first objects of the new management will be the increase of the business, and its development on business lines, while still maintaining the high standard of work for which " Pullars " has always been famed. Great reliance is to be placed on a bold enterprising policy on the commercial side, in which the advice and co-operation of those employed at Perth, as well as Branch Managers in all parts of the country, will be sought and welcomed. The position having been carefully studied in all its bearings, and full allowance having been made for the difficulties which all businesses of this class must meet while the war lasts, the new management look to the future with confidence.

The closing of "Pullars" is therefore no longer in prospect, and it is believed that the foregoing statement will not only be a relief to the large number of workers employed, but will remove the apprehension that has been more or less felt in the City of Perth since the statement Mr. A. E. Pullar made at the Conference, over which His Grace the Duke of Atholl presided, during the Labour trouble in September, 1917.

It is to be clearly understood that, though the control of the business has passed into other hands, it is still to be carried on under the present name of J. Pullar & Sons, Limited, Cleaners and Dyers, Perth.

The Final Statement (PKDLA)

their surprise, it was revealed that Eastman and Son had acquired "a controlling interest" in the firm. Further, the Pullar family "would continue their interest for a time, but would have no responsibility." The news brought a wave of relief to the city - there would be no closure and Pullars' name would be retained. Beyond that, little was known about the "new management."

Within a week A.E. Pullar announced that he would not consider the Union's latest wage demands until he had seen a deputation from the workers.[621] This was a signal for the Dyers' Union to renew their campaign against non-unionists.[622] They issued a statement saying that non-unionists were not entitled to the recent pay rise and warned them that they only had seven days left in which to enrol. A.E. Pullar was furious and he posted a notice advising workers that "We will not distinguish between unionists and non-unionists." He praised "the most pleasing relationship in the Works" and expressed the view "that the British people are free people and the workers are entitled to decide in regard to their membership with trade unions." That this was not popular in some quarters was proved shortly afterwards when the factory walls were disfigured with black, lead pencils.[623] However, it was not till late May, 1918 that the wage claim was heard in Perth before an arbiter.[624]

Finally, on 8 April, 1918 the workers in John Pullar and Sons learned something about their new masters.[625] Eastman and Son, Limited were not amalgamating with Pullars, as many had feared. They were simply providing "new management." Eastman and Son, Limited had a longer history than John Pullar and Son, Limited: founded in 1802 by Thomas McGill at No. 2 Windmill Street, near Tottenham Court Road, London their growth, like so many other firms at that time, was slow. However, in 1840, William T. Eastman, a nephew, became a partner. In 1866 they moved to Burwood Mews, Edgeware Road, London. Seven years later, his son, William Eastman (1844-1919) also became a partner just as they opened a dry-cleaning plant at Kensal New Town. Business was now booming and in 1890 they again moved to larger premises at Latimer Road, Shepherd's Bush, London. The Eastmans now felt that they should concentrate their activities and in 1900 they purchased a 6 1/2 acre site at Acton Vale. A year later dry-cleaning, dry-dyeing and lace-curtain cleaning operated from there. By 1906 Latimer Road had closed and everything was moved to Acton Vale, which, in time, also became over-crowded. At this stage the company was now a serious challenge to John Pullar and Sons, especially as it had 200 branches in the south of England. One of

A. E. Pullar (PKDLA)

H

their interests proved very profitable - the Chemical and Dyeing Company, which operated a wholesale business for upholstery firms and theatres. Much of its success was due to a talented manager for eight years, A.W. Fisher, who was now to assume the same position at Pullars. The Senior Director at Pullars was to be William Eastman who had made his company a limited company in 1908 at which point in time he employed 1,350 staff - 800 in the factory and 550 in offices. There were to be five other Directors for Pullars - Frank and Cyril Eastman, who were to be Works Managers, and their brother, Ralph Eastman, Accountant. The two others were Mr. Bygrave, Secretary and Mr. Bryceson, Assistant Works Manager. The oldest Eastman, Frank, was also the ablest. He was well qualified to be the new Managing Director of John Pullar and Sons. Educated at University School, London he had studied Chemistry and Dyeing at the Yorkshire College, Leeds - attended by R.D. Pullar so many years before. Then he had spent a year as a worker with Mon. Rouchon in Bordeaux. Subsequently, he had worked and studied in Paris, Lyons and Marseilles. By 1895 he was back at Latimer Road, where, for the next five years, he worked in every department of the factory. By 1900 he was Assistant Works Manager and able to boast that "he knew every worker in the premises."

It must have been obvious to most people that the Eastmans were offering the "same enterprising personal management as the Pullars had done in the past." The question was - could they make it work any better?

Footnotes

1. *C* 23/6/1930, 3/2/1930, 16/9/1918
2. Ibid., 10/2/1930
3. *PC* 27/7/1909
4. *PA* 16/3/1876
5. *PC* 12/6/1817
6. Ibid., 12/10/1809
7. Ibid., 15/2/1810
8. Ibid., 3/2/1814
9. *PA* 27/6/1883
10. Ibidl, 25/8/1917, 21/5/1919
11. Ibid., 27/6/1883; *C* 3/2/1930
12. *PC* 10/1/1911
13. Ibid., 30/3/1886
14. Ibid., 21/5/1822
15. Ibid., 7/1/1823
16. *LS* 34; *PA* 29/3/1924
17. *LS* 45; *PA* 19/2/1878
18. LS 55
19. *"Elements of Dyeing"*, C.L. and A.B. Berthollet, London, 1824, Vol. 1, p. 26
20. *PC* 22/4/1830
21. *"Water Power in Scotland 1550-1870"*, John Shaw, J. Donald, Edinburgh, 1984, p. 350
22. *LS* 35; *C* 10/2/1930; *PA* 8/3/1824
23. *LS* 37
24. "An Aspect of Family Enterprise in the Industrial Revolution", Roy A. Church, *B.H.*, Vol IV, 1961, p. 120
25. *PG* 15/4/1825
26. Ibid., 20/4/1826, 19/4/1827, 3/5/1827
27. *LS* 36
28. *PC* 15/11/1827
29. *LS* 11
30. *PC* 4/6/1829
31. Ibid., 10/6/1828
32. Ibid., 5/6/1828
33. Ibid., 24/9/1829
34. Ibid., 14/10/1829, 23/10/1828, 4/12/1828
35. Ibid., 8/1/1829
36. Ibid., 7/1/1830
37. Ibid., 11/2/1830
38. Ibid., 19/11/1835
39. Ibid., 20/11/1834
40. Ibid., 8/9/1831
41. Ibid., 6/10/1831
42. Ibid., 27/10/1831
43. Ibid., 4/9/1834, 20/11/1834, 22/1/1834
44. Ibid., 31/5/1832
45. *LS* 11
46. *PC* 18/3/1830, 22/9/1831, 17/10/1833
47. *PA* 6/6/1833; *PC* 2/1/1834
48. Ibid., 20/11/1835
49. Ibid., 20/11/1834; *PA* 30/10/1834; *PC* 29/10/1835
50. Ibid., 24/11/1836
51. Ibid., 10/11/1836
52. Ibid., 3/11/1836, 9/2/1837
53. Ibid., 29/6/1837
54. *C* 25/4/1838; *PA* 8/3/1838
55. *C* 8/8/1838
56. *PC* 9/8/1838
57. Ibid., 23/7/1840
58. Ibid., 30/5/1844
59. Ibid., 7/7/1885
60. Ibid., 9/1/1845
61. Ibid., 27/8/1846, 14/9/1846
62. *C* 26/2/1912
63. *PC* 16/4/1846
64. *PA* 27/6/1883
65. *PC* 21/5/1846
66. Ibid., 14/5/1846
67. Ibid., 13/5/1847
68. *PA* 29/10/1846, 5/3/1846
69. *C* 4/8/1847
70. *PC* 8/4/1847
71. Ibid., 27/5/1847
72. *PA* 17/6/1847; *PC* 17/6/1847; *C* 1/12/1847; *PA* 9/3/1848
73. *PC* 9/3/1848
74. Ibid., 20/4/1848
75. Ibid., 10/9/1912
76. *LS* 37
77. Ibid., 46
78. *PC* 15/2/1848, 11/9/1851

Footnotes

79. *PA* 30/8/1849
80. *PC* 22/3/1849
81. *LS* 42
82. *PA* 10/1/1850, 10/4/1851
83. *PC* 26/9/1850
84. Ibid., 22/5/1851
85. Ibid., 5/6/1851, 20/11/1851
86. Ibid., 29/4/1852, 6/5/1852
87. Ibid., 27/2/1851
88. *PA* 8/3/1924
89. *PC* 6/3/1851
90. Ibid., 6/11/1851
91. *LS* 37
92. *PC* 26/2/1846, 24/8/1848; *C* 2/8/1848
93. *PC* 7/7/1885
94. Ibid., 25/8/1853, 29/9/1853
95. *PA* 9/12/1852
96. *PC* 11/8/1853
97. Ibid., 16/12/1852
98. Ibid., 2/3/1854, 5/10/1854; *PA* 26/10/1854, 2/11/1854, 9/11/1854
99. *PC* 19/10/1854
100. *PA* 19/10/1854
101. Ibid., 12/7/1855
102. Ibid., 27/3/1856
103. Ibid., 1/5/1856
104. Ibid., 10/5/1856
105. *PC* 27/9/1855
106. *PA* 4/10/1855
107. *PC* 10/1/1856
108. Ibid., 17/1/1856
109. Ibid., 3/4/1856
110. *"The Parcel Post of the British Isles"*, J.A. Mackay, Dumfries, 1982, p. 5
111. *PA* 26/7/1855
112. Ibid., 6/9/1855
113. *PC* 29/5/1856
114. Ibid., 7/8/1856
115. *PA* 16/7/1857
116. *PC* 10/4/1856
117. Ibid., 31/1/1856
118. Ibid., 12/2/1852
119. Ibid., 23/6/1853
120. Ibid., 1/12/1853
121. *PA* 26/5/1859
122. Ibid., 2/1/1851
123. Ibid., 17/4/1851
124. Ibid., 25/8/1910
125. *PC* 8/3/1855
126. *PA* 28/5/1857
127. Draft History of Pullars, April, 1865
128. *PC* 17/9/1918
129. *C* 10/2/1930
130. *PC* 11/6/1856, 14/8/1856, 25/9/1856, 22/7/1858; *PA* 25/11/1858; *PC* 5/3/1861, 9/7/1861
131. *PA* 30/9/1858
132. *PC* 8/4/1858
133. *C* 9/6/1859
134. *PC* 23/6/1859
135. *PA* 16/6/1859
136. Ibid., 9/6/1859
137. *PC* 9/6/1859
138. *C* 22/12/1859
139. *PC* 8/3/1860
140. Ibid., 10/1/1861
141. *PA* 9/7/1859
142. *PC* 3/9/1861
143. *C* 10/10/1861
144. *PC* 31/12/1861
145. Ibid., 10/3/1863
146. *PA* 12/3/1863
147. Ibid., 21/9/1865
148. *PC* 25/11/1862
149. Ibid., 13/6/1865
150. Ibid., 4/2/1862
151. Ibid., 8/3/1864
152. *LS* 46
153. *PC* 24/5/1864
154. Ibid., 1/11/1864
155. Ibid., 30/5/1865
156. Ibid., 14/11/1865
157. *C* 4/1/1866
158. *PA* 7/12/1865
159. Ibid., 27/6/1883
160. Ibid., 26/4/1866

Footnotes

161. Ibid., 6/2/1915
162. *C* 25/1/1866
163. *PA* /8/1866
164. *PC* 16/10/1866
165. *PA* 27/9/1866
166. Ibid., 14/5/1867
167. *C* 17/7/1859
168. *PC* 8/11/1865, 13/11/1866
169. *PA* 22/11/1866
170. *PC* 12/6/1866
171. *PA* 1/2/1866; *C* 15/2/1866; *PA* 5/7/1866, 12/7/1866, 26/7/1866, 13/9/1866
172. Ibid., 1/1/1867
173. *PC* 28/1/1868
174. Ibid., 7/1/1868
175. Ibid., 7/7/1868
176. Ibid., 5/1/1869
177. *PA* 4/4/1867
178. *PC* 10/2/1867
179. *C* 23/8/1880
180. *PA* 28/5/1867
181. *C* 6/6/1867
182. *PC* 12/5/1868
183. *PA* 16/2/1869
184. The Glasgow Herald, 6/4/1966
185. *C* 3/2/1930
186. *PC* 5/3/1867
187. Ibid., 17/9/1867
188. *C* 6/1/1870
189. *PA* 10/2/1870
190. *PC* 5/4/1870, 4/10/1870
191. *PA* 6/10/1870
192. *PC* 4/7/1871
193. *PA* 26/1/1871, 8/6/1871
194. *C* 4/3/1870
195. *PC* 18/10/1870; *PA* 8/11/1870; *PC* 5/11/1871, 9/11/1871
196. Ibid., 20/2/1872
197. Ibid., 13/7/1869
198. Ibid., 20/9/1870
199. *PA* 29/9/1870
200. *C* 20/11/1871
201. *PC* 9/1/1872, 27/2/1872, 4/3/1872
202. Ibid., 8/10/1872
203. *PA* 11/1/1872
204. *PC* 22/10/1872
205. Ibid., 12/11/1872
206. *PA* 21/1/1873; *C* 22/1/1873
207. *PC* 21/1/1873
208. *PA* 7/8/1873
209. *C* 27/12/1875
210. *PA* 4/1/1877, 18/1/1877
211. *PC* 29/12/1874
212. Ibid., 4/8/1874
213. Ibid., 28/7/1874
214. *C* 20/9/1875
215. Ibid., 19/4/1876
216. Ibid., 27/4/1874
217. *PA* 2/1/1873; *PC* 4/2/1873; *PA* 24/7/1873, 4/9/1873; *PC* 28/4/1874, 20/10/1874
218. *"The History of J. Pullar and Sons Ltd"*, H.C. Fisher, Perth, 1967
219. *PC* 20/4/1875, 1/6/1875
220. Ibid., 22/6/1875
221. *C* 24/11/1875
222. *PA* 9/3/1876
223. *PC* 18/1/1875
224. Ibid., 7/3/1876
225. *C* 24/7/1876
226. *PA* 25/5/1876
227. *PC* 3/10/1876
228. *PA* 15/6/1876; *C* 13/12/1876
229. *PA* 12/10/1877; *PC* 9/10/1877
230. *PA* 10/8/1876
231. *C* 24/6/1874; *PA* 29/10/1874
232. Ibid., 1/6/1874
233. *PC* 17/11/1874
234. Ibid., 11/9/1877
235. Ibid., 23/2/1875
236. *C* 24/5/1880
237. *PA* 10/11/1881; *Daily Review*, 31/7/1879
238. *PC* 13/9/1881
239. Ibid., 17/12/1878
240. Ibid., 30/4/1878
241. *PA* 8/8/1878
242. Ibid., 6/2/1879

Footnotes

243. *C* 20/1/1879

244. *PA* 30/6/1881

245. *PC* 25/1/1881; *C* 26/3/1881

246. Ibid., 18/8/1880

247. *PC* 15/4/1879

248. *PA* 22/4/1880; *PC* 27/4/1880

249. Ibid., 26/10/1880, 2/11/1880

250. *C* 26/1/1881

251. Draft History

252. *C* 13/2/1899

253. *LS* 41-42

254. Fisher

255. Mackay, J.A., pp. 9, 13

256. *PC* 1/5/1883

257. Ibid., 8/8/1882

258. *MS* 51/5/5.14

259. *C* 15/1/1883

260. *PA* 23/5/1883; *C* 2/4/1883; *PA* 8/12/1934; *PC* 2/2/1886

261. *C* 2/3/1881

262. *PC* 18/2/1883

263. Ibid., 11/3/1884

264. Ibid., 14/6/1887

265. Ibid., 23/9/1884

266. Ibid., 2/2/1882

267. Fisher

268. *C* 28/12/1885

269. Draft History

270. *C* 29/1/1883

271. *PC* 6/5/1884

272. Ibid., 30/6/1885

273. *C* 14/7/1885

274. *PA* 2/2/1882

275. *PC* 4/7/1882

276. Ibid., 22/11/1882

277. *PA* 27/6/1883

278. *PC* 31/3/1903

279. *LS* 43

280. *PC* 25/9/1917

281. *C* 16/8/1886

282. Draft History

283. *PC* 19/6/1888

284. *C* 10/10/1888; *PC* 15/10/1889

285. *C* 31/12/1888

286. *PC* 4/1/1887

287. Ibid., 11/6/1889

288. Ibid., 14/6/1887

289. *C* 9/6/1886

290. *PC* 27/8/1889

291. Ibid., 25/2/1890

292. *C* 30/4/1890

293. *PA* 24/6/1890

294. *PC* 7/7/1891

295. Ibid., 21/8/1888

296. *C* 13/10/1890

297. *PC* 6/8/1889

298. Ibid., 18/11/1890, 23/12/1890

299. *PA* 26/12/1890

300. *PC* 19/1/1891, 20/1/1891, 17/3/1891, 24/3/1891

301. *PA* 20/5/1890

302. *PC* 2/6/1891

303. Ibid., 16/6/1891, 15/9/1891

304. Fisher

305. *PC* 19/1/1892, 15/8/1893

306. *PA* 18/8/1893

307. *C* 7/2/1894

308. *PC* 6/11/1894

309. Ibid., 6/4/1894, 3/4/1893

310. Ibid., 5/3/1895

311. Ibid., 7/5/1895

312. Ibid., 16/4/1895

313. Ibid., 21/5/1895

314. *C* 29/5/1895

315. *PA* 12/7/1895

316. *PC* 22/1/1895

317. *PA* 6/3/1895

318. Ibid., 8/3/1895

319. Ibid., 10/5/1895

320. *C* 30/12/1895

321. *PA* 20/3/1895

322. Ibid., 29/5/1895

323. Ibid., 19/7/1895

324. *PC* 13/8/1895

325. Ibid., 16/4/1895

326. Ibid., 28/4/1896

Footnotes

327. Ibid., 8/6/1897
328. MS 51/5/5.14
329. *PC* 10/11/1896, 23/12/1898
330. *C* 13/2/1897
331. Ibid., 21/9/1898
332. Ibid., 13/2/1897; *PA* 25/1/1897
333. Ibid., 5/4/1898
334. Ibid., 23/7/1894
335. *C* 27/12/1889
336. *PC* 4/5/1889
337. *C* 27/12/1899
338. Ibid., 28/6/1899
339. *PA* 28/3/1898
340. Fisher
341. *PC* 23/12/1899
342. Ibid., 21/9/1899
343. Draft History
344. *C* 21/1/1901
345. *People's Journal*, 23/3/1903
346. *C* 19/1/1903
347. Ibid., 20/1/1902
348 *PA* 20/1/1902
349. Ibid., 14/5/1900
350. Ibid., 8/8/1900
351. *PC* 30/12/1901, 16/10/1900
352. Ibid., 30/12/1901
353. *PA* 5/1/1903
354. *PC* 23/11/1898
355. *C* 31/10/1900
356. Ibid., 10/4/1901
357. Ibid., 8/3/1901
358. *PC* 23/1/1900
359. Ibid., 6/2/1900
360. Ibid., 1/1/1901
361. PA 19/5/1900
362. Ibid., 16/4/1900
363. *C* 30/6/1902
364. Ibid., 1/10/1902
365. *PA* 1/2/1905
366. Ibid., 24/2/1902
367. *C* 25/3/1903
368. *PA* 22/4/1903
369. Ibid., 19/10/1903; *C* 15/5/1905; *PA* 6/11/
1905
370. *PC* 17/2/1900
371. *PA* 29/2/1904
372. Ibid., 4/3/1901
373. *The Laundry News*, January, 1907
374. Daily Mail, 9/4/1907
375. *PC* 11/2/1902, 26/1/1904
376. Daily Chronicle, 12/2/1904
377. *PC* 21/7/1908
378. *C* 1/2/1909
379. *PC* 11/5/1909
380. *C* 31/12/1900
381. *PA* 1/2/1901
382. Ibid., 9/8/1901
383. Ibid., 21/7/1902
384. Ibid., 10/4/1903
385. *C* 17/6/1903
386. *Power Laundry*, October, 1904
387. *PA* 22/12/1906
388. *PC* 22/5/1906
389. *PA* 2/7/1900
390. *PC* 3/7/1900
391. *PA* 19/5/1905
392. *PC* 1/11/1904
393. *C* 7/2/1900
394. *PC* 5/8/1902
395. *PA* 3/2/1904
396. Ibidl, 8/7/1904, 2/12/1904; *PC* 18/4/1905, 25/5/1905
397. *C* 3/1/1906
398. *PA* 4/7/1906
399. *PC* 23/1/1906; *PA* 29/1/1906
400. Ibid., 20/7/1905
401. Ibid., 6/12/1905
402. *C* 1/1/1906
403. Ibid., 29/1/1906
404. *PC* 2/10/1906
405. *PA* 14/3/1906; *C* 7/2/1906
406. Ibid., 2/1/1907
407. *PC* 1/1/1907
408. *PA* 6/3/1907
409. *Laundry News*, January, 1907
410. Ibid., April, 1907

Footnotes

411. *Our Home*, 20/6/1907
412. *Daily Mail*, 4/2/1907
413. *PC* 28/5/1907
414. *C* 13/5/1907
415. Ibid., 13/3/1907
416. Fisher
417. *PC* 7/1/1908
418. *C* 2/1/1907
419. Ibid., 1/1/1908
420. *PC* 5/1/1909
421. *C* 4/1/1909
422. Ibid., 1/1/1908
423. Ibid., 23/12/1908
424. *PA* 29/11/1909
425. *PC* 3/8/1909
426. Ibid., 7/12/1909
427. Ibid., 28/4/1908
428. Ibid., 3/11/1908
429. *C* 6/1/1908
430. *PC* 7/4/1908
431. *C* 5/2/1908
432. Ibid., 10/3/1909; *PC* 19/4/1909
433. *C* 21/12/1909
434. Ibid., 3/1/1910
435. *PA* 7/9/1910
436. *C* 4/1/1909
437. *PC* 28/4/1910; 28/9/1910; *C* 16/5/1910; *PA* 24/8/1910
438. *C* 4/1/1909
439. Fisher
440. *PA* 11/3/1911
441. *C* 6/4/1910
442. *PC* 3/1/1911
443. *PA* 20/5/1911
444. *PC* 20/9/1910
445. *PA* 21/9/1910
446. *PC* 3/1/1911
447. *C* 2/1/1911
448. *PA* 21/10/1911
449. *PC* 22/8/1911
450. *PA* 25/10/1911
541. *C* 12/1/1910
452. *PC* 18/7/1911
453. *"Dictionary of Labour Biography"*, edit. J.M. Bellamy and J. Saville, Vol. IV, pp. 69-74; Vol. II, pp. 255-260, Macmillan, 1974
454. *PA* 17/5/1911
455. *PC* 22/8/1911; *C* 28/8/1911
456. *PA* 8/4/1911
457. *C* 21/2/1912
458. Ibid., 6/3/1912
459. *PC* 5/3/1912
460. *PA* 9/3/1912
461. *C* 1/1/1912
462. Ibid., 11/3/1912; *PA* 20/3/1912
463. *C* 6/3/1912
464. Ibid., 26/2/1912
465. *PA* 3/6/1912
466. Ibid., 1/6/1912
467. *C* 3/6/1912
468. *PC* 11/6/1912
469. *PA* 8/6/1912
470. *C* 12/6/1912
471. *PA* 22/6/1912
471. *C* 24/6/1912
473. Ibid., 3/7/1912
474. Ibid., 24/6/1912
475. Ibid., 11/9/1912; *PA* 14/9/1912; *C* 16/9/1912; *PC* 17/9/1912
476. *C* 15/7/1912
477. *PA* 13/11/1912
478. Ibid., 23/11/1912
479. *PC* 17/10/1913
480. *C* 1/1/1913
481. *PA* 5/6/1912
482. *PC* 7/1/1913
483. Ibid., 28/1/1913; *PA* 15/2/1913
484. *C* 1/10/1913; *PC* 15/10/1913
485. Ibid., 31/12/1913
486. *PA* 14/6/1913
487. *C* 16/6/1913
488. *PC* 19/8/1913
489. Ibid., 19/5/1914
490. *C* 1/9/1913
491. *PA* 13/9/1913; *C* 6/1/1913, 3/3/1913, 23/

Footnotes

3/1913, 7/4/1913, 21/4/1913, 26/5/1913, 23/6/1913, 10/12/1913

492. Ibid., 4/6/1913, 18/6/1913; *PC* 7/10/1913

493. *C* 2/3/1914

494. Ibid., 14/1/1914

495. *PA* 7/2/1914

496. *C* 11/2/1914, 16/2/1914

497. *PA* 14/2/1914

498. Ibid., 18/2/1914

499. *PC* 31/3/1914

500. Ibid., 3/2/1914

501. *PA* 20/6/1914

502. *PC* 9/6/1914; *C* 4/3/1914, 25/3/1914; *PA* 4/4/1914

503. Ibid., 28/1/1914

504. *C* 8/6/1914

505. *PA* 31/10/1914

506. *PC* 25/8/1914

507. *C* 7/10/1914

508. *PC* 9/2/1915; *C* 22/2/1915

509. Ibid., 28/12/1914

510. *PA* 11/1/1915

511. *C* 20/1/1915

512. *"Who Was Who 1916-1928"*, Adam and Charles Black, London, 1947, p. 951; *"Who Was Who 1941-1951"*, Adam and Charles Black, London 1952, p. 672

513. *PC* 26/1/1915; *PA* 23/1/1915

514. *C* 1/2/1915

515. 1916-1928, pp. 881-882: *PA* 13/2 1915; *C* 15.2.1915

516. *PA* 10/2/1915

517. 1916-1928, p. 989

518. *C* 17/2/1915

519. *PA* 24/3/1915

520. Ibid., 13/3/1915

521. *C* 3/11/1915

522. Ibid., 3/1/1916

523. Ibid., 21/8/1916

524. *PA* 22/7/1916

525. *C* 21/8/1915

526. *PC* 1/12/1914; *PA* 26/12/1914

527. *PC* 14/9/1915

528. *PA* 3/2/1915, 2/10/1915

529. *PC* 28/3/1916; *PA* 11/11/1916

530. Ibid., 10/6/1916

531. Ibid., 11/11/1916, 6/5/1916

532. *C* 7/8/1916, 16/8/1916; *PA* 30/8/1916, 2/9/1916, 14/10/1916

533. *C* 3/1/1916

534. Celtic Annual, 1916

535. *C* 22/7/1916

536. Ibid., 21/8/1916

537. *PA* 23/9/1916

538. *PC* 12/1/1915, 12/10/1915, 14/12/1915

539. *C* 3/2/1915; *PC* 5/10/1915

540. Ibid., 28/9/1915

541. *C* 22/2/1915, 17/3/1915, 28/4/1915, 24/5/1915, 76/7/1915, 29/9/1915

542. *PA* 20/3/1915, 14/4/1915

543. *C* 6/1/1915, 13/1/1915

544. Ibid., 1/2/1915

545. *PC* 1/2/1916

546. *C* 29/3/1915

547. Ibid., 14/6/1915

548. *PA* 14/4/1915

549. *C* 3/3/1915

550. Ibid., 26/4/1915

551. Ibid., 5/4/1915

552. Ibid., 5/2/1917, 19/3/1917 30/5/1917, 4/6/1917, 3/7/1917, 3/10/1917, 19/11/1917

553. Ibid., 22/1/1917

554. Ibid., 2/5/1917, 13/6/1917

555. Ibid., 26/8/1917

556. *PC* 18/5/1915, 13/7/1917

557. *C* 3/1/1916

558. Ibid., 1/1/1917

559. *PC* 16/5/1916; *PA* 1/7/1916

560. Ibid., 11/11/1916

561. Ibid., 27/2/1915

562. *C* 24/1/1917

563. *PC* 28/11/1916

564. Ibid., 21/11/1916

565. *C* 1/1/1917

566. *PA* 20/6/1917

567. *C* 11/6/1917

Footnotes

568. *PA* 9/6/1917
569. *C* 18/6/1917
570. *PC* 23/6/1917
571. *PA* 23/6/1917; *C* 25/6/1917; *PC* 26/6/1917
572. *PA* 30/6/1917
573. Ibid., 7/7/1917
574. *C* 9/7/1917
575. *PA* 7/7/1917
576. Ibid., 25/8/1917
577. *C* 25/7/1917
578. *PA* 25/7/1917
579. Ibid., 25/7/1917
580. *C* 30/7/1917
581. *PA* 18/8/1917
582. *C* 20/8/1917
583. Ibid., 21/8/1917
584. *PA* 22/8/1917
585. *PC* 28/8/1917
586. *PA* 25/8/1917
587. *C* 27/8/1917
588. *PC* 28/8/1917; *PA* 29/8/1917; *C* 29/8/1917
589. *PA* 25/8/1917; *PC* 28/8/1917; *C* 29/8/1917
590. Ibid., 3/9/1917
591. *PA* 1/9/1917
592. Ibid., 5/9/1917
593. *C* 17/10/1917
594. Ibid., 5/9/1917
595. *PA* 29/9/1917; *PC* 2/10/1917, 9/10/1917
596. *C* 10/9/1917
597. *PA* 8/9/1917
598. Ibid., 15/9/1917
599. *C* 17/9/1917
600. *PA* 19/9/1917
601. *C* 19/9/1917
602. *PA* 22/9/1917
603. Ibid., 23/9/1917
604. *C* 24/9/1917
605. *PC* 25/9/1917
606. *PA* 24/9/1917
607. Ibid., 25/9/1917
608. *C* 24/9/1917
609. *PA* 24/9/1917
610. *C* 26/9/1917
611. Ibid., 24/9/1917
612. *PC* 20/10/1917
613. Ibid., 9/10/1917
614. *PA* 10/10/1917
615. Ibid., 15/12/1917
616. *C* 16/1/1918
617. *PA* 12/1/1918
618. Ibid., 19/1/1918
619. *C* 6/3/1918
620. *PA* 13/3/1918
621. *C* 20/3/1918
622. *PA* 27/3/1918
623. *C* 22/4/1918
624. *PA* 5/6/1918
625. *C* 8/4/1918

Chapter IV
Other Business Interests and Investments

"For native-born Scots the expansion of handloom weaving presented a ladder for social and economic advancement."
- "Scottish Textile History", edited John Butt and Kenneth Ponting, Aberdeen University Press, 1987, p. 140.

Although John Pullar and Sons, Dyers and Cleaners, Perth won international fame as a dyeing firm it must never be forgotten that the initial capital came from the hard-earned profits of Robert Pullar, Umbrella and Gingham Manufacturer, Perth.

It was never easy. No sooner had Robert Pullar installed gas lighting for his weavers in 1824[1] than his costs rocketed[2] and the cotton trade plunged yet again into a depression 1825-1826.[3] His workers continued to blame the corn laws[4] and Glasgow.[5] Soon 500 looms were idle and wages fell to a mere 5/6d a week.[6] Pullar's weavers were not immune and some had to go on public works - breaking stones in the Carse of Gowrie[7] or levelling the South Inch.[8] "Trade was never at a lower performance in the town."[9]

By 1828 however, there were signs that the gingham trade was picking up,[10] despite the havoc caused by greedy French, Gloucester and Paisley agents, whose activities fueled speculation.[11] Local manufacturers responded by launching crams with silk webs and sheetings. Together with dawlings, skirtings, cambrics, jaconets, pullicate, damask shawls, zebras, silk plaids, striped and checked ginghams they obtained good prices and a measure of prosperity returned to the town.[12] It seemed an appropriate time to take John Pullar into partnership in Robert Pullar and Son, Umbrella and Gingham Manufacturers, Perth.

Problems soon returned - a shortage of hands in 1830,[13] abandoned looms in the fine summer of 1831,[14] industrial unrest on the eve of the proposed Reform Bill,[15] a drop in the volume of sales[16] and outbreaks of typhus and cholera in 1832.[17] While the Soup Kitchen fed 700 a day[18] the more unfortunate died by the score, unemployed and underfed, caught in the classical illness-poverty trap. Scottish profit margins fell dramatically in 1830[19] as English technology surged ahead. Foolishly, the Scots clung to the narrow market offered by fancies[20] which was unable to adapt to changing fashions.[21] Robert Pullar was forced to turn to London "the crucial focal point in the distribution of cotton."[22] There, discount houses offered cotton at bargain prices.[23]

Another headache was the appearance of a Weavers' Union.[24] They soon forced all the Perth gingham manufacturers to pay by the ell rather than the piece[25] and this may well mark the start of the Pullar antipathy towards Trade Unions. Their advent in Perth in 1834 was certainly marked by "inflamatory demonstrations"[26] and riots.[27] No doubt Robert Pullar, like other Perth employers, was particularly anxious to prevent the Dundee Weavers' Union from getting a hold in Perth.[28].

Throughout 1835 English competition continued to increase while yarn costs rose steadily and supplies from Glasgow virtually evaporated.[29] Perth's weavers, desperately afraid of the threat of power looms,[30] either left for jobs in Paisley[31] or fell prey to "visionary agitators."[32] Soon gingham prices had reached "rock bottom"and the umbrella cloth trade became more and more depressed."[33] Even repeated visits to London by coach did not alleviate the situation for Robert Pullar. Indeed, the long and exhaustive trips simply drained his strength as he struggled to survive in a world of spiralling costs.[34] His health ruined, he died in November, 1835 at the age of 53.

John Pullar now had no option but to devote himself almost exclusively to the weaving side of the family business, as his brother, Laurence, was only 18 years of age and his two sons, Robert and John, just 7 and 5 years. He soon saw that a rail link to the port of Dundee was essential and he played a leading part in the fight for it.[35] He was lucky in that weaving was "brisk again"in 1836[36] and he was able to give his weavers their first rise in wages since 1815.[37] With the craze for tartan handkerchiefs weaving became "even more prosperous"[38] and he was able to purchase "Jacquard machines for umbrella fabrics."[39] Inevitably, the market collapsed again and John Pullar was forced to reduce wages in what was described as "a massive cutback."[40] However, the threat of a strike, organised by the Perth Radical Association, compelled the Perth manufacturers "to restore levels."[41] The whole area was affected - Cromwell Park Spinning Mill was put up for sale; Tulloch and Ruthvenfield Calico Works were closed down; Stanley Cotton Mills went on half time and Stormont Bleachfield was put up for let.[42] By April, 1837 some 200 Perth Weavers were idle and by June, 1837 at least 150 of them were forced to dig for sand and gravel at the harbour.[43] Although trade revived with the summer, weavers could not make more than 10d a day.[44] The winter of 1837-1838 was very hard and those weavers who could not afford bread at 8d a loaf had to clear snow for the Town Council.[45] As before, the market improved with the summer again[46] just as Laurence Pullar reached the age of 21 years and was taken into partnership in Robert Pullar and Sons, Umbrella and Gingham Manufacturers, Perth.[47]

A few days later John Pullar had a surprise [48] - the Handloom Commissioners, Dr J. A. Harding and J. C. Symons, arrived in Perth "to inquire into the conditions of the Hand-loom weavers in the United Kingdom."[49] In the Burgh Court Room from 11 am to 10 pm they levelled questions at groups of weavers and a few employers including John and Laurence Pullar. The long inquiry revealed a mas of information. Although the Pullars exported gingham through Glasgow and Paisley agents there had been a fall in umbrella manufacture since 1833. John Pullar admitted that wages were low, a mere 6/2d a week after deductions, but he stressed that he only employed old men and apprentices. He blamed excessive competition for the run-down of the industry, especially English dyers dyeing their own cloth, while Scots dyers continued the old practice of dying yarn. He felt that there was no alternative to the 13-14 hour day worked by weavers. When asked the reason for the current trade depression he said that on a recent trip to London he found Swiss and German goods were far cheaper. When asked for remedies he suggested the withdrawal of trade restrictions, the establishment of a freer market, the sale of umbrella gingham to France, a system of low wages and cheap food by repealing the Corn Laws.

Although John Pullar and his brother emerged from the inquiry with dignity and even some popularity among the weavers[50] he decided to transfer a substantial amount of his capital to the dyeing side of his interests. The result was an increase in the number of dyers which seemed justified by the dyeing boom of 1840. That John Pullar profited from the latter is proved by his election as a Trustee in the National Security Savings Bank of the City and County of Perth[51] a measure of his growing prosperity and communal acceptance of the fact. Tragically, weaving again went into a serious decline - "The Great Depression."[52] Dunning, Kinross and Milnathort were not spared either.[53] In Perth, the Town Council ran out of money to pay unemployed weavers who were building a curling pond on the North Inch[54] and the local gentry came to the rescue by hiring them to clear their walks.[55] Ironically, wages then rose in the autumn of 1840[56] and by 1841 wages were 21/- a week and hands were in short supply.[57] Then, with the sudden collapse of a major Paisley firm[58] wages fell back to an average of 5/6d weekly. While Perth's six ship-yards closed down[59] John Pullar's weavers were able to earn 6/2d a week thanks to his astute deals in London. A temporary improvement in May, 1842[60] was brought to an end by a drastic fall in the demand for umbrella cloth at the end of the year.[61] The Town Council was forced to send unemployed weavers to Killiecrankie on a tree-planting programme.[62] Even food prices fell and the loaf was down to 4 1/2d.[63]

At this very moment John Pullar displayed his business intuition by purchasing a flax-spinning mill in Paul Street for his brother, Laurence, in December, 1842.[64] Although many no doubt felt it was a foolish risk, John Pullar was convinced it was a bargain. Built in 1840 by a John Cameron it had never been used. By April, 1843 it was producing ladies' skirting.[65] There were now three parts to the Pullar family business, all of which were hard at work throughout 1843.[66] It was not easy. In October, 1843 John Pullar again had trouble with a Paisley firm[67] and in January, 1844 several Dundee weaving firms collapsed.[68] An unpredictable factor saved him - an enormous demand from South America for umbrella cloths.[69] So great was this demand that even U.S. agents came to Perth in 1845 looking for business.[70] John Pullar's weavers soon had 21/- a week[71] and were able to enjoy the celebration of the Corn Laws Repeal[72] especially as Glasgow agents guaranteed a good market for ginghams throughout 1846.[73]

1847 proved to be a good year for Robert Pullar and Sons as the rail link with Dundee's port facilities opened in May and a strong London demand for umbrella ginghams was recorded.[74] Certainly it benefitted John Pullar who was now referred to as "John Pullar, Esquire" rather than simple Mr John Pullar.[75] Then, in the summer of 1847 the cost of living rose and the price of a loaf soared to 10d.[76] By November, 1847 the umbrella cloth market had suffered "a tremendous fall."[77] as more English manufacturers produced their own cloth. The editor of the "Perth Courier" summed it up: "Weaving has suffered a severe and sudden check."[78] Within a month John Pullar had laid off most of his workers.[79] Inevitably, 1848 was a hard year for the city. With bitter winter adding to the problems[80] wages were "fearfully low"[81] by February: by April Glasgow prices were down 50% on the level of the previous year.[82] With workers earning a miserable 6/- a week[83] John Pullar must have been dismayed to read the editorial in the "Perthshire Constitutional": "Making ginghams is now is abeyance as the fabric is no longer fashionable and Manchester makes them more cheaply than Glasgow."[84] This judgment coincided with his decision to take his son, Robert, into partnership in his dyeing concern, John Pullar and Son, Silk Dyers, Perth.

Weavers' wages continued to drop[85] just as cholera ravaged Perth yet again.[86] Although John Pullar had the option to transfer his resources to dyeing he continued to persevere with umbrella ginghams and he even bought new machinery for winding yarn which made his women employees superfluous. Despite all his efforts wages in September, 1849 were still 30% lower than the 1847 level.[87] This see-saw instability of prices and profits continued to vex Robert Pullar and Sons throughout 1850 and John Pullar was forced to cut back wages yet again.[88] With the trade depression lasting to the end of the year[89] and matters made worse by a rail strike[90] he instructed his son to stop all yarn dyeing immediately.[91]

The Great Exhibition of 1851 in the Crystal Palace, London seemed a golden opportunity for John Pullar and he sent representative samples of his products to the south - umbrellas, fancy ginghams, handkerchiefs and woollen derries.[92] He even joined with other manufacturers in the setting up of a society to send workers to London on subsidised fares of 28/6d.[93] Among the seven exhibitors from Perth and the sixteen from the county there was great rivalry for awards - H Sandeman of Tulloch, who sent machines for stretching shrunken cloth, handkerchiefs and coverlets dyed with munjeet; C. Gibon of Pitlochry, who sent dyed wool; P. Imrie and Garvie and Deas of Perth. While steamship companies offered "dock-passage"from Perth to London for 15/-[94] Scottish Central Railway preferred "Exhibition Trains"with a 3rd class return at 30/-[95] "Exhibition Fever"swept the city of Perth as manufacturers rushed to produce more and more "Exhibition Specialities."[96] Finally, in October, 1851 came the results: 3,000 of the 17,000 exhibitors had won either medals of "Honorable Mentions."Sadly, although five of Perthshire's 23 entries were in these categories, R. Pullar and Sons were not.

This must have been a tremendous disappointment to John Pullar, especially as the cheaper parcel post rates introduced in 1851 meant greater business in London and soon after a Royal Warrant as Dyer to the Queen for John Pullar and Son, Silk Dyers. Weaving in Perth suffered another blow in April, 1851 when depression hit Dundee.[97] Wages had to be cut again and even a 14 hour day carried no more than a mere 7/- a week pay. By June, 1851 this was even further reduced to 1/- a day.[98] Many Perth weavers had now had more than enough and their names may be found on the emigration list for Australia.[99] Others determined to stay and fight "the starvation wages" by forming a Trade Union.[100] John Pullar, on the other hand, placed his faith in more and better machines and in 1852 installed power-looms in his factory.[101] Although this increased production and allowed him to increase wages by another 2/6d weekly[102] the collapse of more Dundee weaving firms had an adverse effect on business.[103] The editor of the "Perthshire Advertiser"warned his readers: "Weaving is an illpaid occupation - a dying trade and children should avoid it."[104] Then, as so often in the past, salvation came from an unexpected source - South America again.[105] Big contracts for checks and plaids allowed John Pullar to raise wages to 9/- a week and a few months later to 15/-.[106] By August, 1853 weaving was "relatively prosperous"[107] and John Pullar felt confident enough to begin the production of shoddy (woollen rags).[108]

Progress was cut short by another bout of cholera in 1854[109] which coincided with another fall in wages.[110] This was bitterly resented by the weavers of Perth and they immediately formed the Hand-loom Weavers' Emigration Association in September, 1854.[111] They could scarcely be blamed. Real wages were falling fast while food prices rose by 60%.[112] By January, 1855 wages were only 6/- a week in Perth[113] and even the Town Council condemned the employers who were "accumulating fortunes."The "Perth Courier" joined the campaign of denunciation and blasted "the hard-hearted manufacturers of Perth."[114] Perhaps it was this unfriendly atmosphere that persuaded John Pullar to buy the Keirfield Bleachworks at Bridge of Allan. Of course, his second son, John Pullar, jnr., was now 26 and well able to manage the fourth family unit.

By January, 1856 weavers' wages began to improve[115] and by November some were even "well paid"with 30/- a week.[116] Nonetheless, it was becoming clear to John Pullar that dyeing now offered a far higher return on outlay, especially as his son Robert, had convinced him that the work of Perkins was only the prelude to a vast development in the coming years. Hence John Pullar's unease in February, 1857 when he and his brother Laurence, took out a joint patent on "An Improvement in the Manufacture of Umbrellas and Parasols."[117] Laurence realised this and suggested that they go their separate ways[118] But it was the Commercial Crisis of 1857 which proved the decisive factor;[119] John Shields and Company, Perth went bankrupt, many firms in Dundee were ruined and a Glasgow Bank collapsed. John Pullar now decided to withdraw from Robert Pullar and Sons and close down all weaving in Mill Street immediately. This released capital and space for dyeing while some men and equipment were transferred to Bridge of Allan.[120] There, John Pullar, jnr., was joined by his younger brother, 20 year old Laurence Pullar. Their uncle, Laurence, went off to develop his own firm - Laurence Pullar and Son, Weavers, Paul Street, Perth. As his successive home addresses indicate he certainly succeeded - 36 Mill Street, 18 Marshall Place, Moncrieff Bank and finally, the palatial Boatland House. In weaving he was far more experienced than his brother John having worked for their father 1830-1835 and then for his brother 1835-1858. His real achievement came in 1862 with an exhibition in London [121] which gave him the capital to build the Balhousie Works in Dunkeld Road.[122] This was an expensive outlay - £4,000 for the land and £3,000 for equipment.[123] Indeed, by January, 1868 his total costs were almost £9,000.[124] However, as a prominent shareholder in the Central Bank of Scotland and the Savings Bank of the City and County of Perth he had ample funds.[125] By 1874 he was on the point of retiring[126] when Andrew Coates persuaded him to join him in his new venture as Coates, Pullar and Company, Jute Spinners and Weavers, Balhousie Works, Perth.[127] Huge sums were spent on alterations[128] but the firm was bedevilled by almost continuous strikes.[129] Ill-health finally forced Laurence Pullar to withdraw to Bath 1877, but he maintained an interest in jute spinning and weaving till 1886.[130] He died there at the age of 80 in November, 1897.[131]

Meanwhile John Pullar had poured his capital into dyeing and in 1859 launched his plan for expansion.[132] As John Pullar and Sons, Dyers, Cleaners and Finishers this involved a massive expenditure. Fortunately, the boom periods of 1861 and 1863 had made dyeing increasingly profitable. No doubt it was knowledge of this that made John Pullar's villa at St. Leonard's Bank a tempting target for silver thieves in 1863.[133] As for the Keirfield Bleachworks, they caused nothing but problems, especially after the Bleaching and Dyeing Act of 1860[134] and the subsequent charges of "wage slavery."[135] Naturally, the Civil War in the U. S. A simply made matters worse. [136] Luckily, the revival of cotton in 1865 encouraged John Pullar, to buy a small mill at Ashfield.[137] Thus, while son Robert ran the dyeworks, John, jnr of Keirfield was joined by his brothers, Laurence in 1971 and Edmund in 1877. Like his father, John Pullar, jnr had political aspirations and served as Provost of Bridge of Allan 1870-1873. Sadly, he died prematurely at the age of 53 in April, 1883.[138]

John Pullar, snr. virtually retired from business in 1870 and thereafter spent a great deal of time with his physician son, Alfred, in London. His last business venture was a long, wearisome attempt to buy a gas works in 1870.[139] Perth Gas Company, founded 1822-1826,[140] had a complete

John Pullar (LS)

monopoly over gas supply in the city and "oppressed by its exorbitant charges."Various attempts in 1829 to establish a rival concern fell through till 1844 when the New Perth Gas Company appeared. Thanks to competition prices were reasonable till 1867, when the two companies agreed to "raise their prices considerably" in a secret agreement. Local manufacturers organised the "Gas Movement" and this forced the suppliers to cut prices by 10d. In February, 1871 John Pullar offered to buy one of the gas companies for £2,500 but this was rejected.[141] The then elderly John Pullar set off for London in July, 1871 to seek the backing of the Gas Commissioners.[142] The monopolists fought hard to survive and it was not till January, 1874 that John Pullar completed the deal and purchased Blackfriars Gas Works for £2,200.[143] It was only four years before his death.

Investment had always been important to all the Pullars, but as far as Robert Pullar, who died in 1835, was concerned his financial achievements were very modest. His will, written on 31 January, 1835, ten months before his death,[144] and registered on 16 February, 1837, shows just how modest they were. Carrying a duty of only £30 its terms were simple - from his half share in the business he had to provide for his widow, Elizabeth Black, and his three surviving children, John, Isabella and Laurence. The two boys already had the other half share; Elizabeth was left an annuity of £80 and Isabella £30 "for an outfit on marriage."Laurence was to get a quarter of his father's half share plus a salary of £50 per annum, while John was to get half the profits. On the death of Elizabeth there was to be equal divisions among the survivors. However there was a proviso: "If the business fails, provision must be made for my wife."Obviously, little money was involved and even Robert Pullar was not entirely sure that the firm was strong enough to outlast his demise.

John Pullar's Inventory of Estate is quite different: it is a monument to his solid achievement, confidence and wealth.[145] The total estate was no less than £122, 561 which was divided among his widow, Mary Daniell and his six sons - Robert (dyer), John (bleacher-manufacturer), James (dyer), Laurence (bleacher - manufacturer), Alfred (physician-surgeon) and Edmund (bleacher-manufacturer) and three girls (all married). Although it is not known how this money was divided it consisted of £81, 673 invested in Scotland, of which some £13,775 was invested in Mill Street and £13,185 in Keirfield, an indication of the value that John Pullar placed on cotton right to the end of his life. Banks too had always played a significant part in his business activities and on his death he had

£2,430 in two banks, the Bank of Scotland and the Mercantile Bank of India, London and China. There was also £6,000 in Bank of Scotland stock. John Pullar had, in fact, been a shareholder in the Central Bank of Scotland as early as 1847 and by 1854 often chaired its Annual General Meeting.[146] He even led the 1863 discussions on the effects of the Companies Act upon the bank.[147] He was also involved as a committee member of the Savings Bank of Perth from 1862.[148] His cautious nature is revealed by his £12,556 commitment to two assurance companies - Standard Life Assurance Company and the Scottish Freemasons' Life Association. As one might expect there were also family loans - £1,055 to a son-in-law and £2,511 to Laurence Pullar at Bridge of Allan. The bulk of his money, £17,466 (45% of the Scottish investments), was placed in seven railway companies - (in order of importance) Highland Railway Company; North British Railway Company; Dundee, Perth and Aberdeen Junction Railway Company; City of Glasgow Union Railway Company; Glasgow and South-West Railway Company; Caledonian Railway Company and the Lesmahagow Railway Guaranteed Company. This is hardly surprising as John Pullar had argued vigorously for years on the effects of railways in Scotland [149] and even suggested a "New Town"for Perth.[150] However, it was as Director on the Scottish Central Railway Board that John Pullar made his greatest impact [151] especially when he led the debate on the amalgamation of the Scottish Central Railway and the Caledonian Railway in the year 1865.[152] Gas too was important to him and he invested £5,770 in Glasgow, Aberdeen and Dundee Gas Annuities. Water companies at Edinburgh and Bridge of Allan also attracted his interest as did the Dundee, Perth and London Shipping Company. The remainder of his money in Scotland was invested in Glasgow Corporation, Athole and Strathearn Hydropathic Hotels and the Edinburgh Tramways Company.

In England he had £40,888 invested and some £21,224 of that was to be found in six railway companies, mainly London-based - (in order of importance) London and North-West Railway Company; Great Western Railway Company; Manchester, Sheffield and Lincolnshire Railway Company and the Great Eastern Railway Company. As in Scotland John Pullar worked through two banks - the Bank of New Zealand. A staunch believer in the concept of Empire he had £10,977 invested in three colonies - in Australia £4,427 in Melbourne Hobson's Bay Railway Company and Government Bonds in New South Wales, Queensland and South Australia; in Canada £3,640 in the Great Western Railway of

Canada and in British-Canadian and Canadian Government Bonds; in New Zealand £2,910 in Government Bonds. There was also some £4,223 placed in U. S. Government Bonds as well. The remaining £2,520 was in the Gas Meter Company, Eastern Telegraph Company and the Alum and Ammonia Company.

Robert Pullar, his son, was essentially a dyer. Any money he aquired was directed towards improvements in his North British Dye Works in Perth. Nonetheless, his father did leave him a considerable sum and this he invested in shares. His first commercial venture, outwith dyeing, was in 1864 when he feued land from the Scottish Central Railway for a new street [153] The houses built there however went only to his workers. A more profitable outlay was the actual building of villas in Balhousie Street in 1876[154] and later, in 1881, the flotation of a Limited Liability Company with £7,500 for a new hall in Tay Street.[155] which within three months had a theatre licence.[156] Like all the other members of his family Robert Pullar liked a substantial residence, but his move from 17 Marshall Place to 6 St Leonard's Bank in 1868[157] was nothing compared to his purchase of the splendid Tayside House in the winter of 1879-1880.[158] Banking affairs were well known to Robert Pullar and he usually worked through the Central Bank of Scotland[159] and the Savings Bank of the City and county of Perth.[160] There was however nothing sentimental about his dealings and when his father's favourite hotel, Athole Hydropathic, [161] lost money, he was quick to urge liquidation.[162] Yet, he was not without sympathy for fellow-shareholders as he demonstrated in 1878, when the City of Glasgow Bank failed in October, 1878[163] it was revealed that the jailed directors had misappropriated £6,190,983.[164] Several Perthshire investors were ruined and Robert Pullar proposed a "National Fund for the Relief of Shareholders"and donated £300.[165]

On his death in 1912 Sir Robert Pullar's personal estate in Scotland amounted to £361,690 and in England a further £127,268, a grand total of £488,959 in the U.K. Another £30,716 was invested abroad making an overall total of £519,675. In fact, by the time that all the legal problems had been sorted out, November, 1913, that total had soared to £560,425.[166] The details of the Disposition and Settlement were as follows - Tayside and all its furnishings were offered to Rufus and then Albert "at a reasonable price"; an Annuity of £40,000 was established to pay £200 pa to the three sisters and a sister-in-law; £100 pa to her daughter; legacies, £1,000 to each grandchild, £5,000 to Hillside Home, £5,000 to Barnhill Sanatorium and £500 "to my good friend, Dr. David Halkett."The remainder was to be divided equally among the sons. Dated 30 February, 1907 the will had a codicil added, dated 22 March, 1910 increasing Mrs. Elizabeth Keyworth's annuity to £600 pa. This took time to confirm, hence the delayed settlement.

Only 12.8% of the total estate (£69,802) was held in the North British Dye Works, mainly in £10 shares. Like his father, Sir Robert dealt through the Bank of Scotland, which held £16,136 of his money. The other bank, through which he conducted his foreign business, the Chartered Bank of India, Australia and China held £2,014, a joint total of £18,150 in banks. A firm believer in assurance Sir Robert had £19,798. The bulk of his investments, £148,834, was in railways - 9 English, 9 Scottish, 5 Canadian, 5 American and 2 in exotic locations, 30 in all. The Scottish rail investment amounted to £60,020 by far the majority of which, £20,653, was with the Caledonian Railway Company. The others (in order) were - the Highland Railway Company; Glasgow and South-West Railway Company; North British Railway Company; Portpatrick of Wigtonshire Railway Company and the Solway Railway Company. The English rail investment amounted to £37,492 and were (in order) the North-Eastern Railway Company; London and North-western Railway Company; Great Western Railway Company; Midland Railway Company; Great Northern Railway Company; Lancashire and Yorkshire Railway Company; Great Central Railway Company; London, Brighton and South Coast Railway Company and the South-Eastern Railway Company. In other words, a total of £95,512 in British railway companies. Canadian railway companies accounted for £46,711 with the Canadian Pacific Railway Company taking a massive £37,185. The others (in order) were - the Canadian North Railway Company; Grand Trunk Railway Company of Canada; Manitoba South-West Colonization Railway Company and the Montreal Street Railway Company. In contrast, U.S. rail companiess only involved £6,031 - (in order): Union Pacific Railway Company; Illinois Railway Company; Baltimore and Ohio Railway Company; Minneapolis S. S. Marie and Atlantic Railway Company; and the Norfolk and Western Railway Company. The other two companies in exotic regions both lost money and jointly were worth no more than £147 - the Quayaquie and Quito Railway Company in Peru and the Honduras Government Railway.

Sir Robert was interested in four gas concerns to the value of £5,948 - Edinburgh and Leith Gas Company; Gas Light and Coke Company; Aberdeen Gas Company and the Gas, Water and general Investment Trust Company. There were only two water holdings - Dundee Water

Annuity and the Edinburgh and District Water Works covering £4,793. Shipping attracted £13,546 in five companies, the most important of which was the Dundee, Perth and London Shipping Line with £6,565. The others, (in order) were - Cormack and Company, Leith; Cunard Steam Ship Company; Royal Mail Steam Packet Company and the Palace Shipping Company. Five corporations also enjoyed Sir Robert's patronage to the sum of £35,301. Glasgow and Perth dominated with £14,338 and £12,105 respectively. The others (in order) were - John Shields and Company; Macdonald Fraser and Company; Garvie and Deas; Perth Lodging House Company; Perth Creamery Company, Craigiehall Golf Club and King James VI Golf Club. Rented property in Perth - shops in Scott Street, villas in Balhousie Street and other houses in Strathmore Street and the Isla Road was worth £31,124, 16 of them to Perth citizens. There were only two hotels in his portfolio - Strathearn Hydropathic and Peebles Hydropathic worth £1,462. Basic industries to the sum of £22, 821 revolved mainly around J. P. Coates and Company with £18,471. The others (in order) were - Coltness Iron Company; Bradford Dyers' Association and the Warwickshire Coal Company.

Canada was clearly the most important of the colonies - £61,714. Apart from the five railway companies there were Government Stocks, two loan companies, two investment companies and two general companies in Montreal to the value of £15,003. Australia was next with £12,891 in Government Stock in Queensland, Victoria, New South Wales and South Australia. The remainder was placed with a bank and an investment company. India, with shares in Government Stocks and a bank, was worth £5,341. South Africa, with only two companies, was only valued at £1, 589. Sir Robert's favourite investment area was the U.S.A. where he had £34,731. Apart from the five railway companies his investments covered six trust and investment companies together with money in the New York Telephone Company and the American Thread Company, to the sum of £28,700. There was also money placed in five other countries - Sweden, Equador, Peru and Honduras to the value of £4,948. The bulk of this cash was held by three companies in the Argentine - £4,234. As for Sir Robert's other shares - some eight trust companies in the U. K. worth £23,688. The remaining £27,702 was spread over 14 companies ranging from Nobel's Explosive Company to the Eastern Telegraph Company.

Rufus D. Pullar was also exclusively a dyer. On his death on 22 September, 1917 he left a personal estate in Scotland valued at £181,158 and a further £59,282 in England, a total of £240,440 in the United

Kingdom. His will was very simple: the Brahan and its furniture as well as an Annuity of £400 plus one-third of the residue of the estate were to go to his widow, Rose Lindsay Pullar; the rest was to be divided between his two sons - R. M. Pullar and J. L. Pullar [167]

Unlike his father the bulk of Rufus D. Pullar's holdings, some £58,084 or 24.12% of the total, was lodged with the firm. On the other hand, he followed his father's example and dealt with the Bank of Scotland, which held £5,995 of his money in Scotland and £469 in London, a total of £6,464. There were no other bank holdings. However, there were two insurance policies for £4,599. Railways still played a prominent part in the Pullar portfolio although the number of railway companies was much reduced - 17 in fact - 8 Scottish, 7 English and 2 Canadian to the sum of £55, 788 or 23% of the total. The railway companies in Scotland involved £40,067, the major part of which was with the Caledonian Railway Company - £12,595. The others (in order) were - Highland Railway Company; Portpatrick and Wigtonshire Railway Company; Great North of Scotland Railway Company. The English Investment was only £10,316 and included (in order) - North-East Railway Company; Great Western Railway Company; London, Brighton and South Coast Railway Company and the Great Central Railway Company. In other words, 15 railway companies in the U.K. absorbed £50,383. The two Canadian railway companies totalled a mere £5,405 - Canadian Pacific Railway Company and Canadian North Ontario Railway Company.

R. D. Pullar was interested in only two gas companies - Aberdeen Gas Annuities and Gas, Light and Coke which took £2,598. There was only one water works - Edinburgh and District Water Works Authority which took only £567. In shipping there was £2,936 in two companies - Dundee, Perth, London Shipping Line and the Royal Main Steam Packet Company. Three corporations enjoyed support to the tune of £11,675 - Glasgow, Perth and Edinburgh, while Government War Stocks attracted £21,234 or 8.8% of the total. Perth city only enjoyed £11,119 - three loans valued at £535, 11 bonds at £8,833 to various joiners, architects, cutlers, butchers, etc. Seven Perth companies had £1,751 (in order) - Coates and Company; McDonald Fraser and Company; Perth Lodging House Company; John Shields and Company; Perth Creamery Company; Craigie Hill Golf Club; Garvie and Deas. There were three hotels in the portfolio and these (in order) were - Peebles Hydropathic; Elie Hotel Company Limited and Frederick Hotels Limited to the sum of £690. Basic industries revolved around three companies - J. and P. Coats; Bradford Dyers'

Association and British Aluminium Company and amounted ot £8,808.

Canada was still the most important of the colonial links as far as the Pullars are concerned. There R. D. Pullar had £10,122 invested in two railway companies and £4,717 in Government Stock and the City of Montreal. Indian Government Stock amounted to £3,037, while Queensland and South Australian Government stocks were estimated at £1,710. The U.S.A. was still a favourite investment attraction with £9,665 in five companies (in order) - First Scottish-American Trust Company; North American Trust Company; Scottish-American Investment Company; British and American Mortgage Company; American Investment Company. The Argentine only had two companies to the sum of £1,980 - the River Plate Trust Loan and Agency Company and the Argentine Stone and Brick Company, which was losing money. Six trust companies in the U. K. involved £5,750 (in order) - British Investment Trust Company; British Assests Trust Company; Calendonian Trust Company; Stock Conversion and Investment Trust Company; British Trust Company; General Scottish Trust Company. The remaining £5,138 was spread over 13 companies ranging from the Tyne Improvement Company to the First Garden City Limited. Some of these investments however were only for nominal sums - Golf Club and Country House Limited; Royal Automobile Club Buildings Company; Ideal Studios Limited; Royal Societies Club; British Dyewood and Chemical Company. Others were actually losing money - Town and Gown Association and the Scottish Home Industries Association.

Such wealth, common to all the members of the Pullar family,[168] guaranteed them a life-style far removed from the humble tedium of their employees. This is best seen by examining the details of Sir Robert's residence, Tayside House, on the banks of the Tay. Purchased in the winter of 1879-1880[169] he determined to turn it into a magnificent show-piece. Accordingly, architect John Young was hired "to make changes, alter and extend the house and improve the grounds." The best tradesmen in the city were used - T. Readdie, mason; C. S. Whittet, joiner; Frew and Sons, plumbers; Annan and Sons, plasterers; Stalker and Boyd, painters. Money was no object and for six months the very best of materials made their way to Tayside. A new dining-room was added, together with a billiard room, two towers, a verandah with mosaic titles and tinted glass roof, arches and columns as well as a splendid entrance hall. Inside there was "an elegant staircase" with wainscoted rail and balustrade specially designed by Messer. Craig of Glasgow. The panelling designs in fruit and flowers illuminated by stained glass windows created in Edinburgh. All the rooms, lined with wood in the finest baronial style, were furnished with new ceilings. At the end of the billiard room a French casement window led to the grounds. On the terrace there was a large conservatory or "winter garden", a full 100 yards under cover. There were greenhouses, vineries, plant houses, even an orchard house 85' by 20', all heated by hot water pipes, forming a promenade and cared for by W. McDonald, Head Gardener. In the centre of the 120' long conservatory was an Abyssinian Banana and nearby - a Sago Palm, an Indian River Tree and New Zealand tree ferns. There was even a hawthorn tree reputed to be over 300 years old. Everywhere there were banks of fushias, pelargomiums, begonias, azaleas, camilias, mosses, ferns and heaths, together with waterfalls, groups of statuary, miniature fountains, rock-garden and a large rustic summer-house with mirrors. On the riverbank there was a paved promenade leading to a covered harbour. New walls were built around the estate and even new pavements outside. As for the kitchen garden it was described as "simply huge."

Footnotes

1. *PC* 12/11/1824
2. Ibid., 4/1/1825
3. "Marketing Organisation and Policy in the Cotton Trade: McConnel and Kennedy of Manchester 1795-1835", C. H. Lee, B. H., Vol. X, 1968, p. 91; "Risk, Specialisation and Profit in the Mercantile Sector of the 19the c. Cotton Trade: Alexander Brown and Sons 1820-1880". John Kellick, *B. H.*, Vol. XVI, 1974, 0. 3; *PC* 27/7/1826
4. Ibid., 23/6/1826
5. Ibid., 6/4/1826
6. Ibid., 8/6/1826
7. Ibid., 15/6/1826
8. Ibid., 22/6/1826
9. Ibid., 27/7/1826
10. Ibid., 22/5/1828
11. Ibid., 4/12/1828, 11/12/ 1828, 8/1/1829
12. Ibid., 29/10/1829, 12/11/1829
13. Ibid., 27/5/1830
14. Ibid., 3/11/1831
15. Ibid., 16/6/1831
16. Ibid., 24/11/1831
17. Ibid., 19/1/1832, 3/5/1832, 17/5/1832, 21/6/1832; *LS* 14
18. *PC* 1/3/1832
19. "The Decline of the Scottish Cotton Industry 1860-1914", A. J. Robertson, *B. H.*, Vol. XII, 1970, p. 116
20. *"Scotland since 1707 - the Rise of an Industrial Society"*, R.H. Campbell, J. McDonald, Edinburgh, 1965, pp. 109-110
21. Robertson, A. J. P. 119
22. *"The Growth of the British Cotton Trade 1780-1815"*, Michael M. Edwards, Manchester University Press, 1967, p. 163
23. Ibid., pp. 109, 148; Lee, C. H., p. 91
24. *PC* 15/4/1825
25. Ibid., 29/8/1833
26. Ibid., 20/2/1834, 13/3/1834
27. Ibid., 17/4/1834 15/5/1834, 22/5/1834, 15/1/1835, 12/3/1835
28. Ibid., 12/6/1834
29. *PA* 29/1/1835
30. Ibid, 3/10/1833
31. Ibid., 7/12/1833
32. *PC* 20/2/1834
33. *PA* 26/2/1835, 5/3/1835
34. *LS* 12
35. *C* 13/11/1835
36. *PC* 14/1/1836
37. *PA* 23/6/1836
38. *PC* 24/11/1836
39. *PA* 1/12/1836
40. *PC* 9/3/1837
41. Ibid., 9/2/1837, 16/2/1837
42. Ibid., 2/2/1837; *C* 19/4/1837; *PC* 1/6/1837, 13/10/1837
43. *PA* 22/6/1838
44. *PC* 29/6/1837
45. Ibid., 22/3/1838
46. *PA* 21/6/1838
47. *C* 8/8/1838
48. Ibid., 1/8/1838
49. *PC* 9/8/1838
50. Ibid., 10/1/1839
51. Ibid., 6/2/1840
52. Ibid., 20/2/1840
53. *PA* 26/3/1840
54. *C* 15/1/1840; *PA* 23/7/1840
55. Ibid., 14/5/1840, 21/5/1840
56. *PC* 16/9/1840
57. Ibid., 14/10/1841
58. Ibid., 2/12/1841
59. Ibid., 9/12/1841
60. *PA* 12/5/1842
61. *PC* 8/12/1842
62. Ibid., 30/3/1843
63. Ibid., 3/11/1843
64. *C* 19/4/1842
65. *PC* 26/1/1901

Footnotes

66. Ibid., 28/6/1843
67. *C* 18/10/11843
68. Ibid., 31/1/1844
69. *PC* 1/8/1844
70. Ibid., 13/2/1845
71. Ibid., 11/9/1845
72. *PA* 2/7/1846
73. *PC* 19/2/1846
74. Ibid., 15/4/1847
75. *C* 24/2/1847
76. *PC* 24/6/1847
77. Ibid., 11/11/1847
78. Ibid., 18/11/1847
79. *PA* 3/2/1848
80. *PC* 20/2/1848
81. *PA* 3/2/1848
82. *C* 12/4/1848
83. Ibid., 31/5/1848
84. Ibid., 29/11/1848
85. *PC* 6/9/1849
86. *PA* 27/9/1849
87. Ibid., 6/9/1849
88. *C* 30/1/1850
89. *PA* 27/9/1850
90. *C* 13/3/1850
91. *LS* 42
92. *PC* 22/5/1851
93. Ibid., 27/2/1851
94. Ibid., 8/5/1851
95. *PA* 5/6/1851
96. *PC* 23/10/1851
97. Ibid., 1/4/1851
98. *PA* 26/6/1851
99. *PC* 7/8/1851
100. Ibid., 13/11/1851
101. *LS* 38
102. *PC* 18/11/1852
103. Ibid., 1/4/1852
104. *PA* 3/6/1852
105. *PC* 2/12/1852
106. *PA* 14/4/1853
107. *PC* 25/8/1853
108. Ibid., 13/1/1853
109. *PA* 16/3/1854
110. Ibid., 19/1/1854
111. Ibid., 28/9/1854
112. *PC* 6/4/1854
113. *PA* 11/1/1855
114. *PC* 4/1/1855
115. Ibid., 10/1/1856
116. Ibid., 20/11/1856
117. MS 51/5/5.14
118. *C* 5/4/1866
119. *PA* 19/11/1857
120. *LS* 84
121. *PC* 1/4/1862
122. Ibid., 3/3/1863
123. *PA* 21/7/1864
124. *C* 23/1/1868
125. *PC* 17/2/1863
126. Ibid., 1/9/1874
127. *C* 12/2/1900
128. *PC* 11/8/1874
129. Ibid., 25/5/1875
130. Ibid., 8/6/1886
131. *C* 29/11/1897
132. *PC* 9/6/1859
133. Ibid., 7/4/1863
134. *PA* 5/7/1860
135. Ibid., 5/7/1862
136. *LS* 89
137. *PA* 22/9/1870
138. Ibid., 25/4/1883
139. *PC* 4/10/1870
140. *C* 13/2/1871
141. *PC* 2/2/1871
142. Ibid., 7/11/1871
143. *PA* 28/1/1874
144. Commissariot of Perthshire Book of Inventories and Wills, Vol. 18, SC 49/31/23

Footnotes

145. Ibid., Vol. 102, SC 49/31/109

146. *PC* 10/8/1854

147. Ibid., 24/2/1863

148. *C* 20/2/1862

149. Ibid., 4/10/1848

150. *PA* 8/3/1849

151. *PC* 7/3/1850

152. Ibid., 20/6/1865

153. Ibid., 29/3/1881

154. Ibid., 16/5/1876

155. Ibid., 29/3/1881

156. *C* 13/6/1881

157. Post Office Directories 1862-1863, 1865

158. *C* 29/6/1880

159. *PA* 16/7/1868

160. Ibid., 7/3/1878

161. *PC* 28/5/1878

162. *C* 25/1/1856

163. Ibid., 7/10/1878

164. Ibid., 21/10/1878, 23/10/1878

165. Ibid., 18/11/1878

166. Ibid., 19/11/1913

167. Commissariot Vol. 225, SC 49/32/24

168. The only other partner who died before 1918 was James F. Pullar and he left an estate valued at £17,502. Some £120,757 was located in Scotland and of that £42,147 or 26.4% of the total estate was lodged with the firm. The remaining £53,745 was invested either in England or abroad. Like his father, brother and nephew, J. F. Pullar favoured the same kind of portfolio, viz., railways and trust companies. Commissariot, Vol. 214, SC 49/32/13

169. *PA* 30/6/1881; *C* 29/6/1881

Chapter V
Involvement in Municipal Affairs

"Perth was 'a sleepy hollow' till Lord
Provost Pullar arrived."
- PC 20/5/1915

Robert Pullar 1782-1835

The earliest reference to Robert Pullar, outwith his business affairs, comes from 1817, when he was Vice-President of the Perthshire Auxilliary Bible Society.[1] Described as "a wise and judicious Christian", who audited the books of the Baptist Church,[2] he was known to be a man who steadfastly placed duty before personal safety or even reputation. This he proved as a Visitor for the Destitute Sick Society in 1832.[3] At a time when cholera raged in Perth and his own son was desperately ill, Robert Pullar visited the sick and the dying in Guard Vennel, the Skinnnergate, Castlegable and Curfew Row — an area choked with slums and infested with disease. However, he was never a generous man and his name is absent from the lists of those who subscribed to the Relief of Weaver Membership.[4] He never showed any interest in the Mechanics' Institute nor in a school for Weavers' children as did his business rivals, Cornfute, Blair and Cleland.[5] He did not even attend any of the lectures on chemistry at a time when he was running his son's dyeing business.[6] Only the Anti-Cholera Campaign of 1832 excited his sympathy and support.[7] Neither did he ever attempt to cut a figure socially as did dyer James McLeish, who made so much of his donations to the infirmary.[8]

In 1832 he openly revealed his political convictions when he joined the Perth Reform Association and fought for Lord James Stuart, a Whig, who failed to become Perth City's first M. P.[9] His own sally into local politics was restricted to an attempt to represent Ward 4 (Castlegable to Charlotte Street) in October, 1833.[10] The ward required six representatives and 11 local businessmen were nominated, including Robert Pullar and dyers, James McLeish and Peter Campbell. All three got on the leet. On Tuesday, 5 November, 1833 the election was held in the Methodist Church, South Street. All Perth was interested in the outcome as Ward

4 had the largest vote in the city, some 150, and 125 of these voted. The number of votes for the successful candidates ranged from 101 to 66 and McLeish was in this group with 91. Robert Pullar and Peter Campbell both failed with 58 and 20 respectively.

John Pullar 1803-1878

John Pullar was a much more substantial figure than his father, and was, indeed, one of the best known faces in Perth. Not only did he guide his firm for 50 years, but he was also a Town Councillor 1847-1851 and Lord Provost 1867-1873, during which time he showed himself to be "enterprising, untiring, and of indomitable perseverance." His particular gifts lay in the field of finance and he helped resolve the city's fiscal problems during his terms of office, as well as playing a prominent part in London in shaping the Burgh Financial Act. In 1851 he resigned as a Town Councillor in order to help the Scottish Central Railway Company sort out its monetary difficulties. He enhanced the city's reputation for honest administration and integrity and made it a better place in which to live.

Like his father, John Pullar displayed a spartan devotion to his religious beliefs, which were so central to his life - a convinced Baptist, regular churchgoer and devoted Christian. As a Dissenter he argued that Laymen should be allowed to talk about religion in public halls[11] and that the Town Council should not send representatives to the General Assembly of the Church of Scotland.[12] He also believed that University Tests should be abolished and nothing be taught against the Bible.[13] He even objected to the use of public money for religious education.[14] There were two themes on which he was adamant: respect for the Sabbath and distrust of Roman Catholicism. Even before the railways came to Perth he argued that "the Sabbath must be preserved from desecration."[15] The greatest outcry in Perth came in October, 1849[16] when the public condemned the Post Office for working on Sundays.[17] John Pullar and Lord Provost Dewar were nominated at a public meeting to journey to London as a delegation and tell Lord John Russell of the city's disapproval.[18] They had barely reached Edinburgh when they were told that Russell would see no more delegations on the matter. They returned home. A few months later the issue was revived.[19] This time the duo actually reached London and met Sir George Grey at the Home Office. However, it was his fear of Roman Catholicism that disturbed him most. While a bailie in January, 1851 he organised a meeting in the City Hall attended by 2,000 citizens to discuss the proposition that "Roman Catholicism is a threat to the State."[20] Here he seconded the motion that "Popery is a system of superstition and idolatry - which subverts public liberty."Later, he chaired meetings of the Anti-State Church Association to explore the dangers presented by Roman Catholics.[21] Even as late as 1876 he lectured the London Missionary Society on this very point.[22] Hence his interest in Continental Protestantism[23] and his support for the Waldensians.[24] His most fervent wish was to see Italy evangelised.[25] Not only did John Pullar back a whole range of religious groups - the Religious Tract Society and the Evangelical Protestant Deaconesses' Institution - but he lectured to Perth City Mission and the Y.M.C.A. as well as clearing the debt owed by the Evangelical Union Chapel.[26] All of John Pullar's life was spent in close contact with religion in Perth, as a Committee Member of Perthshire Bible Society in 1828[27] and as an organiser of a series of lectures by Robert Moffat, Missionary, in 1873.[28]

Another passion in the life of John Pullar was politics. Despite his poor health in 1832 he joined the Perth Reform Association[29] and was soon invited as guest speaker at a dinner for Sir Henry Parnell in the Trades Hall, Dundee.[30] Having revealed himself as a Radical Whig he was appointed to Lord James Stuart's General Committee in Whig campaign to win Perth.[31] Unfortunately, they failed. Perth was too staunchly Tory. Nonetheless, he had drawn himself to the attention of the Whig leaders as a man of intelligence and integrity. The short-term outcome was an appointment as Water Commissioner for Ward 5.[33] Although this was useful to him as a dyer, the important result was that it gave him a taste for political battle, a taste which he found far more exhilarating than dyeing. Business concerns interrupted his political activities till 1837 when he campaigned for the Hon. A. Kinnaird.[34] Soon he was Police Commssioner[35] a post much-desired by his fellow-dyers, James McLeish, Archibald Campbell and Andrew Miller, all liberals too. By 1852 John Pullar had rejected the Hon A. Kinnaird: "I do not think he has progressed with the times,"[36] and had moved to the more extreme wing of Radical Liberalism. Hence his support for Charles Gilpin of London and his campaign against "the Yoke of Toryism."It was not till 1859 that he and Kinnaird were reconciled,[37] after having worked particularly hard for William Stirling of Keir.[38] One ambition seemed to elude him: the acceptance of W. E. Gladstone, his hero, of the Freedom of the City of Perth. The offer was declined in September, 1871[39] and again in August, 1872.[40] Finally, in October, 1872, and to John Pullar's infinite delight,

Gladstone accepted.[41]

John Pullar's foresight was ably demonstrated as early as November, 1835 when he urged a rail link from Perth to Dundee harbour.[42] The harbour-river vested interest pointed out that it would cost at least £160,000 to lay a line through the Carse of Gowrie and that it made more sense to dredge the Tay and improve harbour facilities at Perth.[43] Lord Kinnaird, principle landlord in the Carse, was bitterly opposed to the idea of a track through his lands and he denounced the proposal.[44] There seemed to be substance in his view. The river was certainly well used: in June, 1836 the steamer "Hero" brought 400 visitors to Perth, while, a month later, the steamer "The Tay" brought another 750.[45] The harbour too seemed to be booming - 700 ships used the harbour in 1836 and 78 of these were registered in Perth.[46] An iron steamer, 115' long and 17' wide with a 70 HP engine, had been built in Perth and launched in 1836.[47] Its trials in 1837 were a great success.[48] On the basis of this new confidence a Steamship Company was formed in the Guild Hall in December, 1837 to sail regularly from Perth to London.[49] John Pullar was quick to point out that the biggest ship in the harbour, "The Five Brothers", weighed only 170 tons and that to dredge the river for bigger ships would be enormously expensive.[50] Such remarks were scorned and dredging began at the rate of 600 tons a day.[51] However, this did not deter the demand for a railway[52] and by 1844 many letters were appearing in the press urging an immediate rail connection with Dundee, including those written by prominent industrialists, W. S. Turnbull of Huntingtower and J. Marshall of Luncarty.[53] Despite fears that the South Inch might be required for a terminus[54] the Town Council decided to buy shares in the Scottish Central Railway Company.[55] Not that everybody wanted a railway in Perth. In fact, railways were actually unpopular - between March and May, 1846 Six navvies were killed in rail construction work at Perth and many felt that this was too high a price to pay.[56] Worse still, when their weekly pay was late, in July, 1846 the navies rioted and hordes of drunken Irish labourers rampaged through the streets terrifying the citizens[57] and severe punishments did not discourage another riot over late pay in September, 1846.[58] Nevertheless, John Pullar was not discouraged and even argued for another line to Edinburgh with the prospect of cheap coal and stone.[59] Finally, in May, 1847 the rail link to Dundee officially opened.[60] The results were dramatic: The river-harbour group was shattered as were their hopes for a deepened Tay and mighty harbour. It was also a death-blow to the stage-coach industry. The Perth-Dundee line closed immediately

K

and the only survivor was one coach a week from Aberdeen to Edinburgh.[61] The four carrier firms that ran carts to Dundee, 20 daily, were all ruined. There was even a question mark on the steamers to Dundee and the two weekly lighters to London. Most important of all, the railway signalled a saving of time, greater mobility, cheaper travel and better communications, which were destined to shatter Scottish parochialism. Some of the benefits were quite astonishing - fish caught off Arbroath in the morning were on Perth dining tables by noon.[62] Day-trippers - 700 from the Wallace and Lilybank Foundries, Dundee poured into Perth in June, 1847 from 23 carriages pulled by two engines - eager to spend their money in Perth's shops.[63] Further navy riots in 1847-1848 did not deter John Pullar and he demanded an immediate link to Edinburgh.[64] His reasoning was simple: the Town Council were already committed as they had bought shares in this southern line in 1846 and again in 1847. Furthermore, coal in Perth at 11/- a ton would be replaced by Bannockburn coal at 3/6d a ton, an annual saving of £22,000 for the city. That a southern line was advantageous to Perth was obvious by June, 1848 when 1,000 workers from the Carron Iron Works in 33 carriages steamed into the city.[65] Of course, there were risks and John Pullar warned the community to reject overtures from the Scottish Central Railway Company for the South Inch.[66] He even warned of the danger of railway monopoly through mergers[67] and suggested that the development of the harbour might be a wise precaution.[68] However, his proposal for a rail-link to Perth harbour was rejected, despite his trip to London to seek the backing of the Marquis of Breadalbane.[69] He was also anxious to establish a new suburb or "New Town" in the west of the city[70] with access to the General Station from the Glasgow Road.[71] Although he feared that a rail-bridge over the Tay at Dundee might mean that trade would by-pass Perth[72] he never lost his interest in railways - opening a new Refreshement Room in Perth Station, meeting the first gas-lit train arriving from Edinburgh and attending the annual festivals of the Servants of the Scottish Central Railway.[73]

Although John Pullar once said, "I do not profess to be a tea-totaller, but I sympathise with the Temperance Movement",[74] his fight against "the evils of drink"[75] was more in the nature of a crusade. He demonstrated this early when he encouraged his workers to have tea-breaks in 1839.[76] The Perth Tea-Total Society had an enormous task to face in Perth - 31 spirit agents, 8 wine merchants, 10 taverns, 59 public houses and 50 tippling houses.[77] In the "Hungry Forties" drinking increased and by 1847 there were no fewer than 250 licensed establishments ie one for every 84 residents.[78] The evidence was in the streets - 37 in High Street, 32 South Street, 11 Methven Street, 10 each of in Watergate and Bridgend, 8 Canal Street, 6 in each in the Castlegable, Kirkside and Lime Shore, 5 Skinnergate, 4 Meal Vennel, Speygate, North Port, Princes Street and George Street. The annual outlay on drink was estimated at £50,000 a year. The consequences were equally serious - in August, 1847 the unpaid navvies again rioted,[79] a situation aggravated by the railway management's policy of paying off in bad weather;[80] in January, 1848 drunken soldiers rioted when one of their number was arrested[81] only to be followed by an orgy of destruction by the navvies again at the end of the month;[82] other serious disorders occurred in June and September, 1848.[83] Not surprisingly, John Pullar stood for the Town Council on "the drink issue." Strong for law and order he declared himself opposed to the drink trade, which by 1850 had as many as 308 licenses in Perth, 40 in one street.[84] Thus, when in the Town Council he banned the sale of spirits in booths at the North Inch Races and when a petition, purporting to be from 280 spirit-dealers, protested this action he cleverly demonstrated that it was a forgery from only 2-3 hands.[85] Although the Forbes-Mackenzie Act of 1853 had raised the duty on distilled whisky from 3/6d to 10/- a bottle and had slashed the number of licensed premises in Perth to 131 - 34 inns, 64 pubs, 33 spirit-dealers,[86] "intemperence was still a dreadful curse."[87] John Pullar was convinced that a deadly equation was at work - Drink equalled Intemperance, which equalled Poverty. When he was appointed Commissioner of the Peace in July, 1866 he redoubled his efforts.[88] His target was now Sunday drinking[89] and when a deputation of irate citizens petitioned him in April 1868 that the number of licensed premises had risen to 140 ie one for every 85 residents, much worse than Glasgow with its one to every 240 residents, he too was furious.[90] Among the first to feel his wrath was a Mrs. Christie of the Black Bull Inn, Kirkgate, who was warned that any breach of the licensing law would see her premises closed down for good.[91] So determined was John Pullar to stamp out excessive drinking and gambling that he banned both in his Peoples' Club and Institute for the Working Classes.

Determined to fight "the drink menace" John Pullar stood as a "Dissenter-Whig Radical" for the Town Council in 1847 along with solicitor, John Kemp.[92] Only Ward 3 was available and their two opponents were formidable - Lord Provost Sidey and Bailie Wallace, coach-builder and the city's biggest employer. The results saw Kemp with 58 votes, Pullar 53, Sidey 42 and Wallace 34. The "New Men" had won. As far as the editor of the "Perthshire Advertiser"was concerned: "Mr Pullar is a gentleman of high character and respectability who has been long known as a Liberal, at once thorough-going, and yet safe and moderate in his sentiments and he has moreover that stake in the welfare of the community which is derived from a very large and flourishing business."[93] This victory opened doors for John Pullar and he made close friends of prominent Councillors - Peter Graham, shipbuilder; Archibald Turnbull of Bellwood; William Richardson, shawl manufacturer and Andrew Heiton, architect.[94] At their first meeting on 5 November, 1847 David Ross, merchant, proposed John Pullar as bailie and Kirkwood Howat, candlemaker, seconded this extraordinary compliment. John Pullar, however, refused - he was "too inexperienced."[95] But, he did agree to join the Education and Sanitary Committees. He soon showed his integrity at the monthly meetings. When a discussion arose on the let of the City Hall it transpired that the Total Abstainers' Society had been promised the lease of one night for 10/-. Later, another party offered 30/- and some Councillors were tempted to alter the lease. John Pullar was adamant: "Promises must be kept!" There was much that irritated him, especially the "secrecy of transactions",[96] the lack of consideration for the public[97] and the "disorderly proceedings."[98] His fresh, honest and forthright manner together with his obvious distaste for red tape made him much appreciated. The editor of the "Perthshire Advertiser"called him "temperate and judicious"although he rarely spoke in public debate. When he did, it was intelligent and to the point because he hated rambling ditherers like the bailie who spoke 21 times on the same topic.[99] Not surpisingly, he was 4th bailie by November, 1848.[100] His early concerns were control over Tay flooding, [101] the need for more Dissenter kirk sites,[102] the danger of inadequate drains and sewers.[103] On wider issues he also showed his concern - possible abuses in the new Lunacy Bill and the need for a Financial Reform Association in Perth.[104] By November, 1849 he was 3rd bailie.[105] His tenacity was now famous. In May, 1850 for instance, he argued for the removal of the horse-market from the South Street as it blocked traffic.[106] His suggestion of Victoria Street was rejected by the public by 330 to 139.[107] A month later he had succeeded in reversing the verdict by four votes.[108] On another occasion, in February, 1851 he said that Perth's petty customs on wool were too high and he was "hissed by the audience."[109] Yet, a week later, his judgement was accepted by a large majority.[110] In September, 1851 he warned the Town Council that he intended to retire and this he did in November, 1851.[111]

John Pullar did not return to active politics till June, 1867 when he received a requisition from all 26 Town Councillors and 114 electors to be Lord Provost as "a man possessed of business talents and ability."[112] The city's leading men initiated this invitation - John Shields, manufacturer; G.L. Cornfute, manufacturer; W. Frew, plumber; D. Stirling, M.D.; T. Miller, Rector, Perth Academy. The newspapers endorsed the choice - "an eminent citizen" said the "Perth Courier"; "we are exceedingly glad" said the "Perthshire Constitutional"; "he is a tried man and has a name and reputation in Perth and beyond."[113] On 15 June, 1867 he accepted - he was 64 years old. Unfortunately, there was no election till November, 1867 and business took him off to England. But, before he left he announced that he would stand for Ward 1. This was the signal for anonymous enemies to launch an attack on what they sneeringly called "the Civic Farce."[114] CIVIS, AN ELECTOR, AB, FIRST WARD and AM all asked the same question - why stand for Ward 1 when there was a vacancy in Ward 4? They were unanimous in their view - it was a squalid political move to oust Dean of Guild Thomas Robertson from Ward 1. John Pullar hurried home to issue a statement to the effect that 242 electors in Ward 1 had petitioned him to represent them.[115] One last attempt was made to sabotage his chances. James Graham denounced his plans for Tay Street as "the dyke by the river costing £2,000 and yet only a church is to be built - sheer nonsense." It was to no avail. John Pullar received 240 votes and Thomas Robertson 224 with the result that he became Lord Provost of Perth.[116] He soon proved his worth - in the Council Offices every day at noon;[117] never missing a monthly Town Council meeting; careful attention to the work of the Burgh Valuation Court.[118] The verdict of the electorate was unanimous - "a gentleman who discharges his duties in a faithful, open and straight-forward manner."[119] One objective he was determined to achieve - the widening of Perth Bridge. Built 1766-1771 it had become too narrow for the wheeled traffic of 1841, but the estimated costs for widening were considered to be too high. It was the same in 1862. However, in January, 1868 John Pullar revived the idea and said that it would only cost £1,400 and he donated £100. The Earl of Mansfield then gave £300 and the Earl of Kinnoull another £200. Because public contributions were slow to appear John Pullar donated another £400 to get the project underway. The editor of the "Perthshire Advertiser" summed it up neatly: "The Bridge would not have been done, but for the public spirit and energy of the Lord Provost."[120] Almost immediately, John Pullar held a Grand Bazaar to raise funds for a new organ in the City

Hall.[121] At the same time he did not neglect the working class - he sympathised with the Early Closing protesters,[122] ordered the Registrar to remain open in the evenings "for the sake of the working men,"[123] and continually urged the Working Man's Association to build their own houses.[124] CIVIS, however, was soon on the rampage again with the libel that John Pullar had discouraged Gilroy of Dundee from opening a factory in Perth in order to keep down labour costs. Fortunately, John Pullar was able to prove that it had nothing to do with him, but rather the agents of the Earl of Kinnoull.[125] This vindication resulted in another request to serve again as Lord Provost.[126] This time John Pullar was determined to get much wider support and he announced that he would only serve again if permitted to pursue his "six aims" - finish the north end of Tay Street; join Scott Street to Kinnoull Street; build a new Police Office in Tay Street; erect a new Gas Works in Canal Street; merge the Water and Police Commissions and end the anomaly of gas prices. Instantly, another critic appeared. NO TRUCKLER launched a savage attack by calling John Pullar "a dictator" and accused him of bullying other Councillors to take steps that would only benefit his firm at public expense. Even CIVIS chipped in with taunts of "bad taste."[127] John Pullar's friends rushed to his side. Bailie Hewat's view was that "he did not seem to have any selfish end in view and all that he had done had been for the public good"[128] - making Tay Street "one of the finest promenades in Britain"; raising the rateable value of the city by £10,000; extending the Infirmary and Wellshill Cemetery; reducing disease by better drainage; widening Perth Bridge; installing new heating in the City Hall and giving the city cheaper gas. Hewat even suggested that a street be named after him. John Pullar just laughed: "I have no wish to see my name plastered up at the end of a street."[129] Luckily, John Pullar did stand again and although his second term of office was much less dramatic many of his projects came to fruition. The pomp and pageantry of office pleased him, especially when he had to go to the Central Station dressed in his red robes to welcome the Circuit Court judges and return to the Council Chambers escorted by a troop of Scots Greys[130] as did the solemnity of religious occasions, especially when the colours of the 90th Foot were presented to St. John's Kirk for safe-keeping.[131] By 1873 he was ready to retire[132] and his last official act was formally to open Tay Street in November, 1873.

The environment was always important to John Pullar, hence his desire "to improve the city, both from a sanitary and ornamental point of view."[133] As early as October, 1848 he warned the Town Council about the need for better drains and sewers and he condemned the open drains of Clayholes[134] and the smallpox-ridden slums of Shuttlefield Close.[135] Hence his attempts to ban rubbish thrown into the streets[136] or allowing cess pools to run into "the filthy Lade."[137] Despite this, cholera killed 151 in 1849[138] only to return in 1854 with another 25 deaths.[139] The 1865-1866 outbreaks were only controlled by the presence of the new Infectious Diseases wing of the Infirmary.[140] John Pullar knew this only too well and regularly contributed £100 towards its support.[141] As for the Lade itself, claiming at least 8 lives every three years,[142] there was little that could be done[143] apart from raising the protecting wall.[144] Like all Perth dyers John Pullar was continually being blamed for the pollution in the Tay.[145] But he knew that the absence of a good drainage system and the presence of too many curriers and tanners was the real cause of pollution.[146] For this reason he urged the closure of "the killing houses" in the Newrow, Fleshmarket Close and Mill Street and the construction of a municipal abattoir outwith the city at the Shore. In 1846 the Public Baths opened and he gave constant support[147] firmly believing that "better health comes through bathing and exercise" on a regular basis.[148] Thus his presidency of the Public Baths and patronage of the Tay Regatta.[149] As for the aesthetic appearance of Perth John Pullar had argued for Tay Street since 1839.[150] Although work started in 1846 he continually had to press for its completion.[151] The Inches were of particular concern[152] and he protected them against thoughtless riders,[153] tree vandals[154] and military encampments.[155] He believed that they were for the leisure of Perth citizens, hence his backing for a North Inch Skating Pond.[156] By 1863 he was even suggesting a new bridge across the Tay from Tay Street.[157] Two of his projects attracted much criticism - the improved alignment of Union Street[158] and the Historical Tablets scattered throughout the city.[159] Perhaps because of this he was never able to complete his plans to link Scott Street with Kinnoull Street, even though he offered £4,000 to help the scheme forward.

Another area in which he made a considerable impact to the benefit of the city was gas. Early in 1844 he warned of the need for a Gas Company owned by the public - "Gas should be in the hands of a public company."[160] The stiff rise in the price of gas in 1867 vindicated his warning. Soon he was launching a campaign to fight the monopolistic gas companies and he contributed £100 to the fund.[161] It was a long fight that took John Pullar to London to the Board of Trade and brought the Gas Commissioners to Perth.[162] His efforts brought him petty retribution from his opponents. In

March, 1871 he was blackballed by the Royal Perth Golfing Club and refused membership.[163] Despite an apology from almost all the club members he refused to reapply. His satisfaction lay in the fact that the city now had its own Gas Works. Another field of interest, although with a personal dimension, was fire fighting. The local Fire Brigade was quite inadequate for its task and John Pullar had to strive hard to reorganise it while in the Town Council. This he did by pointing out that it would be more economical and efficient to transfer control to the Police Commissioner.[165] Recognition came in 1854 when he was asked to select a fire engine for the city.[166]

Although a convinced believer in the concept of "self-help" in the struggle for better housing, clothing and food, John Pullar was always sympathetic towards the poor and unemployed. His support for unemployed weavers as well as his denunciation of the Corn Laws and demand for cheap food made him very popular with the working classes.[167] He often attended Chartist meetings[168] and in 1844 at an Anti-Corn Law League Rally he shared the platform with Richard Cobden and John Bright.[169] He also played a prominent part in the July, 1846 celebrations for the Repeal of the Corn Laws on the North Inch.[170] Yet, it was his chairmanship of the Parochial board, where he "promised to study economy",[171] that attracted most attention. Perth was inundated with swarms of vagrants from the Highlands and Ireland[172] but only had places for 35 in the Cutlog Vennel Poorhouse.[173] For this reason John Pullar argued for a new Poorhouse based on the Stirling design[174] and he frequently entertained the inmates.[175] Perth's two Soup Kitchens regularly enjoyed his support and he even managed the South Street Soup Kitchen.[176] Many other charities received gifts: Perth Model Lodging House, Perth Ladies' House of Refuge for Destitute Girls, Destitution in the Highlands Fund and the Indigent Old Men's Society.[177] To co-ordinate municipal effort he suggested an Association for Improving the Condition of the Poor as in Edinburgh. Law and order, of course, was important and he proposed a reorganization of the city's Peace Officers[178] as well as the work of the County Prison Board for Perthshire.

As a member of the Town Council Education Committee John Pullar believed that "Education is vital."[179] Hence the need to have trained teachers and good equipment.[180] Like all Dissenters John Pullar felt that all Parish Schools were inadequate and he pleaded for an extension of the National Schools System.[181] Much of his time was spent in visiting the Deaf and Dumb School, Fechney Boys' School, Wellshill Girls' School, Perth School of Art, Newrow National School and the Farm School for the Ragged Poor.[182] He even entertained boys from the "Mars" Training Ship, Dundee.[183] John Pullar also had intellectual interests: the Philosophical and Scientific Institution, the Literary and Antiquarian Society and the Perthshire Society of Natural Science. He attended many lectures on the American Civil War and Female Suffrage and he even invited the British Association to Perth.[184] His patriotism and belief in the value of the British Empire were well known in Perth, especially his financial aid to the widows of the Crimean War and Indian Mutiny.[185] Every royal occasion was duly celebrated and he played a leading part in funding the Prince Albert Memorial.[186] His compassion for others was also marked - the distressed Lancashire Cotton Workers, the captives held in Abyssinia, Shipwrecked Mariners and the victims of the Chicago Fire. Unfortunately, his Aid to the Sick and Wounded in the Franco-Prussian War Fund left him open to the criticism that he was pro-German because his daughter-in-law was herself German.[187] He was eventually forced to issue a statment that "We are not partisan in this War." Finally, although a prominent Liberal many Tories sought his company at the dinner-table - the Master of Dupplin, Lord Panmure, Marquis of Breadalbane and Sir Alexander Muir-Mackenzie. His obvious good-will made him a charming companion and his involvement in the presentation of the Freedom of the City to men like Sir John Hope and Alexander Mackenzie helped to give prestige to his home city.

Robert Pullar 1828-1912

Of all the members of the Pullar dynasty Robert Pullar alone has to be seen against a national canvas. Not for him the local hustings and service on the Town Council nor even any ambition to represent the City of Perth as Lord Provost. Instead, he played his part on a grander stage - in Edinburgh, London and even abroad. In many ways he was luckier than his father in that he had fewer enemies and they were far less dangerous. He did not have to fight for access to railways or control of gas or even fire appliances. His great advantage, apart from a bottomless compassion, was his wealth, a wealth that allowed him to lavish gifts upon the people of his home-town. His energy was phenomenal - opening bazaars, presenting prizes, attending sales of work organising meetings, making speeches and even going to Parliament at the age of 80 - "the oldest new member in History." Yet, he was a man with lots of ideas, many in advance of contemporary opinion - he was one of the earliest advocates of a "Scotch

Sir Robert Pullar (The Story of Pullars, 1937)

Department";[188] he pleaded for Home Rule for Ireland;[189] he urged the formation of a Woman's Branch in the Liberal Party;[190] he supported the idea of triennial parliaments;[191] and he denounced the House of Lords as "a misfortune where the members live forever."[192] He argued for a place in schools for French and German if exports were ever to succeed;[193] he prophecied that "horseless carriages" were inevitable;[194] he hoped that Evolution would be examined and assessed and not thoughtlessly rejected;[195] and he helped finance the renovation of tenements as a step towards better housing.[196] Overcrowding, he believed, was the real cause of TB and he condemned ruthless landlords: "We do not need to go to the heart of Africa to find savages when there are such places as this in our very midst."[197] He disliked militarism and conscription in any shape or form and feared a drift to war unless they were checked.[198] But, above all, he loved the city of his birth and was convinced that Perth should have the same status as Dundee.[199]

Religion, naturally, was the motivating force in his life and he was devoted to certain religious societies. One, Perth City Mission, had been his mother's favourite and it was the first to which his name is attached. In fact, he eventually bought the Baptist Church in South Street in 1891 for the Mission. His own particular favourite was the Perth Working Boys' and Girls' Religious Society and nothing delighted him more than to take their services, often to as many as 860 youngsters on a Sunday morning.[200] They also enjoyed his financial support and received a hall in Tay Street, which could seat 700.[201] The YMCA were also highly favoured and in 1899 they too acquired new premises. There were many others - the Religious Tract Society, Perth Bible Society, Perthshire Bible Association and the Young Men's Guild. Individual churches could always look to him for regular gifts - the Wesleyan Church, the Knox Free Church, the Bridgend United Presbyterian, St. John's Kirk, Wilson Church and North United Presbyterian. Of course, he had two famous themes which always aroused his interest and sympathy - Disestablishment[202] and Sabbath Labour.[203] The latter especially fuelled his anger in October, 1905 when the "Sunday Cars Controversy" was at its height - should trams run on Sundays? Like all 19th century believers Robert Pullar was passionately keen on missionary work, particularly in India. In 1905 he supported the Zenana Mission and gifted a whole dispensary to Berhamphore. The periodic bouts of Indian Famine in 1874, 1877 and 1897 resulted in substantial donations. Turkish atrocities in 1876 against the Bulgars and in 1895 against the Armenians moved him so much that he sent a telegram to Lord Salisbury demanding British intervention. In 1868 he helped to finance the Palestine Exploration Society dedicated to finding lost biblical sites. Every year cheques were sent to a wide range of missionary groups, especially the Edinburgh Missionary Medical Society and he was thrilled to play a part in the 1910 World Missionary Conference. Scarcely a month went by without his attendance at lectures on "Medical Missions in China" or "China is awakening." In fact, Robert Pullar was at his happiest playing host to any kind of religious gathering.

Probably his next great passion was his interest in politics. Yet, it started in a very humble way, when he was appointed to a Ward 4 Committee "to investigate the activities of the Town Council."[204] He did not seem to be over-impressed, because the only office he ever held was Water Commissioner for Ward 5 in 1869 and he duly resigned in 1874.[205] His venture into School Board politics was "frustrated by denominational pressure" and he withdrew in disgust.[206] Another unfortunate experience came in 1874 when he was accused of influencing his workers on how to vote.[207] This offended him deeply, although many said that "Robert Pullar is a man of honourable neutrality and it is a disgraceful allegation." From thenceforth, he was careful to invite all prospective parliamentary candidates to visit his factory at the same time.[208] Slowly, he built up experience working with candidates - the Hon. A. Kinnaird in 1874[209] and C.S. Parker in 1880.[210] The latter, who came from Largs and was an Oxford graduate, was faced with a formidable Tory, ex-soldier, Col D.R. Williamson of Lawers. Robert Pullar did his work well and Parker won a resounding victory with a majority of 1,541.[211] Sadly, it was not long before many regretted their choice and Robert Pullar wrote to Parker asking him to come out strongly in support of the "local option" against the drink trade.[212] Parker felt that the proposal was unrealistic and he fudged the issue. The result was a split in the Perth Liberal camp - the Liberal Committee, including Robert Pullar, who gave Parker the benefit of the doubt, and the Liberal Association, who were bitterly anti-Parker. While Robert Pullar tried to reconcile these factions Parker's attempts to exclude Bradlaugh from the Commons infuriated the Liberal Association.[213] It was the same with his views on Ireland.[214] Nonetheless, by October, 1882 Robert Pullar had had some success and the reconciled group was called the Perth United Liberal Association. At this stage Parker returned to Perth to state his case and 2,000 people heard him steadfastly refuse to support the Local Veto (Scotland) Bill.[215] The argument dragged on[216] with Robert Pullar urging a Temperance Register for Perth as a compromise.[217] Membership among the Liberals began to decline, even in the Perth United Liberal Association, and Robert Pullar had to face many "stormy gatherings."[218] By now, Parker was being attacked for almost all his views - Land Laws and Pensions. One speaker denounced him as "a slippery gentleman who usually votes Tory and is out of harmony with his constituents." In Perth, Parker could only get "a hostile reception"[219] even from the Disestablishment Association.[220] Despite the patronage of Robert Pullar he was "frequently hissed in the streets." The split came to a head in May, 1884 when Parker told 300 members in Exchange Hall that "banning drink was totally unrealistic."[221] Gladstone was so worried by these events that he hurried to Perth to investigate.[222] Robert Pullar expressed his confidence in Parker and said that he would continue to support him.[223] This was not to be enough and the Perth United Liberal Association at their AGM passed a resolution "expressing dissatisfaction with C.S. Parker as M.P."[224] Robert Pullar had no option - he resigned. The anti-Parker faction quickly put up a challenger - A. McDougall of Manchester. Thus the Liberals were divided on the eve of an election. Desperately, Robert Pullar arranged a public debate in the City Hall.[225] It was a bad mistake - they savaged each other like gladiators in a Roman arena before an "uproarious meeting" of 2,000. Parker won 1,652 votes at the hustings, McDougall 967 and Chisholm, the Unionist, 1,099. In other words, the Liberal vote had fallen by almost 1,000 and Parker's personal vote by 663. It was a bad omen. Parker realised this and at a celebratory banquet confessed that he owed his victory to Robert Pullar.[226] He was right. Within the next few months both the Liberal Committee and the Disestablishment Committee turned against C.S. Parker over his views on Ireland.[227] In the 1886 election his majority against an obscure Liberal-Unionist, W. Fowler, slumped to 453. Behind the scenes Robert Pullar worked furiously to repair the damage[228] and by June, 1887 had persuaded 60 activists from the United Liberal Association and the Liberal Committee to form a new group to which he was elected President - the Perth Liberal Club.[229] For the first time talk was heard of making Robert Pullar the MP for Perth, but he declined. Meanwhile, he launched an attack on the Liberal Unionists as "more Tory than the Tories."[230] He seemed to be making steady progress till Parker publicly ignored the vote on Free Education.[231] Robert Pullar was deeply offended and demanded an explanation.[232] At anti-Parker meetings in December, 1889[233] demands were made that "Radical of Radicals, Robert Pullar, be our M.P." and as for C.S. Parker - "We have tried him for 16 years and made nothing of him - absolute stereotyped." Within a month a requisition, signed by 2,050 citizens, was presented to

Robert Pullar begging him to stand as M.P.[234] To the admiration of even the Tories, he refused. However, he did resign from Parker's Committee[235] and this gave him the opportunity to criticise Parkers' attitudes to Free Education.[236] At this point a new anti-Parker group emerged, the Liberal and Radical Association, which asked Robert Pullar to be its President.[237] Although he refused, the news brought Parker scurrying back to Perth to announce that he had changed his view and would now vote for Free Education. The Perth Liberal and Radical Association were not impressed and they passed a resolution that "C.S. Parker is not fit and proper."[238] Letters began to appear in the press claiming that "Parker had fooled Pullar."[239] Then, from London, came James Woollen, "an extreme Radical", whose aim was to challenge Parker.[240] More letters appeared in the newspapers revealing Parker's dismal voting record in Parliament and an open invitation to Robert Pullar to support the Perth Liberal and Radical Association and join Woollen's Committee "because C.S. Parker is a carpet-bagger."[242] Again Robert Pullar refused and continued to support Parker canvassing for him with the approaching election in mind.[243] Then, the impossible happened - the Tories won Perth with a slender majority of 227.[244] Robert Pullar was shattered as he realised that if it had not been for the Woollen-Parker split Perth would have been held with a clear 688 votes. Gladstone was furious and labelled the episode as "deplorable proceedings." Woollen made haste to justify himself by pointing out that Parker was solely to blame and that his three last election results proved this - the 1880 majority 1,570; the 1885 only 907 and the 1886 a mere 453. Unfortunately, he also hinted that Robert Pullar had paid his costs, but had then, unexpectedly, switched sides again. Once more Gladstone came to Perth to investigate the truth of the matter in July, 1892.[245] Evidence was produced that Robert Pullar had never supported Woollen nor the Liberal and Radical Association[246] and this compelled Woollen to blame Robert Pullar openly.[247] This was obviously absurd, but Robert Pullar was deeply hurt and it took a full six months before he recovered his composure.

Having again refused to stand as MP for the Radical Liberals in February, 1893[248] Robert Pullar bought new premises for the Liberal Club in Tay Street and proposed Robert Wallace, QC from London as "a reconciliation candidate."[249] He also formed yet another grouping, the New Liberal Association, and accepted the post of chairman.[250] Both he and Wallace worked hard to heal the political breach and launched a series of rallies which ended in December, 1894 with a "Monster Liberal

Rally" attended by 3,000.[251] Of course, some criticised the choice of Wallace[252] and he and Robert Pullar decided to win popular support by releasing a statement demanding local control over the drink traffic.[253] Unfortunately, May, 1895 was the moment chosen by Asquith to put forward his Factories and Workshops Bill banning overtime for dyeworkers under 18 "under any circumstances."[254] Robert Pullar, hearing that the local MP, William Whitelaw, had denounced the proposal as "a liberal ploy to win public sympathy and thus votes," had dashed off to London to advise Asquith. Whitelaw, on the other hand, returned to Perth and at a public meeting said that Robert Pullar had paid off in winter when work was slack and that he gave poor wages.[255] Robert Pullar was very angry and considered libel action. Luckily, better sense prevailed. Then, in a debate in the House of Commons, it was disclosed that J. F. Pullar, Chairman of the Perth Conservative Club, had actually been a member of a deputation to the Home Secretary and had expressed views entirely opposite to those of Robert Pullar.[256] This "enormous embarrassment" was made worse by the additional news that H. S. Pullar was also against the Bill. Then came the final blow. It was revealed in the press that for the coming 1895 election R. Wallace had been proposed by Robert Pullar and W. Whitelaw by J. F. Pullar.[257] Clearly the Pullar family was in grave danger of ridicule and J. F. resolved the matter by slipping off quietly for a holiday in Germany, while Robert Pullar was addressing 3,000 in the City Hall.[258] Never had there been such an exciting election in Perth. Both candidates hired cyclists to rouse voters from their firesides. Robert Pullar played his part to the full and spent an exhausting day visiting every poll-station. It was not in vain - Wallace defeated Whitelaw and Perth was liberal again. Asquith himself came to the city to join the celebrations. Tory analysts, on the other hand, pointed out that 374 was the smallest liberal majority in 21 years and that the 1895 split "had started a steady swing to the Conservatives."[259] Days later, Robert Pullar was knighted amid rumours that it was a reward for paying Wallace"s election costs.[260] The latter rejected the charge as "an unmitigated lie" and even the Tories found "the allegation repugnant." However, they were growing in strength as their Fair City Habitation of Primrose League, founded in 1881, was able to attract 3,000 entrance-paying citizens to a rally in the City Hall, including, not only the Duke of Atholl, the Earl of Kinnoull and Lord Hay of Kinfauns, but every member of the Pullar family except Sir Robert and his wife.[261] This must have been a bitter blow to his pride and news that a further 5,000 attended the Conservative

James F. Pullar (LS)

Rally at Huntingtower could not have helped.[262] Gladstone realised that the Liberal grasp on Perth was slipping and he made two more visits to the city in 1897.[263] His death, not long after, was a deep, personal blow to Sir Robert, who attended the funeral in Westminster and later, with his wife, visited the grave at Chester. While Wallace continued to be active[264] and although he was himself a friend of the new liberal leader, Sir Henry Campbell-Bannerman, Sir Robert kept a low profile politically and almost no part in the 1900 election, which Wallace won with a reduced majority of 344.[265] But it did not bring unity to the party. Another faction emerged who were critical of Campbell-Bannerman[266] and it took Sir Robert some time to defeat them. More and more he was acclaimed as "an Advanced Liberal"[267] who was a friend of Lloyd George[268] and host to Campbell-Bannerman.[269] These contacts gave Sir Robert enough confidence to revive his views on Free Trade and with R. B. Haldane condemn Chamberlain and Protectionism.[270] The Tories were scornful - "The German trade threat is very real and that is why Free Trade does not work."[271]Because of his wife's death Sir Robert did not take up the challenge.

After an absence of almost two years Sir Robert returned to Perth to find Wallace plagued with suffragettes[272] and the Tories well organised.[273] At this moment Wallace announced that he had obtained a position at Clerkenwell Sessions and intended to resign from Parliament. The Liberals were now faced with a dilemma. A new candidate had to be acceptable to the two wings of the party at Perth - the liberal Club and the Liberal Association - and had to be able to match the growing popularity of the Conservatives. Only Sir Robert's "characteristic sagacity" was praised and he was described as "the ideal candidate."[274] He also had had plenty of experience working with Kinnaird, Parker and Wallace. Even his opponents admitted that "he never jibbed nor trimmed to please a friend or foe."[275] Even his age was not against him because of his "marvellous juvenility."[276] The choice of Sir Robert was a blow to the Tories, but they decided to accept the fait accompli[277] because they knew that none could match him at the polls, whatever their political views. On 18 February, 1907 Sir Robert was introduced to the House of Commons by the Master of Elibank and John A. Dewar. However, Sir Robert was neither fluent nor eloquent and spoke, but rarely. Only in the Small Landholders (Scotland) Bill did he have much to contribute.[278]Despite this Campbell-Bannerman called him "my old friend."[279] Two years later he had had enough and decided to retire. When he returned to Perth to attend an

L

Perth Unionism-"I thought I might get a seat when the gent with the carpet bag left, but now I suppose courtesy demands that I shall hang on a bit longer."
A 1907 Cartoon (PKDLA)

election rally he was greeted with "a storm of applause" and hailed as "a unique phenomenon in British politics."[280] His successor, Alex F. Whyte, won with a majority of 738.[281] A few months later, at yet another election, this was increased to 974.[282] It seemed as if the long self-inflicted wounds of the Liberal Party were over. It was only fitting therefore that Sir Robert's life came to a close shortly after receiving the highest accolade for a Perth-born man - Freedom of the City in April, 1911.[283]

Robert Pullar's membership of the Licensing Court in 1876 and his experiences in the Temperance Society in 1888 convinced him that "Immorality and Crime are due to drink."[284] In 1881 therefore he led his first "campaign against strong drink."[285] The Rev. Mr. Addie of Wilson Church condemned Perth as "degraded" and he condemned those who were making money from the miseries of others. Sabbath drinking was particularly offensive to Robert Pullar as a Christian and the high rate of absenteeism on Monday mornings concerned him as an employer. In 1905 he shared a platform with General Booth and expressed the view that "the Scottish Working Class spend too much on drink."[286] The Rev. Mr Knight of St Leonard's U. F. Church also denounced "darkest Perth" with "its selfish landlords"[287] He even established that Perth had a rat population of almost two million, but that this was nothing compared to drink, "the real threat to the community."[288] He estimated that £4.6.0. per annum per person in Perth went on drink - £2,000 per week.[289] 1906 saw "an epidemic of drunkenness" in Perth[290] and he persuaded R. Haldane M.P. to speak in the City Hall on the drink menace in the city.[291] By the 1909 the situation had deteriorated with "drunkenness on the increase and drunks causing many unnecessary fires in which people died."[292] Robert Pullar's crusade against intemperance had failed.

Health was vital as far as Robert Pullar was concerned, hence his interest in rowing regattas and gardening.[293] In 1886 he started the Swimming Bath Movement with a grant of £250 and four years later cleared it debt of £500. The infirmary also received a great deal of attention with gifts of cash and food. From 1868 he never missed an AGM and he was proud to be elected a Director in 1908. Convinced that TB was on the increase[294] he donated £3,000 to buy land at Barnhill for the erection of cottages for the victims and in 1901 a further £3,000 to the Relief of Incurables and Treatment of Chronic Disease. Although he did much for the Nurse's Home and the Friarton Fever Hospital, his main interest lay with the Hillside Home for the Chronically Sick. Here, he personally showed magic slides and donated beds to celebrate the Queen's

Diamond Jubilee. In 1901 he gifted £8,000 for general upkeep and a few months later, a further £10,000 for roads and shelters.[295]

Although he lived in considerable splendour at Tayside, Robert Pullar never forgot the less fortunate. From 1855 he contributed regularly to the Soup Kitchens, which by 1900 were giving out 17,000 free meals a year. For the Indigent Old Men's Society he was a visitor and frequently entertained its members to meals. The Association for Improving the Condition of the Poor attracted his support as early as 1876 and by 1901 some 336 persons were receiving free coal on a regular basis. The Poorhouse residents were often the recipients of his generosity as when he took 200 of them to Broughty Ferry by steamer. As a Perth bailie commented: "I don't know what Perth would be like without the Messrs. Pullar." Several times he cleared the debt of the Relief of the Destitute and the Unemployed Society as he did with the Model Lodging House. Two more of his favourite charities were the Discharged Prisoners' Aid Society and the Night Shelter for Women. He also helped the Sick Poor Nursing Society, which had 75 patients in 1885 and 473 by 1900. Even the Provident Society in Perth owed its growth to Robert Pullar.

Robert Pullar once said - "My aim is to assist in promoting the good of my native city."[296] Sometimes, of course, people objected. For instance, in 1895 he held public meetings to argue for a new bridge across the Tay. Fishing interests objected[297] but these were overruled when Sir Robert donated £2,500 to the Bridge Fund. By October, 1900 the Victoria Bridge opened at a cost of £29,333 and the protest of some ratepayers.[298] The trees on the South Inch had his protection as had Moncreiffe Island and a 4 acre allotment near the Lade for the Perth Working Men's Association.[299] A footpath was built in 1901 from Craigie to Cherrybank and he saved Jeanfield Park for the public in 1911. In 1904 he opened Perth's 50-stall public wash-house which had cost him £8,500.[300] He had proposed a Free Library in 1892 and he watched Lord Rosebery open the Sandeman Library in 1896.[301] The list of his endowments is almost endless - £500 to the City Hall Organ Fund, a stained glass window for the Municipal Chambers, a hall to the Scotch Girls' Friendly Society, £100 to the Victoria Institute in Dovecotland, Kinnoull Recreation Club and a Town Band. No wonder Bailie Watson commented in 1901: "He is the beau ideal of a citizen and the Grand Old Man of the City of Perth."[302]

Hardly an intellectual Robert Pullar advocated a City Museum as early as 1877 and gave £500 to start off its Fund. As Vice-President of the Society for Natural Science he was particularly fond of lectures on the

Antarctic and the American Rockies. A member of the Literary and Antiquarian Society he was famous for his Penny Readings and participation in the Parliamentary Debating Society. Patriotism was one of his favourite topics and he regularly sent royal addresses to the Queen. Old soldiers from the Crimea and South Africa could count on him for employment and support, while Festivals of Empire never passed without his full involvement. Robert Pullar's compassion was not only directed to the Lancashire Cotton Distress Fund, the Railway Benevolent Fund, the Lifeboat Institution, the S. S. P. C. A., Bankfoot Orphanage, but to foreign misadventures - victims of the Seige of Paris, the Newfoundland Fires, etc., His interests were wide-ranging - the Boys' Brigade, Gaelic Mods, the Young Scots Society, the Franco-Scottish Society and the Photographic Society. As for education - he helped found the Perth School of Art and as a Governor of Sharp's Institution gave £6,000 for a Science Extension in 1897. Fechney Industrial School for Boys received a new wing in 1889 and a gymnasium and baths in 1893, while he served as a Director at the Wellshill Industrial School for Girls. Not only did he open two new schools, Caledonian Road School in 1892 and Southern District School in 1899, but he was actively involved in the School for the Blind, the Deaf and Dumb School and the Rescue Tinkers' Children Movement. Higher education was not neglected - Christian Women's Educational Union, Perth Educational Trust, the Duncan Bequest and the Scottish Technical Education Committee. But it was as Governor of University College, Dundee that he received his most valued recognition - an L.L.D. from the University of St Andrews.[303]

But it was the social life of Robert Pullar and his wife that captured the imagination of the citizens of Perth. Well might Andrew Coates comment: "Robert Pullar has a larger place in the hearts of his fellow-citizens than any individual of the present generation."[304] He had his portrait painted by Sir John Millais and he was sculpted by John Tweed; he dined with the Earl of Rosebery, the Marquis of Breadalbane and Sir Henry Campbell-Bannerman; he attended the Prince of Wales' Levee and Holyrood Palace Garden Parties. A close friend of the millionaire Andrew Carnegie he enjoyed the London Season, admired the Fleet at the Spithead Naval Review and danced at the United States Ambassador's Receptions. His wealth enabled him to holiday in exotic parts of the world and every little detail appeared in the press to be avidly read by his fellow-citizens and workers. A member of the Reform Club, the National Liberal Club, the Glasgow Liberal Club and the Edinburgh Scottish Liberal Club he was as much at home in Paris or Berlin as he was in Edinburgh or in London. The huge turnout at his funeral was an indication of how much he was admired by the people of Perth who never doubted his oft-expressed love for his place of birth.

James F Pullar 1835-1912 and Rufus D. Pullar 1861-1917

Both James F. Pulllar and his nephew Rufus D. Pullar were much less significant figures than their three predecessors - James F. Pullar because of his personality and Rufus D. Pullar because of his short life overshadowed by the War.

James F. Pullar was a man of retiring disposition and he hated publicity of any kind. The great love of his life was music and he did much to leave his mark on the city's musical scene. He sponsored Perth Musical Society, organised Pullars' Works Road, financed the North Inch Bandstand, gifted instruments to the Salvation Army and donated organs both to Kinnoull Church and St Andrew Church. He was a golfer of some merit and played regularly at the Royal and Ancient, St. Andrews, Perth Golfing Society and King James VI Club. A measure of his "quiet humility" is the fact that he enlisted in the ranks of the 1st Perth Rifles and rose to be an officer at the famous Edinburgh Review of 1860. The needy always attracted his compassionate aid, whether in the Poorhouse or in the Society for Improving the Condition of the Poor. For years he was an unobtrusive supporter of the Soup Kitchens, Industrial Schools and Working Boys' and Girls' Religious Society. His favourite charity however was the Night Shelter for Women, which he had built on the site of the Old Burns Tavern in the Watergate. Much of his time was spent on the affairs of the Infirmary and the City Mission, which both enjoyed many gifts from him over the years. With his brother he contributed large sums of money for Kinnoull Street and the Victoria Bridge and he played a leading part in determining the future of the Swimming Baths and the Museum. Together they presented an organ to the City Hall and gifted funds to refurbish it.

Rufus D. Pullar was regarded as "clever and cultured" by all who knew him and in all probability he was the most professional dyer of all the Pullars. His skill was certainly acclaimed by his colleagues, who elected him President of the Dyers' and Colourists' Society. In the community he played a prominent role and held a wide range of offices - Sub-Commissioner in Perthshire for National Service, a post which often required his presence in London; President of the Perth Brotherhood; President of Perth Indigent Society; Vice-President of the Perthshire Bible Society; the City Mission; the Association for Improving the Condition of the Poor; the Perth Working Boys' and Girls' Religious Society and Perth Soup

Kitchen; Governor of the Educational Trust and Sharp's Institution; Chairman of the Sick Poor Nursing Society and Tibbermore School Board; Director of Hillside Homes and the Murray Royal Hospital; a member of the Perthshire Secondary Education Committee; the County Appeal Tribunal and the Financial Committee of Perth Royal Infirmary; and an Elder in Bridgend UF Church. Devoid of any political ambition he refused to be Lord Provost of Perth or to stand for the Town Council.

All members of the Pullar family felt that they had an obligation to the City of Perth and its inhabitants and their contribution to the community was enormous - A. E. Pullar, H. S. Pullar, Laurence Pullar and R. M. Pullar. Their wives and sisters shared this motivation, especially Lady Pullar and Mrs R. D. Pullar. Together, they left an imprint on Perth.

Footnotes

1. *PC* 2/1/1817
2. *LS* 10
3. *PC* 16/12/1832
4. Ibid., 9/8/1822, 23/5/1823, 21/9/1826, 28/9/1826
5. Ibid., 30/9/1830, 31/7/1834
6. Ibid., 19/4/1832
7. Ibid., 29/3/1832
8. Ibid., 22/1/1835
9. Ibid., 5/7/1832, 6/12/1832
10. Ibid., 24/10/1833, 31/10/1833, 7/11/1833
11. *C* 5/3/1851
12. *PA* 10/4/1851
13. *PC* 26/6 /1851
14. *PA* 18/4/1872
15. Ibid., 29/4/1847; *PC* 13/5/1847
16. *PA* 15/2/1849. 19/4/1849. 7/2/1850
17. Ibid., 25/20/1849
18. Ibid., 1/11/1849
19. Ibid., 11/7/1850
20. Ibid., 2/1/1851
21. Ibid., 27/11/1851
22. Ibid., 15/12/1867
23. Ibid., 28/8/1856
24. Ibid., 2/7/1857; *PC* 14/3/1871
25. *PA* 15/9/1870
26. Ibid., 2/11/1871; *PC* 28/2/1865
27. Ibid., 2/10/1828
28. Ibid., 1/7/1873
29. Ibid., 5/7/1832
30. Ibid., 21/11/1832
31. Ibid., 6/12/1832
32. Ibid., 27/12/1832
33. Ibid., 20/11/1834
34. Ibid., 24/8/1837
35. *C* 1/11/1837
36. *PC* 1/4/1852
37. *C* 28/4/1859
38. *PA* 2/4/1857, 5/5/1959
39. Ibid., 15/10/1872
40. *PC* 13/8/1872
41. Ibid., 15/10/1872
42. *C* 13/11/1835
43. Ibid., 14/2/1835
44. Ibid., 5/12/1836
45. *PC* 23/6/1836; *C* 10/7/1836
46. *PC* 23/6/1897
47. *C* 3/8/1836
48. Ibid., 22/2/1837
49. Ibid., 20/12/1837
50. Ibid., 28/4/1930
51. Ibid., 18/9/1835
52. Ibid., 21/11/1838
53. *PC* 21/3/1844. 6/6/1844
54. *C* 5/3/1845, 21/1/1846
55. Ibid., 29/1/1845
56. Ibid., 11/3/1846, 27/5/1846
57. *PC* 9/7/1846
58. Ibid., 13/8/1846, 3/9/1846
59. Ibid., 8/4/1847
60. Ibid., 27/5/1847
61. *LS* 65
62. *PA* 24/6/1847
63. *PC* 3/6/1847
64. *PA* 9/3/1848
65. Ibid., 15/6/1848
66. *C* 8/4/1930
67. Ibid., 6/12/1848
68. *PA* 7/12/1848
69. *C* 21/5/1851
70. *PA* 7/9/1848
71. Ibid., 17/10/1850
72. Ibid., 17/11/1864, 13/12/1864
73. Ibid., 4/8/1859, 11/12/1862, 29/12/1863
74. Ibid., 2/2/1871
75. Ibid., 6/3/1851
76. *PC* 3/1/1839
77. Ibid., 22/11/1841
78. *C* 7/3/1923
79. *PC* 5/81847

Footnotes

80. *C* 17/11/1847
81. Ibid., 5/1/1848
82. Ibid., 19/1/1848
83. Ibid., 21/6/1848, 27/9/1848
84. *PA* 4/4/1850
85. Ibid., 10/10/1850
86. Ibid., 1/5/1856
87. Ibid., 25/1/1855
88. *C* 19/7/1866
89. *PC* 2/10/1860
90. Ibid., 14/4/1868
91. Ibid., 19/4/1870
92. *C* 15/9/1847
93. *PA* 4/11/1847
94. *C* 10/11/1847
95. *PA* 11/11/1847
96. *PC* 9/12/1848
97. *C* 9/2/1847
98. *PA* 10/2/1848
99. *PC* 30/3/1848
100. *PA* 16/11/1848
101. Ibid., 6/1/1848; *PC* 26/9/1850
102. *C* 6/1/1848
103. *PA* 10/10/101848, 7/3/1850
104. Ibid., 12/7/1849
105. Ibid., 15/11/1849
106. *PC* 7/5/1850
107. Ibid., 8/8/1850
108. Ibid., 5/9/1850
109. *PA* 20/2/1851
110. Ibid., 27/2/1851
111. *PC* 6/11/1851
112. Ibid., 18/6/1867, *PA* 20/6/1867
113. *C* 20/8/1867
114. *PC* 20/9/1867
115. Ibid., 5/11/1867
116. Ibid., 12/11/1867
117. *LS* 52
118. *PC* 21/9/1868
119. Ibid., 4/6/1868
120. *PA* 8/2/1870
121. Ibid., 20/12/1869
122. Ibid., 7/4/1870
123. *PC* 3/5/1870
124. *PA* 14/7/1870
125. *PC* 2/8/1870
126. Ibid., 19/7/1870
127. Ibid., 16/8/1870
128. Ibid., 6/9/1870
129. *PA* 15/6/1871
130. *PC* 23/4/1872
131. *C* 1/7/1872
132. Ibid., 12/12/1873
133. *PC* 12/11/1867
134. *PA* 7/3/1870
135. *PC* 4/3/1862
136. *C* 17/7/1889
137. *PC* 9/6/1859 *C* 25/12/1859
138. *PA* 7/11/1849
139. Ibid., 14/9/1854
140. *C* 1/6/1885
141. *PC* 14/5/1867
142. *PA* 11/7/1834
143. *C* 6/1/1870
144. *PA* 10/1/1850
145. *PC* 7/7/1885; *PA* 22/9/1870
146. *LS* 61, 63
147. *PC* 27/2/1845, 7/5/1849
148. *PA* 29/1/1857
149. *C* 5/9/1867
150. *PC* 10/10/1839
151. Ibid., 7/9/1848, *PA* 8/3/1849, *PC* 26/9/1850, 16/12/1851
152. *PA* 5/6/1851
153. Ibid., 7/9/1891
154. *C* 24/4/1872
155. *PC* 13/5/1873
156. *PA* 11/1/1872
157. Ibid., 8/1/1863
158. Ibid., 21/12/1871

Footnotes

159. *C* 11 /10/ 1876
160. *PC* 14/3/1844
161. *PA* 30/12/1869
162. *PC* 28/3/1871, 7/11/1871
163. *PA* 9/3/1871
164. *PC* 12/9/1844, 4/12/1845
165. *PA* 6/12/1849
166. *C* 3 /7/1845
167. *PA* 3/ 8 /1837
168. Ibid., 31/1/1839, 25/6/1840
169. Ibid., 18/1/1844
170. Ibid., 2/7/1846
171. *PC* 17/12/1867, *PA* 11/1/1849
172. Ibid., 7/3/1850
173. Ibid., 11/7/1850, *PC* 26/9/1850
174. Ibid., 11/3/1858
175. Ibid., 19/12/1871
176. *PA* 14/11/1870
177. Ibid., 20/1/1848, *PC* 18/2/1847, 30/11/1848
178. Ibid., 31/12/1867
179. *C* 5/7/1848
180. *PA* 10/8/1848
181. Ibid., 16//1850. Founded in 1811 as the National Society for the Education of the Poor it decided in 1839 to allow dissenters' children to withdraw from religious lessons in their schools.
182. Ibid., 28/6/1849, 12/8/1869, 22/9/1864, 26/7/1847, *C* 27/3/1850
183. *PC* 23/7/1872
184. Ibid., 20/8/1867
185. *PA* 19/7/1855,15/10/1857
186. Ibid., 30/1/1862
187. *PC* 13/9/1870
188. *C* 25/44/1883
189. Ibid., 2/1/1888, 21/2/1888
190. *PC* 25/4/1883
191. *PA* 4/1/1895
192. Ibid., 14/3/1899
193. Ibid., 28/6/1895
194. *C* 25/11/1895
195. *PA* 31/12/1895
196. *C* 28/10/1896
197. *PC* 18/10/1898
198. *PA* 16/8/1905
199. Ibid., 4/9/1908
200. Ibid., 14/3/1883
201. *PC* 3/5/1881
202. *C* 19/2/1883
203. *PA* 11/12/1893
204. Ibid., 1/11/1866
205. *C* 18/11/1869, 11/11/1874
206. *PA* 27/3/1873, 10/4/1873
207. *PC* 3/2/1874
208. *C* 21/1/1878
209. Ibid., 2/2/1874
210. *PC* 23/3/1880
211. *C* 5/4/1880
212. *PC* 14/6/1881
213. *C* 15/3/1882
214. Ibid., 15/5/1882
215. Ibid., 20312/1882
216. *PC* 18/12/1883
217. *C* 30/1/1884
218. Ibid., 26/3/1884
219. *PC* 22/1/1884
220. *C* 16/4/1884
221. Ibid., 7/5/1884
222. *PC* 30/9/1884
223. *C* 28/1/1885
224. Ibid., 12/10/1885
225. Ibid., 21/10/1885
226. Ibid., 25/11/1885
227. Ibid., 4/6/1886
228. *PC* 31/5/1887
229. Ibid., 7/6/1887
230. *PA* 27/3/1889
231. *PC* 16/4/1889
232. *C* 24/4/1889
233. *PC* 17/12/1889

Footnotes

234. Ibid., 14/1/1890

235. Ibid., 4/3/1890

236. *PA* 15/4/1890

237. Ibid., 2/5/1890

238. Ibid., 29/9/1890

239. *PC* 9/6/1891

240. *C* 21/9/1891

241. *PC* 29/3/1892

242. Ibid., 19/4/1892, 3/5/1892

243. *PA* 24/6/1892

244. *PC* 12/7/1892

245. Ibid., 26/7/1892

246. Ibid., 9/8/1892

247. Ibid., 16/8/1892

248. Ibid., 25/2/1893

249. Ibid., 9/5/1893, 23/5/1893

250. *PA* 23/10/1893

251. *PC* 3/4/1894, 4/12/1894

252. *PA* 4/1/1895

253. Ibid., 11/1/1895

254. *PC* 7/5/1895

255. Ibid., 23/4/1895

256. *C* 29/5/1895

257. *PC* 21/5/1895

258. Ibid., 9/7/1895

259. *C* 15/7/1895

260. *PC* 23/7/1895; *C* 13/4/1896

261. *PC* 21/4/1896

262. *C* 21/9/1896

263. *PC* 31/8/1897, 3/10/1897

264. *PA* 12/4/1898; *PC* 3/1/1899

265. Ibid., 3/10/1900

266. *PA* 17/2/1902

267. *PC* 10/3/1903

268. Ibid., 27/1/1903

269. Ibid., 9/6/1903

270. *C* 26/10/1903

271. Ibid., 8/7/1906

272. Ibid., 24/12/1906

273. Ibid., 1/1/1906

274. Ibid., 4/2/1907

275. *PA* 13/2/1907

276. *PC* 5/2/1907

277. *PA* 6/2/1907

278. *PC* 2/7/1907, 9/7/1907

279. Ibid., 8/10/1907

280. *PA* 12/1/1910

281. *C* 19/1/1910

282. *PC* 6/12/1910

283. *PA* 8/4/1911

284. *PC* 7/2/1893

285. *PA* 10/2/1881

286. Ibid., 9/10/1905

287. *C* 6/11/1905

288. Ibid., 6/12/1905, *PA* 14/3/1906

289. *C* 7/2/1906

290. Ibid., 16/7/1906

291. *PA* 30/9/1908

292. Ibid., 8/1/1909, *PC* 15/6/1909

293. Ibid., 15/8/1905

294. Ibid., 5/4/1898

295. Ibid., 7/10/1901; *PA* 12/2/1902

296. *PC* 15/11/1887

297. Ibid., 3/2/1897

298. *PA* 12/10/1900

299. *C* 8/101873; *PA* 25/4/1890, 31/3/1891

300. *C* 20/7/1903

301. *PC* 14/10/1896

302. *PA* 20/12/1901

303. Ibid., 18/10/1905

304. *PC* 20/8/1895

Evaluation

Were the Pullars "good managers" or simply "robber-barons"?

Managers have certain clearly defined functions among which are making a profit for the firm's owners or shareholders, establishing the reputation of the company in the the eyes of both public and competitors and showing consideration for the workforce. "Good managers" will do so by exercising compassion, honesty and integrity. "Robber-barons", on the other hand, are only interested in profit and are quite willing to cheat their competitors, delude the public and exploit their workforce. Into which of these two catagories do the Pullars fall?

They certainly made enormous profits by their managerial skills. They could anticipate public demand for specific colours and shades; they invested huge sums in the most up-to-date machinery; and they made full use of advertising as well as rail and telephone communications to guarantee a highly efficient turnover in the volume of their trade. By 1885 "Pullars of Perth" was not only a slogan, but a synonym for the highest standard of dyeing and cleaning. Not only were the North British Dye Works world famous, but they had become a tourist attraction for curious aristocrats, envious businessmen and general admirers. Clearly, the public was well satisfied with what was on offer. As for competitors most had fallen by the wayside and those giants that had survived, like P. and P. Campbell of Perth had close contacts with the Pullars and judged them to be of the highest level of professionalism, reputable and honest. That leaves the workforce.

The Pullars, from the very earliest days, made certain demands upon all their employees - they had to be of good character, able to work hard and accept firm discipline, not addicted to drink, and above all, able to demonstrate loyalty. In return the Pullars promised secure employment without lay-offs or cut-backs, steady wages and the prospect of promotion from the shop-floor to managerial status. The result was that people clamoured to get jobs in the North British Dye Works and there was always a waiting list. The firm however went further - preference was given to employees' children and relatives and long years of service virtually assured a pension of sorts. Those fortunate enough to obtain employment there found it easy to get credit with any merchant in Perth and also to find accommodation. The staff knew that they were lucky compared to many segments of the local working class population. The North British Dye Works was also one of the safest places to work in the city having a very low accident rate throughout the 19th century. Indeed, the first works fatality did not come until 1902. Again, the Pullars were the only large-scale employers in Perth not fined for breach of the 1856 laws on "employment of the young" or the 1867 Workshop Acts. It was scarcely surprising therefore that H. M. I. F. in 1875 could state that they "provided the best working conditions in their industry." In 1869, for instance, they made Saturday afternoons free for women and children; in 1873 they introduced a 51 hour week; in 1895 they banned overtime for the young; in 1907 long service workers got holidays with pay and in 1910 they started a 45 hour week. There were other advantages; in 1856 they encouraged soirées; in 1872 they extended meal-breaks and promoted departmental parties; in 1880 they had seaside excursions, free concerts, Works' Band and all kinds of clubs - swimming, football, cricket and cycling; in 1888 they established canteen facilities and Rest Rooms; and at Tulloch there were houses, a school and even a farm. All those of course have to be seen, not against modern working conditions, but in comparison to contemporary situations - lay-offs in slack seasons, longer hours, dangerous working environments and absolutely no prospects of advancement. To secure a job in the North British Dye Works was the heartfelt ambition of most workers in the 19th century Perth.

How then did the slur of "robber-barons" arise? The Pullars, especially John Pullar, had made many enemies in their time - the river-harbour vested interest group, the stage-coach proprietors, the carriers, the steamer owners, the drink trade, landlords. They had even been wrongly blamed for other firms deciding not to come to Perth. However, the "robber-barons" allegation comes from none of these. It was the sole result of the bitter quarrel with the Amalgamated Society of Dyers and Bleachers who condemned the Pullars for refusing to accept their Trade Union in the works and for sacking 27 of their leading activists. They accused the Pullars of ignoring the huge rise in the cost of living for workers and of trying to avoid paying the additional war wages, which might well have resolved the problem. In the propaganda generated by the conflict the Amalgamated Society of Dyers and Bleachers were clearly more adept. They whipped up mass emotions that frequently verged on hysteria and even hinted darkly at the suspect Pullar pro-German sympathies during the 1914-1918 War. The astonishing fact of the matter is that after 70 years the allegation of "robber-barons" can still be heard, despite the evidence of the previous century.

Why were Pullars so late in switching all their resources from
cotton spinning to dyeing and cleaning?

This question, first asked in Perth newspapers c.1858, is essentially misconceived in that the Pullars never did transfer all their resources to dyeing and cleaning. Indeed, as was revealed in 1878 in the Inventory of John Pullar he had as much money invested in cotton spinning and weaving at Keirfield and Ashfield as he had in dyeing and cleaning at Perth. Nonetheless, it seems pertinent given the poor performance of cotton in 19th century Perth.

Whatever the story elsewhere the faults of cotton in Perth sprang from the practice of operating through agents from Glasgow and Paisley. This encouraged speculation with inevitable results - sudden collapse of markets, unsure supplies, unstable yarn prices and wages and even unpredictable demand. There were bad years - 1825-1826, 1831, 1840 and 1857 - and there were good years - 1835, 1844 and 1852. A. J. Robertson[1] has traced the overall picture for Scotland after 1835 when "capital and enterprise seem to have begun to leave the cotton industry for more profitable fields." While John Pullar installed Jacquard Machines in 1836, Houldsworth, Glasgow cotton manufacturer, moved into iron and Findlay and Company put up Catrine, Deanston and Ballindalloch for sale and moved into calico-printing as did Gunn and Company at Thornliebank. Despite English competition after 1847 John Pullar persisted and installed power-looms in 1852 and bought Keirfield in 1855. Many thought that the Commercial Crisis of 1857 would be the last straw. With unsettled conditions in the U.S.A. and "credit structures overstrained" the high cost of cotton in Glasgow depressed profits. Over-production helped to bring prices down and this, together with the fact that cotton was no longer fashionable with the rich, led to "excessive speculation and abuse of credit."[2] In Glasgow the muslin trade collapsed and Monteith and Company as well as McDonald and Company went to the wall. While John Pullar closed down cotton operations in Perth he continued them at Keirfield. Was this an error of judgment? Plainly no, because cotton recovered in 1860 and actually enjoyed a boom in 1861. Although the U.S. Civil War produced the "cotton famine" leading to many closures and short-time its effect was less damaging than popularly supposed. Even though operating through Liverpool after 1865 raised costs, by 1867 the cotton trade was not only "back to normal", it was "healthier than it had been in 1861." The real decline only began in the 1870's with technology falling behind leaving archaic machinery and low productivity. By the time of John Pullar's death foreign competition was also being felt. John Pullar had responded to all these changes by buying Ashfield in 1865 and retaining to the end of his days his high esteem for the value of cotton.

II.

How did they invest their profits and just how innovative were they in the field?

Given that the capital value of John Pullar and Son, Dyers, Perth in 1848 was a mere £500 and given the vast sums spent on the huge programme of expansion after 1859 the profits of the North British Dye Works must have been very high. Their investments too must have given a good to fair return considering that John Pullar left £122,561, while Sir Robert Pullar left £519,675 and Rufus D. Pullar left £240,440. There is not a great deal of difference in their portfolios and clearly the pattern was laid down by John Pullar. His son and grandson, generally speaking, followed his example. Sir Robert achieved the most, but he had easier problems to face than either his father or his son and he did most of his work at a time when the economy was in good heart. It is significant to note that John Pullar only had 11.2% of his total resources invested in dyeing and cleaning. Robert Pullar increased it slightly to 12.8%, but Rufus Pullar was committed to the tune of 24.1%. This substantiates his explanation to the workforce that the works was absorbing too much of his capital. Much of their wealth, particularly that of Sir Robert, went on civic improvements and help for the poor and the needy and of course gave no return. Of their investment portfolios all shared a heavy involvement with railways, both at home and abroad, with John Pullar investing in 13, Sir Robert in 30 and Rufus Pullar in 17. They seem to have become a poor proposition by the time of Rufus Pullar, yet he kept as much as £55,788 in railways. Both John Pullar and his son carried heavy assurances, but not Rufus Pullar. Only Sir Robert scattered his investments over water, gas, hotels, corporations, loans and investment companies, government stocks and trusts. All of the Pullars were firm believers in the British Empire and Canada had pride of place in their affection followed then by Australia and India. Another area warmly regarded by the family was the U.S.A.

Nevertheless, the Pullars were not as innovative as many have thought. For example, the stories, found in many books, that they were responsible for the development of Perkins' work on synthetic dyes in 1856 and the discovery of dry-cleaning in 1866, are really myths, Strangely, they still survive.

The success of Pullar enterprises lay in a combination of two things; an uncanny accuracy in predicting the colour whims of a fickle public and tremendous organising skill which enabled them to adapt new ideas speedily and efficiently. These were first noticeable as early as 1828 when the Pullars moved into rural areas and in the 1830's when they suddenly grasped the significance of the power of advertising. It was the same with the arrival of railways. They realised that rail communication opened up distant markets in the south, especially after the introduction of cheap parcel rates in 1851. The Pullars began garment cleaning in 1849 and this became their central activity. The winning of a Royal Warrant in 1852 was widely advertised on their horse-drawn vans and their name soon spread throughout east central Scotland. The "passing trade of rail trippers" was organised on a regular basis in 1853 with the opening of branch offices within a 30 mile radius of Perth. Of course, speedy turnover was paramount and this led to purchase of specific machines for that purpose in 1855. By 1858 the introduction of ready-made clothing opened up the prospect of working-class customers, who often needed repair on their clothing. The Pullars met this by acquiring a large number of sewing-machines from the U.S.A., which meant an enormous expansion in the size of their finishing departments. With the 1860's came "the invasion of England" and the concentration on the huge market in the London area. Although dry-cleaning techniques came from Berlin the Pullars had the foresight to send some of their best workers there to learn the new skills. By 1868 settling ponds, tanks and sieves finally solved the age-old problem of pollution and the introduction of laboratories made dyeing and cleaning a far more scientific process. By 1878 telephones, electric bells and hoists were commonplace and with the U.S. improvements brought back by Robert Pullar in 1880 the North British Dye Works led the field in modern technology. This was advanced further in 1881 by an admirable new ventilation system and the start of trunk calls in 1884. Already a complex network was spreading across the whole of the U.K. Workers were not forgotten; in 1888 came the Rest Rooms and by 1896 hot-air drying had revolutionised the traditional dye-house with its clouds of steam. The works laboratory by this stage was even producing its own synthetics, dyes by the hundred. By the 1890's the Pullars and their senior managers were scouring Europe for new ideas. The best workers were rewarded by trips to Paris in 1900 and by 1901 the complexity of the Pullar Empire was breath-taking - 22 Receiving Offices, 24 Departments, 300 Branches, 2,600 Staff and 4,000 Agencies. Motor vans rapidly replaced horses by 1905 as the Pullars continued to rely on their key market - London. On the eve of World War 1 the parcel post organisation at Pullars was the envy of the GPO.

III

What style of management did they pursue and did it vary with the personality of the chairman of the firm?

Between 1824 and 1918 the Pullar style of management hardly changed. It was consistently paternalistic and occasionally authoritarian. Continually stressing the virtues of "being a family firm" the Pullar Directors all believed in the worth of moral discipline. They prided themselves on knowing the family background of their employees and it was the boast of Sir Robert that he had known their fathers and even grandfathers too. Because of this they constantly harangued the workforce to avoid strong drink, practise thrift and make proper use of leisure. As the staff rose in number to well over 2,000 this close personal contact was lost and a new style of management technique was needed. Unfortunately, the Pullars found this difficult to achieve and worker-resentment increased. As the firm grew bigger the concept of loyalty slowly eroded and was replaced by organised demands for wage scales, shop stewards and Trade Union rights.

Although there are signs of the notorious "three-generation syndrome" in operation, all of the Pullars were men of remarkable ability, enterprise and foresight, whether working in linen, cotton or dyes. Yet, despite this, they were all different in their personalities.

Robert Pullar, who financed the original dye-works in 1824, was the toughest - hard, inflexible and dour, not an easy man to like nor with whom to work. John Pullar was the most intelligent - clever, shrewd, essentially honest. Sir Robert was the most compassionate and religious - a man with a deep-rooted need to be loved and admired. His brother, James F. Pullar, was the most cultured - a man who shunned the glare of publicity. Ironically, Rufus D. Pullar, the man who failed, was the best educated and the best dyer.

M

Why were they unable to confront the Trade Unions and why did they eventually succumb to the merger?

The Pullars were united in their dislike for and distrust of Trade Unions. Shared power was an affront to their hard work and risk-taking and from 1869 they tried hard, but unsuccessfully, to develop the Working Men's Association as an alternative. Their business history seemd to substantiate their prejudice - in 1834 the Dundee Weavers' Union had tried to organise the Perth workers in a wave of demonstrations, petitions, rallies and riots; in 1850 a rail strike had nearly put paid to the Pullar plans for expansion; in 1869 their building schedule had been plagued by strikes and nearly abandoned. The year 1872 in particular had been a year of violence with mass meetings at the North British Dye Works and demands for shorter hours and higher rates. Only Robert Pullar's skilled efforts produced a compromise. Another rail strike in 1890 exposed the weakness in Pullar's position and this was followed in 1892-1894 by a Trade Union drive to attract female labour. The arrival of the well-known orators, Tom Mann and Ben Tillett, in 1894, was immediately followed by further wage demands in 1895. Even Robert Pullar could not handle the 1907 wage protests and the surge in living costs in 1909 and 1911 simply made matters worse. The arrival of the Labour Party in Perth in 1910 must have been seen as an ominous sign by the Pullars and especially when the Amalgamated Society of Dyers and Bleachers sent a team to organise the city in 1911. With the National Insurance Act in force the Trade Union demanded a wage scale, an end to seven year apprenticeships and "good will" increments. Before any settlement could be reached the 1912 strike by railmen and miners disrupted business to such an extent that fuel costs soared and the plant was put on short-time and even temporarily closed. No sooner had this been resolved than 500 struck over the non-appearance of the traditional June increment. Although Trade Union unity dissolved quickly enough the Pullars felt betrayed. Despite the fact that Rufus Pullar refrained from sackings and conceded a wage scale in 1913 he was then faced with a further demand for a national minimum wage. Angered by shop steward activities he demanded a Petition of Loyalty and dismissed 27 of the dissidents' leaders. By now the War with short-time, lack of coal and dyes, combined with a slump in trade, which the workforce disputed, decided Rufus Pullar to reject the 1917 War Wages Scheme. Instantly, he became a national target for the Dyers' Union. The constant warring broke the Pullars' spirit and in the face of tremendous opposition they sold out to Eastman. Both sides felt betrayed and the bitterness lingered for decades.

Although the Pullars "sold out" to Eastman of London in 1918 they did, in fact, retain some holdings in the new company. It was, therefore, in some ways, a form of merger. As N. A. Utton[3] has proved, mergers were quite common in the dyeing industry after 1898. For instance, in that year the Bradford Dyers' Association absorbed 22 firms covering 90% of the industry; in 1899 the Yorkshire Indigo, Scarlet and Colour Dyers absorbed 11 firms; in 1899 the English Velvet and Cord Dyers absorbed 46 firms covering 85% of their branch of the trade; in 1900 the Bleachers' Association some 10 firms. Thus, merging with another firm to secure wider outlets was a common practice and an obvious choice for Pullars.

V
How did they come to dominate the city of Perth so completely and did they do so by exploiting local politics?

The Pullar family dominated Perth for just under 50 years from. c.1867-1912. Both before and after these years their influence was negligible.

Although a self-confessed Radical Whig in 1832 Robert Pullar never attempted to cut a social figure and probably would have had nothing but contempt for those who did so. Perth was a Tory burgh and he was a Dissenter with a middle-class clientele, not a promising equation for social success. Even John Pullar, although exhilarated by politics, had little success while in the Town Council 1847-1850 and for the next 17 years was far too busy with his affairs to run for office. It was only in 1867 when he was asked to serve as Lord Provost that he showed himself as a man who could challenge vested interests with courage and win. His platform was simple - he had concern for the urban environment, he deplored drink and he wanted cheaper gas for all. It revealed him as intelligent, energetic and honourable. Some would have disagreed - publicans, certain landlords, gas company proprietors and even some ratepayers. Generally, they were people who had lost money through his reforms. Spiteful malice was their typical response and his political rivals were by far the worst. They accused him of being autocratic - a man, who, despite some civic improvements, ruthlessly got his own way. This is blatantly untrue. He never saw the Scott Street-Kinnoull Street link, nor the union of George Street and Mill Street, both of which would have been beneficial for his personal business. Neither did he succeed in having "that old warship", the Old Council House, demolished, nor even a New

Public Hall for the city. It was left therefore to his son to make the greatest impact upon Perth and its citizens. Yet, Robert Pullar never served on the Town Council nor was he ever Lord Provost. His personality made him popular and his generosity made him loved. His lavish life-style made him the obvious "Merchant Prince of Perth", a man from whom all blessings might flow. Significantly, after his death in 1912 Pullar influence quickly evaporated.

Did the Pullars exploit local politics to dominate Perth? There is no evidence that they did so. Like all their rivals, Campbell, McLeish, Braid and Miller, they were anxious to have a say on the Water Commission, so essential to their survival as dyers. Widening their social contacts through public office and the free publicity which this entailed were legitimate activities. They certainly never made any money from any of their commitments. In fact, the opposite was the case. Anyway, involvement in local politics was a common practice among the successful 19th century entrepreneurs.[4]

VI

Did they make any specific errors of judgment or was the firm simply doomed by its geography?

At first sight all the mistakes seem to have been made by Rufus Pullar in 1917. In fact, there were at least three long-term fundamental errors of judgment stretching back as far as 1872.

Although the Pullars disliked and distrusted Trade Unions, events in 1872, when the workforce demanded shorter hours and higher overtime rates, should have warned Robert Pullar that the time had come to consider the option of accepting Trade Unions. Unfortunately, his poor health in 1902 and the death of his wife in 1904 blunted his awareness and his clumsy handling of the 1907 wage protest suggests a fading interest.

As early as 1866 British dyers became aware of the economics threat from Germany. The Pullars, especially Robert and James, with their intimate knowledge of what was going on there, should have begun long-term planning to meet this growing menace. Instead, they seem to have been blinded by their admiration for teutonic efficiency. Others saw the danger quite plainly and criticised the Pullars 1893-1895. Anti-German feeling in Perth was strong by 1904 when it became obvious that the Germans were cheating to evade British Patent Acts. Still the Pullars made no response. By 1909 when German industrial spying had reached its height the Pullars continued to mouth Free Trade platitudes.

The third long-term error in judgment should have been spotted as far back as 1903. The year before had seen confident predictions made by the Pullars that the North British Dye Works might soon have a workforce of 6,000. This was quite unrealistic. The bulk of their trade, unlike that of P. and P. Campbell, lay in the south of England, in fact, London, and there were at least 660 London dyeworks alone competing for business, not to mention the two giant firms, Eastman and Son, Acton Vale and Johnson Bros., Bootle. By 1910 the drop in trade was quite marked and this should have forced a re-think of policy and direction.

That none of these three factors was really considered is a charge that must be laid at the feet of Sir Robert Pullar.

Then there were the factors over which the Pullars had absolutely no control, factors which, separately, might have been soluble, but in combination were overwhelming. The first was the unexpected rise in the cost of living, especially in the years 1909 and 1911. The Pullars clearly regarded this as an aberration which would soon adjust itself. The second was the consequences of the National Insurance Act 1911 which they had not fully thought out. The third was the rise of the National Federation of Women Workers together with more strident demands made by females all over the country for better pay, rights and prospects, and on a parallel course the increasingly aggressive style of the Amalgamated Society of Dyers and Bleachers with their demands for a national minimum wage and recognition of shop stewards. Fourth was the advent of War with its dislocation of communications and shortages of coal and dyes.

Finally, there are the specific errors of judgment which were spread over a very short space of time and all of these were the responsibility of a flustered and confused Rufus Pullar. Despite his attempts to modernise management-worker relationships he singularly failed to explain to his workforce the significance of the firm's decision to become a Joint Stock Company in 1911 and particularly the new financial year arrangments. It was the same with the effects of the National Insurance Act 1911 and his cancellation of the old Sickness Benefit Society. Anything that followed this breakdown of communication was seen by the workers as malicious punishment. Another mistake was not to explain earlier that greater competition was causing the firm to lose money and that the cut in the summer holiday was necessary to win back production levels after the rail strike. By the time he started to demand a Petition of Loyalty and sack Trade Union activists he had lost control and panic was taking over.

This is shown by his most fatal error of judgment - refusal to accept the 1917 War Wages Scheme. The summons for the Lanarkshire Mounted Police to win the Battle of the Gates was therefore inevitable. It gave Rushworth an opportunity to contrast the Pullars' lavish life-style and big mansions - Tayside, the Durn, Rosebank and Ochil Villa with the plea for an extra 10/- a week.

Despite these long-term and short-term specific errors the Pullars were, in fact, doomed by their geography. Their physical isolation and virtual remoteness from their main market, London, meant that they could never really compete with their southern competitors on equal terms. Their life-line was the rail system and a series of strikes between 1891 and 1912 should have convinced them just how vulnerable their position was. The 1912 Rail Strike in particular disrupted their complex organisational arrangements and doubled their costs in fuel, packaging and insurance. It was only a matter of time before this would have caught up with them, even without the War of 1914-1918.

VII
Do the Pullars fit the classical pattern of 19th century entrepreneurs?

First, we must ask what entrepreneurs? Although selections would vary with individuals the following are surely the most outstanding by any criteria - Thomas Holloway (1800-1883), proprietory medicines; Sir Titus Salt (1803-1876), textiles; Samuel Morley (1809-1886), stockings and underwear; George Palmer (1818-1897), biscuits; Jeremiah J. Colman (1830-1898), mustard; Andrew Carnegie (1836-1919), steel; George Cadbury (1839-1922), chocolates; Joseph Rowntree (1836-1925), cocoa and chocolates; Jesse Boot (1850-1931), chemist and W.H. Lever (1851-1925), soap.[5] These were men who created mass markets by their willingness to take risks and make decisions - Palmer, who recognised that the fall in the price of wheat in 1846 gave him a chance to produce biscuits on a large scale; Lever and Cadbury, who took advantage of the removal of excise duty on soap and the reduced import duty on cocoa beans in 1853 to mass-produce soap and chocolates; and Holloway and Boot, who used cheap, mass-circulation papers to advertise their products after the 1853 abolition of the high tax on advertisements and the later abolition of stamp duty and excise charges on paper; or Colman, who had free rein for his mustard after the Sale of Food and Drugs Act 1875 and the Trade Marks Act 1875. In the main they operated between 1850 and

1880 when the U.K. economy was dynamic, when the nation's Gross National Income doubled, when the population rose by 25%, when there was a massive shift from the countryside to the towns and when there was a steady rise in real wages. They made full use of the railways which drastically reduced their transport costs and eased distribution. They functioned in a period when Trade Unions were weak and the rising standards of living for workers created a generally optimistic and co-operative outlook with relatively few strikes, demarcation disputes or restrictive practices. In an age when there was no Welfare State they had endless scope for philanthropy if they so desired - in education, health care and social services.

All this being so, it must be possible to construct a profile of the "classical pattern" for a 19th century entrepreneur.[6] Many of them left school at an early age and had little formal education. But, they did have those characteristics so familiar to Max Weber and Richard Tawney - they were relentlessly hard-working, willing to suffer a punishing work load and always at their work-place early; they were methodical, regular and thrifty with temperate, self-improving attitudes to almost all problems and never anything but self-disciplined; they were sober, temperate, honest and straightforward. But they were also cultivated and cultured men with open minds, who were interested in aesthetics and politics. Nonetheless, religion was the dominant force in their lives, hence their warmth, compassion and determination to improve the lives of their fellow-men. This sense of purpose and deep faith gave them drive, enterprise and courage. Dedicated nonconformists they were vigorous individuals with almost a reforming zeal.

As managers they had a flair for sensing the changing tastes of their customers and intuitively responding to them. When they identified a market they sought out the latest ideas and looked for new materials. They saw that advertising was the key to success and they welcomed change and challenge even more. Their organisations were of the highest quality as were the trusted workers they selected for important positions. They generally distrusted Trade Unions and liked to work through networks of agents. Always paternalistic, stern but kind, they could on occasion, be autocratic. Benevolent and patriarchial they showered their employees with moral exhortation and advice.

In their mills and factories therefore they tried to provide a total environment for their workers in an attempt to create virtually self-sufficient communities. Their concern for worker welfare stretched from housing to health and from education to recreation. Most of them lavished a great deal upon their work-places to make them architecturally magnificent. Within they organised excursions to the seaside, tea parties, cricket matches and visits by distinguished personages. Their pensions to retired workers, their sick funds, their savings' banks, their works' kitchens and their welfare schemes were the envy of less fortunate mortals. Among the first to provide Saturday afternoons off they usually gave holidays with pay to celebrate major national events to the astonishment of their competitors.

Their philosophy was essentially what is called Victorian Liberalism - a belief in Free Trade, self-help, minimum government interference, internationalism and radical social reform. Convinced that wealth carried a moral responsibility to the less fortunate they deplored the polarisation of Capital and Labour. They saw a harmony of interests between worker and manager as partners in a great enterprise. They urged war on poverty, a campaign for better housing, a drive against drink through local options and free entertainment to replace the attraction of the pub. Dedicated to the concept of self-improvement, they encouraged emigration, practised philanthropy and invested in railways.

Almost to a man they were Liberals with ardent admiration for Gladstone. Many of them were M.P.'s or else in Town Councils. There their main concern was to fight for better drainage and sanitation and to encourage public bathing as a safeguard to health. Young people were never far from their thoughts and they donated large sums of money to schools and youth movements. In most cases their liberality guaranteed their complete dominance of the towns in which they lived and worked. Finally, in the main, they were well-liked and much admired as men of genius.

Although they shared so many characteristics there were differences - Samuel Morley supported Trade Unions, Joseph T. Colman refused a title, Andrew Carnegie was a hard employer and Jesse Boot had a simple life-style. Nonetheless, their pattern is obvious and the Pullars clearly deserve a place in their ranks.

Footnotes

1. "The Decline of the Scottish Cotton Industry 1860-1914", A.J. Robertson, *B.H.*, Vol. XII, 1970, pp. 117, 118, 119-120

2. "The Western Bank and the Crisis of 1857", Margaret A. Whitehead, M. Litt. (Strathclyde), 1978; *"The Development of the West of Scotland 1760-1960"*, A. Slaven, Routledge and Kegan Paul, 1975.

3. "Some Features of the Early Merger Movements in British Manufacturing Industry", M.A. Utton, *B.H.*, Vol. XIV, 1972, pp. 52-53; *"Retail Trading in Britain 1850-1950"*, James B. Jeffreys, Cambridge University Press, 1954.

4. "Public Pursuit of Private Profit? Liberal Businessmen and Municipal Politics in Birmingham 1865-1900", Linda J. Jones, *B.H.*, Vol. XXV, 1983, p.240; *"Economic and Social Change in a Midland Town: Victorian Nottingham"*, Roy A. Church, Cassell, London, 1965.

5. *"Enlightened Entrepreneurs"*, Ian C. Bradley, Weidenfeld and Nicolson, 1987.

6. *"The Entrepreneurs"*, Elizabeth Hennessey, Scope Books, 1980.

Bibliography

Note

Hard facts about dyeing are elusive. For instance, the 3 volumes of the Proceedings of the Society of Antiquarians of Scotland 1851-1981 have only two references to dyeing and the Scottish Historical Review 1904-1928 has only one. Even the Short-Title Catalogue of Books Printed in Scotland 1475-1640 has only three entries and this from an author catalogue of 26,143 items. Between 1500-1946 only 199 books about dyeing were published in the U.K. Given these facts it is clear that a full history of dyeing will never be written.

Annual Reports

Association for Improving the Condition of the Poor 1876-1901
Bridgend Institute 1884-1920
Discharged Prisoners' Aid Society 1896-1091
Fechney Industrial School 1856-1900
Perth City Mission 1881-1893
Perth County and City Savings Bank 1839-1918; Centenary Issue 1815-1915
Perth Infirmary 1847-1911
Perth Ladies' House of Refuge 1845-1904
Perth Sick Poor Nursing Society 1885-1901
Perth Society for the Relief of Incurables 1877-1927
Perth Society for the Relief of Indigent Old Men 1880-1909
Perth Working Boys' and Girls' Religious Society 1874-1896

Directories

The Commercial Directory of Ireland and Scotland, T. Wilkinson, Edinburgh, 1820
New Commercial Directory of Scotland, Pigot and Company, Edinburgh, 1826
Perth Post Office Directories 1837-1891
Pigot and Company's National Commercial Directory of Scotland, 1837
Slater's Royal National Commercial Directory and Topography of Scotland, London, 1840

Encyclopedias

Encyclopedia Perthensis, Vol. 6, Perth, 1807
Encyclopedia Britannica, Vol. 2, 1771; Vol. 7, 1823; Vol. 8, 1842
Edinburgh Encyclopedia, Vol. 8, Edinburgh, 1830

Guides

Guides to City and County of Perth 1805-1851
Perth: A Town Survey, Civic Trust, 1972

Newspapers and Magazines

Daily Chronicle 12/2/1904, 12/2/1912
Daily Mail 28/6/1902, 9/4/1907
Glasgow Herald 10/9/1912, 6/4/1912, 6/4/1966
Laundry News January, 1907
Our Home 20/6/1907
People's Journal 23/5/1903
Perth Courier 1809-1929
Perthshire Advertiser 1829-1984 (missing 1829-1832, 1884-1886, 1888, 1896)
Perthshire Constitutional 1835-1951 (missing 1841, 1842, 1849, 1853-1858, 1864-1865)
Power Laundry October, 1904
The Scotsman 10/9/1912

The Scottish Philanthropist September, 1912
Celtic Annual 1916

Pamphlets

Perth Pamphlets, edited R.S. Fittis, Vols. 1 and 3, 1898

Parliamentary Papers

Reports of the Assistant Hand-Loom Weavers' Commission, 1839

Pullar Papers

The Story of Pullars, 1937
Draft History of Pullars, April, 1965
Memorial on Pullar Family, PKDLA MS 51/5/5.14
Newspaper Cuttings Book 1890-1926, PAU MS 51/5/2.3
Tulloch Farm Report Book 1883-1916

Registers

Morison's Register 1854-1892
Perth Register 1823-1916

Statistical Account

OSA Perth 1796, Vol. 11, pp.468-518
NSA Perth 1844

Town Council Minutes

Perth Town Council Minutes 1884-1894

Wills

Commissariat of Perthshire Book of Inventories and Wills SC 49/31/23 Vol. 18; SC 49/31/109 Vol. 102; SC 49/32/24 Vol. 225
Scottish Record Office SC 49/31/218

Articles

B.W.E. Alford, Entrepreneurship, Business Performance and Industrial Development, *B.H.*, Vol. XIX, 1977, pp. 116-133

T.S. Ashton, Business History, *B.H.*, Vol. 1, 1958, pp. 1-2

J. Baddiley, The Rise and Development of Wool Dyes; A Brief Historical Survey, *J.S.D.C.*, Vol. 67, No. 12, 1951

T.C. Barker, Business History and the Business-Man, *B.H.*, Vol. 1, 1958, pp. 16-20

John J. Beer, The Emergence of the German Dye Industry, *Illinois Studies in Social Sciences*, Vol. XIV, 1959

A.H. Brewis, Hosiery and Finishing, *J.S.D.C.*, Jubilee Issue, 1934 Asa Briggs, Trade Union History and Labour History, *B.H.*, Vol. VIII, 1966, pp. 39-47

A.M. Brown, Business History and Management Education, *B.H.*, Vol. XVII, 1975, pp. 17-25

A.K. Cairncross, The British Economy 1850-1860, *B.H.*, Vol. V, 1962 pp. 54-56

Roy A. Church, An Aspect of Family Enterprise in the Industrial Revolution, *B.H.*, vol. IV, 1961, pp.120-125

Family Firms and Managerial Capitalism: The Case of the International Motor Industry, *B.H.*, Vol. XXVIII, 1986, pp. 155-180

C.O. Clark, John Wilson, the first British Dyer of Turkey Red, *J.S.D.C.*, Vol. 66, No. 10, 1950

The Earliest Record of Indigo Dyeing in England, *J.S.D.C.*, Vol. 70, No. 11, 1954

W.H. Cliffe, In the Footsteps of Perkin, *J.S.D.C.*, Vol. 72, No. 12, 1956

The Dyemaking Works of Perkin and Son, *J.S.D.C.*, Vol. 73, No. 7, 1957

An Historical Approach to the Dyestuff Industry, *J.S.D.C.*, Vol. 79, No. 8, 1963

T.C. Cochran, Entrepreneurial History, *Bulletin of the Business Historical Society*, Vol. XXIV, No. 3, 1950, pp. 114-115

P.N. Davies, Business Success and the Role of Chance: The Extraordinary Philipps Brothers, *B.H.*, Vol. XXIII, 1981, pp. 208-232

W.V. Farrer, Synthetic Dyes before 1860, Endeavour, No. 120, p. 149

R. Forman, There is no future for Business History: A Reply, *B.H.*, Vol. XXII, 1980, pp. 100-102

S.D. Forrester, The History of the Development of the Light Fastness Testing of Dyed Fabrics up to 1902, *Journal Textile*, Vol. 6, 1975

D.W.F. Hardie, The Emergence of the German Dye Industry, *B.H.*, Vol. V, 1962, pp. 118-122

H. Holmes and H. Muff, The Perils of Entrepreneurial History, *B.H.*, Vol. XVII, 1975, pp. 26-43

J. Hubner, A Contribution to the History of Dyeing with Special Reference to Scotland, *J.S.D.C.*, Vol. 30, 1914

Francis E. Hyde, Economic Theory of Business History, *B.H.*, Vol. V, 1962, pp.

R.J. Irving, British Railway Investment and Innovation 1900-1914, *B.H.*, Vol XIII, 1971, pp. 1-10

David J. Jeremy, Anatomy of the British Business Elite 1860-1980, *B.H.*, Vol. XXVI, 1984, pp. 39-63

Linda J. Jones, Public Pursuit of Private Profit? Liberal Businessmen and Municipal Politics in Birmingham 1865-1900, *B.H.*, Vol. XXV, 1983, pp. 240-259

John Killick, Risk, Speculation and Profit in the Mercantile Sector of the 19thc Cotton Trade: Alexander Brown and Sons 1820-1880, *B.H.*, Vol. XVI, 1974, pp.

C.H. Lee, Marketing Organisation and Policy in the Cotton Trade: McConnel and Kennedy of Manchester 1795-1835, *B.H.*, Vol. X, 1968, pp. 89-100

B. Lenman and K. Donaldson, Partners' Incomes, Investments and Diversification in the Scottish Linen Area 1850-1921, *B.H.*, Vol. XIII, 1971, pp. 1-18

R. Lloyd-Jones and A.A. Le Roux, Marshall and the Birth and Death of Firms: The Growth and Size Distribution of Firms in the early 19thc Cotton Industry, *B.H.*, Vol. XXIV, 1982, pp. 141-155

P. Matthias, Business History and Management Education, *B.H.*, Vol. XVII, 1975, pp. 3-16

J. Morton, History of the Development of Fast Dyeing and Dyes, *Journal Royal Society of Arts*, Vol. 77, 1928-1929

M.S. Moss and J.R. Hume, Business Failures in Scotland 1839-1913: A Research Note, *B.H.*, Vol. XXV, 1983, pp. 3-10

C.W. Munn, Scottish Provincial Banking Companies: An Assessment, *B.H.*, Vol. XXIII, 1981, pp. 19-41

W.H. Perkin, Presidential Address to the Society of Chemical Industry, *Journal of the Society of Chemical Industry*, Vol. 4, 1885

J.H. Porter, Skill and the Struggle for Power at the Workplace, *B.H.*, vol. XXIII, 1981, pp. 359-364

A.J. Robertson, The Decline of the Scottish Cotton Industry 1860-1914, *B.H.*, Vol. XII, 1970, pp. 117-120

E. Robinson, The International Exchange of Men and Machines 1750-1800, *B.H.*, Vol. 1, 1958, pp. 3-15

R.G. Rodger, Business Failure in Scotland 1839-1913, *B.H.*, Vol. XXVII, 1985, pp. 75-99

B.E. Supple, American Business History - a Survey, *B.H.*, Vol. 1, 1958, pp. 63-76

The Uses of Business History, *B.H.*, Vol. IV, 1961, pp. 81-90

Merab Tauman, A Critical Comment on Australian Business Histories, *Bulletin of the Business Archives Council of Australia*, 1, No. 9, 1961, p. 59

K.A. Tucker, Business History: Some Proposals for Aims and Methology, *B.H.*, Vol. XIV, 1972, pp. 1-16

Michael Turner, There is no future for Business History, *B.H.*, Vol. XX, 1978, pp.

A Refutation Refuted, *B.H.*, Vol. XXII, 1980, p. 235-239

M.A. Utton, Some Features of the Early Merger Movements in British Manufacturing Industry, *B.H.*, Vol. XIV, 1972, pp. 51-60

Clarence C. Walton, Business History: Some Major Challenges, *B.H. Review*, 36, 1962, p. 26

Peter L. Payne, The Uses of Business History: A Contribution to the Discussion, *B.H.*, Vol. V, 1962, pp. 11-21

Books

Anon., *Frederick Pattison Pullar*, (pub. privately, 1901)

Who Was Who 1897-1916, (A. and C. Black, London, 1920)

1916-1928, (London, 1947)

1929-1940, (London, 1941)

1941-1951, (London, 1952)

E. Bancroft, *Experimental Researches concerning the philosophy of permanent colours and the best means of producing them by dyeing, calico printing, etc.*, Vol. 1, (London, 1974)

T. C. Barker, R. H. Campbell and P. Mattias, *Business History*, (Historical Association, 1960)

J. N. Barlett, *Carpeting the Millions — The Growth of Britain's Carpet Industry*, (Edinburgh, N. D.)

P. Baxter, *Perth: Past and Present*, (Perth, 1928)

Perth's Old Time Trades and Trading, (Perth, 1930)

Perth: Its Weavers and Weaving and the Weaver Incorporation of Perth, (Perth 1936)

W. H. Beaule, *Romance of Great Businesses*, Vol. 2, (London, 1926)

J. J. Beer, *The Emergence of the German Dye Industry*, (Illinois, 1959)

J. M. Bellamy and J. Saville, *Dictionary of Labour Biography*, Vols. 2 and 4, (Macmillan, 1974)

C. L. and A. B. Berthollet, *Elements of Dyeing*, 2 vols., (London, 1824) H. Blackshaw and R. Brightman, *Dictionary of Dyeing and Textile Printing*, (London, 1961)

N. Blair, *The Postal History of Perth*, (Perth 1976)

W. Braant, *Practical Scourer and Garment Dyer*, (London, 1893)

F. Bradbury, *Carpet Manufacture*, (Boston, 1904)

Ian C. Bradley, *Enlightened Entrepreneurs*, (Weidenfeld and Nicolson, 1987)

D. Bremner, *The Industries of Scotland, their Rise, Progress and Present Condition*, (Edinburgh, 1869)

Asa Biggs, *Friends of the People*, (Batsford, 1956)

The Age of Improvement 1783-1867, (Longman, 1979)

W. B. Bruce, *Sketches of Dunblane: A Guide*, (Dublane, 1900)

J. Butt, *The Industrial Archaeology of Scotland*, (Newton Abbot, 1967)

J. Butt and I. Donnachie, *Industrial Archaeology in the British Isles*, (Slek, London, 1979)

J. Butt and K. Ponting, *Scottish Textile History*, (Aberdeen University Press, 1987)

R. H. Campbell, *Scotland since 1707 — the Rise of an Industrial Scotland,* (J. Donald, Edinburgh, 1965)

The Dynamics of Victorian Business; Problems and Perspectives to the 1870's, (J. Donald, Edinburgh, 1965)

The Rise and Fall of Scottish Industry 1707-1939, (J. Donald, Edinburgh, 1980)

W. A. Campbell, *The Chemical Industry,* (Longman, 1971)

J. Grant, *Memorabilia of the City of Perth,* (Perth, 1806)

R. Chambers, *The Gazetteer of Scotland,* 2 vols., (Edinburgh, 1832)

S. D. Checkland, *Scottish Banking: A History 1695-1973,* (Collins, 1975)

S. and O. Checkland, *Industry and Ethos, Scotland 1832-1914,* (Edward Arnold, 1984)

G. Christie, *Crieff Hydro 1868-1968,* (Edinburgh, 1967)

Roy A. Church, *Economic and Social Charge in a Midland Town — Victorian Nottingham,* (Cassell, 1965)

Kendricksin Hardware, A Family Business 1791-1966, (David and Charles, 1969)

L. J. Clark, *The Craftsman in Textiles,* (Bell, London, 1968)

Philip Clarke, *Small Businesses,* (David and Charles, 1972)

J. E. Clapham, *An Economic History of Modern Britain: The Early Railway Age 1820-1850,* (Cambridge University Press, 1959)

A. and N. Clow, *The Chemical Revolution,* (London, 1952)

S. R. Crockett, *Dyeing and Printing,* (Pitman, 1964)

A. Cooke, *Stanley — Its History and Development,* (University of Dundee, 1977)

S. Cowan, *The Ancient Capital of Scotland,* 2. vols., (London, 1904)

W. Crookes, *Practical Handbook of Dyeing and Calico-Printing,* (London, 1874)

Dyeing and Tissue Printing, (London, 1882)

Phyllis Deane, *The First Industrial Revolution,* (Cambridge University Press, 1979)

P. Deane and W. A. Cole, *British Economic Growth 1688-1959,* (Cambridge University Press, 1969)

T. K. Derry and T. C. Williams, *A Short History of Technology to 1900,* (Oxford University Press, 1960)

Peter F. Drucker, *Innovation and Entrepreneurship,* (Heinemann, 1985)

H. Dussance, *Complete Treatise on the Art of Dyeing,* (Philadelphia, 1863)

Michael M. Edwards, *The Growth of the British Cotton Trade 1780-1815,* (Manchester University Press, 1967)

R. M. Ferguson, *Logie: A Parish History,* (Paisley, 1905)

G. H. C. Fisher, *The History of J. Pullar and Sons Ltd.,* (Perth, 1924)

M. Freeman and D. Aldcroft, *The Atlas of British Railway History,* (Cromm Helm, 1985)

E. Gale, *From Fibres to Fabrics,* (Allman, 1968)

J. Gardner, *Bleaching, Dyeing and Calico-Printing,* (London, 1884)

Francis Godall, *A Bibliography of British Business Studies,* (Gower, 1987)

J. Goodwin, *A Dyer's Manual,* (Pelham, 1982)

George Gordon, *Perspectives of the Scottish City,* (Aberdeen University Press, 1985)

H. G. Graham, *Social Life of Scotland in the 18th Century,* (London, 1901)

F. H. Groome, *Ordnance Gazetteer of Scotland,* 3 vols., (London, 1893)

C. Gulvin, *The Tweedmakers: A History of the Scottish Fancy Woollen Industry 1600-1914,* (Newton Abbot, 1973)

L. F. Haber, *The Chemical History during the 19th Century,* (Oxford University Press, 1958)

A. J. Hall, *Textile Science*, (Allman, London, 1963)

The Standard Book of Textiles, (Newnes-Butterworths, London, 1975)

Henry Hamilton, *An Economic History of Scotland in the 18th Century*, (Oxford University Press, 1963)

The Industrial Revolution in Scotland, (Oxford University Press, 1932) D. W. F. Hardie and J. D. Pratt, *A History of Modern British Chemical Industry*, (Pergamon, Oxford, 1966)

W. C. Henderson, *The Rise of German Industrial Power 1834-1914*, (Temple Smith, 1975)

Elizabeth Hennessey, *The Entrepreneurs*, (Scope Books, 1980)

S. H. Higgins, *Dyeing in Germany and America,* 2 vols., (London, 1907. 1916)

A History of Bleaching, (London, 1924)

W. S. Howe, *Industrial Economics*, (Macmillan, 1978)

J.R. Hume and M.S. Moss, *Beardmore: The History of a Scottish Industrial Giant*, (Heinemann, 1979)

J.J. Hummel, *Dyeing of Textile Fabrics*, (London, 1896)

G.H. Hurst, *Silk Dyeing and Finishing*, (London, 1892)

Handbook of Garment Industry and Cleaning, (London, 1895)

Dictionary of Coal Tar Colours, (London, 1896)

I.C.G. Hutchison, *A Political History of Scotland 1832-1924*, (J. Donald, Edinburgh, 1896)

James B. Jeffreys, *Retail Trading in Britain 1850-1950*, (Cambridge University Press, 1954)

A.E. Johnson, *Drycleaning*, (Merrow, 1971)

R. Kerr, *Essays on New Method of Bleaching*, (Edinburgh, 1791)

E. Knecht, *Manual of Dyeing,* 3 Vols., (London, 1893)

E. Lipson, *The History of the Woollen and Worsted Industries*, (London, 1950)

T. Love, *The Art of Cleaning, Dyeing, Scouring and Finishing*, (London, 1854)

S.G. Lythe and J. Butt, *An Economic History of Scotland 1100-1939*, (Blackie, 1975)

J.A. Mackay, *The Parcel Post of the British Isles*, (Dumfries, 1982)

E. Maclean, *Bridge of Allan - the rise of a village*, (Alloa, 1970)

J. McDowall, *The People's History of Glasgow*, (Glasgow, 1899)

J. Maidment, *The Chronicle of Perth 1210-1668*, (Edinburgh, 1831)

T.B. Marwick, *Economic Development in Victorian Scotland*, Kelley, (U.S.A. 1936)

E. von Meyer, *A History of Chemistry*, (Macmillan, 1891)

T.D. Miller, *The History of the Royal Perth Golfing Society*, (Perth, 1935)

A.S. Milward and S.B. Saul, *The Development of the Economics of Continental Europe 1850-1914*, (Allen and Unwin, 1977)

A. Morison, *Modern Bridge of Allan and Some of its Makers*, (Stirling, 1927)

W. Morris, *Of Dyeing as an Art*, (London, 1893)

J. Morton, *Three Generations in a Family Textile Firm*, (London, 1971)

J. Napier, *A Manual of the Art of Dyeing*, (Glasgow, 1853)

A Manual of Dyeing Receipts, (London, 1855)

C. O'Neill, *Dictionary of Calico-Printing and Dyeing*, (London, 1862)

The Practice and Principles of Calico-Printing, Bleaching and Dyeing, (Manchester, 1878)

E. Ostick, *Textiles for Salesmen*, (Pitman, 1931)

W. Partridge, *A Practical Treatise on Dyeing*, (Pasold Research Fund, 1873)

D. Paterson, *Colour-Matching on Textiles*, (London, 1901)

P.L. Payne, *Studies in Scottish Business History*, (Cass, London, 1967)

The Early Scottish Limited Companies 1856-1895, (Scottish Academic Press, 1980)

D. Peacock, *Perth: Its Annals and its Archives*, (Perth, 1849)

B. Piper, *Fibres and Fabrics*, (Longman, 1970)

K.G. Ponting, *A Dictionary of Dyes and Dyeing*, (Bell and Hyman, London, 1980)

L. Pullar, *Lengthening Shadows*, (pub. privately, 1910)

H. Reimann, *Aniline and its Derivatives*, (London, 1868)

G.M.J. Richardson, *Understanding Industry Today*, (David and Charles, 1984)

S. Robinson, *A History of Dyed and Printed Textiles*, (London, 1974)

C. Rogers, *Social Life in Scotland*, 3 vols., (Edinburgh, 1884)

A. Sansone, *Printing of Cotton Fabrics*, (Manchester, 1887)

Dyeing, 2 vols., (Manchester, 1888)

W.R. Scott, *The Records of New Mills Cloth Manufactory 1681-1703*, (Scottish Historical Society, 1905)

J. Shaw, *Water-power in Scotland 1550-1870*, (J. Donald, Edinburgh, 1984)

T. Sims, *Dyeing and Bleaching*, (London, 1877)

C. Singer, *History of Technology*, 5 vols., (Oxford University Press, 1954-1958)

J.W. Slater, *Manual of Colours and Dye Wares*, (London, 1882)

A. Slaven and S. Checkland, *Dictionary of Scottish Business Biography 1860-1960*, Vol. 1: (Staple Industries, Aberdeen University Press, 1986)

D. Smith, *Practical Dyers' Guide*, (London, 1849)

Dyers' Instructor, (London, 1876)

English Dyer, (Manchester, 1882)

T.C. Smout, *Scottish Trade on the Eve of Union 1660-1707*, (Oliver and Boyd, 1963)

A History of the Scottish People 1560-1830, (Collins, London, 1969)

J. Storey, *Dyes and Fabrics*, (Thames and Hudson, 1978)

Barry Supple, *Royal Exchange Assurance*, (Cambridge University Press, 1970)

Essays in British History, (Clarendon Press, 1977)

F.S. Taylor, *A History of Industrial Chemistry*, (Heinemann, London, 1957)

H. Thomson, *Fibres and Fabrics of Today*, (Heinemann, 1972)

J.M. Thomson, *Practical Dyer's Assistant*, (London, 1849)

F. Thomson, *Harris Tweed*, (David and Charles, 1969)

Violetta Thurston, *The Uses of Vegetable Dyes*, (Dryad Press, London)

K.A. Tucker, *Business History: Selected Headings*, (Cass, 1977)

J. Turnbull, *A History of the Calico-Printing Industry of Great Britain*, (Altrincham, 1951)

A.R. Urquhart, *Auld Perth*, (Perth, 1906)

A.J. Warden, *Burgh Laws of Dundee*, (London, 1872)

J.M. Wilson, *The Imperial Gazeteer of Scotland*, 2 vols., (Edinburgh, 1854)

Theses

John C. Logan, The Dumbarton Glass Work Company, 1777-1850, M. Litt. (Strathclyde), 1970

Anne M.C. MacEwan, The Shotts Iron Company, 1800-1850, M. Litt. (Strathclyde), 1972

Margaret A. Whitehead, The Western Bank and the Crisis of 1857, M. Litt. (Strathclyde), 1978